Embodiment and the Cosmic Perspective in Twentieth-Century Fiction

In dialogue with groundbreaking technologies and scientific models, twentieth-century fiction presents readers with a vast mosaic of perspectives on the cosmos. The literary imagination of the world beyond the human scale, however, faces a fundamental difficulty: if, as researchers in both cognitive science and narrative theory argue, fiction is a practice geared toward the human embodied mind, how can it cope with scientific theories and concepts—the Big Bang, quantum physics, evolutionary biology, and so on—that resist our common-sense intuitions and appear discontinuous, in spatial as well as temporal terms, with our bodies? This book sets out to answer this question by showing how the embodiment of mind continues to matter even as writers—and readers—are pushed out of their terrestrial comfort zone. Offering thoughtful commentary on work by both mainstream literary authors and science fiction writers (from Primo Levi to Jeanette Winterson, from Olaf Stapledon to Pamela Zoline), *Embodiment and the Cosmic Perspective in Twentieth-Century Fiction* explores the multiple ways in which narrative can radically defamiliarize our bodily experience and bridge the gap with cosmic realities. This investigation affords an opportunity to reflect on the role of literature as it engages with science and charts its epistemological and ethical ramifications.

Marco Caracciolo received a PhD in Comparative Literature from the University of Bologna, Italy, in 2012. He is an Associate Professor of English and Literary Theory at Ghent University in Belgium, where he leads "Narrating the Mesh," a collaborative project on contemporary narrative and the nonhuman. His work has appeared in journals such as *New Literary History*, *Contemporary Literature*, *Poetics Today*, and *Narrative*. He is the author of three books: *The Experientiality of Narrative: An Enactivist Approach* (De Gruyter, 2014; honorable mention for the Perkins Prize of the International Society for the Study of Narrative), *Strange Narrators in Contemporary Fiction* (University of Nebraska Press, 2016), and *A Passion for Specificity* (co-authored with psychologist Russell Hurlburt; Ohio State University Press, 2016).

Routledge Studies in Twentieth-Century Literature

Baroque Lorca
An Archaist Playwright for the New Stage
Andrés Pérez-Simón

Hope and Aesthetic Utility in Modernist Literature
Tim DeJong

Exploring the Horror of Supernatural Fiction
Ray Bradbury's Elliott Family
Edited by Miranda Corcoran and Steve Gronert Ellerhoff

Aesthetic and Philosophical Reflections on Mood
Stimmung and Modernity
Birgit Breidenbach

Modernism and Modernity in British Women's Magazines
Alice Wood

Queering Modernist Translation
The Poetics of Race, Gender, and Queerness
Christian Bancroft

Modernist Literature and European Identity
Birgit Van Puymbroeck

Embodiment and the Cosmic Perspective in Twentieth-Century Fiction
Marco Caracciolo

For more information about this series, please visit: https://www.routledge.com

Embodiment and the Cosmic Perspective in Twentieth-Century Fiction

Marco Caracciolo

Routledge
Taylor & Francis Group

NEW YORK AND LONDON

First published 2020
by Routledge
52 Vanderbilt Avenue, New York, NY 10017

and by Routledge
2 Park Square, Milton Park, Abingdon, Oxon, OX14 4RN

*Routledge is an imprint of the Taylor & Francis Group, an
informa business*

© 2020 Taylor & Francis

Library of Congress Cataloging-in-Publication Data
A catalog record for this title has been requested

ISBN: 978-0-367-51720-5 (hbk)
ISBN: 978-1-003-05493-1 (ebk)

Typeset in Sabon
by codeMantra

Contents

Acknowledgments   vii

Introduction: Living within Narrow Limits   1

1 Strange Spaces   25

2 The Cosmology of Everyday Life   51

3 Sex and the Cosmos   81

4 Posthuman Time Faces the Hard Problem   109

5 Bodies from Outer Space   141

6 The Wide, Wide Cosmos   169

Coda: And So What?   199

References   205
Index   221

Acknowledgments

The first draft of this book was completed during a fellowship at the Freiburg Institute for Advanced Studies (FRIAS), University of Freiburg, Germany. I am grateful to the Alexander von Humboldt Foundation for making my stay at FRIAS possible. As for Alexander von Humboldt himself—the German naturalist to whom we owe the word "cosmos" in its modern usage—I can hardly hope to have done justice to his startling vision of the totality of things. But FRIAS proved to be an immensely productive context in which to worry about Humboldt's legacy. It has been a pleasure to spend close to two years in such a stimulating and friendly environment, under the gentle shade of the nearby Black Forest. Thanks go to the director of FRIAS, Bernd Kortmann, and the institute's Fellows in 2015–17, particularly Alice Blumenthal-Dramé, Luca Corlatti, Benoît Dillet, Julia Elsky, Sabine Hake, Kate Rigby, and Evi Zemanek. I was lucky enough to be a member of this interdisciplinary community and participate in many inspiring and wide-ranging conversations—some of them about issues discussed in this book. I would also like to thank the administrative team (in particular, Nik Binder, Petra Fischer, Britta Küst, Helen Pert, and Katharina Seibel) for their patience, humor, and keen interest in the Fellows' ideas and background.

Many friends and colleagues in the field of narrative theory contributed, directly or indirectly, to the ideas laid out in this book. Monika Fludernik, my Humboldt host, was truly a wonderful host both personally and intellectually. Porter Abbott offered—as ever—insightful comments on parts of this book; conversations or correspondence with Ridvan Askin, Lars Bernaerts, Marco Bernini, David Herman, Luc Herman, Liesbeth Korthals Altes, Karin Kukkonen, Merja Polvinen, David Rodriguez, Bart Vervaeck, and Eva von Contzen shaped my understanding of narrative, embodiment, and the nonhuman in ways that can undoubtedly be traced in these pages.

Sections of Chapter 4 build on my article "Posthuman Narration as a Test Bed for Experientiality: The Case of Kurt Vonnegut's *Galápagos*," which appeared in *Partial Answers* 16, no. 2 (2018). Mark Harman graciously granted me permission to use his translation of Franz Kafka's

"A Message from the Emperor" in this book's introduction. The translation, which first appeared in *The New York Review of Books* in 2011, is forthcoming in Harman's *Annotated Kafka* (Harvard University Press).

I put together the final version of this manuscript while at Ghent University. I would like to acknowledge the European Research Council for funding "Narrating the Mesh," my current research project, which was conceived in Freiburg alongside this book and develops its focus on the narrative imagination of the nonhuman. I am grateful to Shannon Lambert for her thoughtful comments on this book and to many other colleagues at Ghent University for creating such an enjoyable and welcoming academic environment. Over the course of this book's somewhat complicated peer review history, four anonymous readers offered perceptive feedback. At Routledge, Michelle Salyga's enthusiasm and professionalism provided key encouragement to bring this project to fruition.

Above all, I am indebted to Wibke Schniedermann for getting me out of the carp pond.

Introduction
Living within Narrow Limits

> He was quick and alert in the things of life, but only in the things, and not in the significances. Fifty degrees below zero meant eighty-odd degrees of frost. Such fact impressed him as being cold and uncomfortable, and that was all. It did not lead him to meditate upon his frailty as a creature of temperature, and upon man's frailty in general, able only to live within certain narrow limits of heat and cold; and from there on it did not lead him to the conjectural field of immortality and man's place in the universe.
>
> (London 1998, 342)

Jack London's "To Build a Fire" tells the story of a man who sets out to explore the Yukon Territories in the dead of winter, accompanied only by a husky. The man experiences the extreme cold but fails to realize how life-threatening it can be; his foolish decision to venture out in this frozen landscape results, in the space of a few pages, in an unceremonious death under the dog's puzzled gaze. In the above-quoted passage, London explicates the man's recklessness via two linked counterfactual scenarios ("It did not lead him...and from there on it did not lead him..."). The man's fate is doubly defined by his failures: first, the failure to acknowledge the physical limits of his body, and how even minor variations in temperature pose a mortal danger to the kind of animals that we are; and second, the failure to abstract from this condition and appreciate "his frailty as a creature of temperature."

The physical constraints that determine the man's death reflect the evolutionary history of our species: natural selection fine-tuned our bodies to survive not just on Earth, but on a fraction of its crust at (or close to) sea level. Even in less dramatic circumstances than those faced by London's character, our experience of the body is, fundamentally, an experience of "narrow limits." We can push back some of these limits—we can learn to swim, for example, and we can probably train our bodies to run a marathon—but whatever progress we make remains, in the grand scheme of things, quite modest: without technology augmenting our bodies, we can't run as fast as cheetahs, or extract oxygen from water like fish, or take flight like birds. Throughout our lives, our bodies are defined by what we *cannot* do. This applies to the able-bodied and individuals with a disability alike, even though societal norms and structures make the experience of narrow limits far more pressing and painful for the latter.

The second failure of London's character is an imaginative one: unable to come to grips with his own mortality, he does not raise the question of "man's place in the universe." His mind is too obtuse to wonder at the scale and role of human life from a cosmic perspective. Yet, as London's story suggests, such imaginative acts are closely bound up with our bodily limits. It is precisely through appreciation of our vulnerability that we have developed imaginative abilities to extricate ourselves from our physical surroundings. From an evolutionary perspective, Conrad Montell draws a direct connection between awareness of mortality and the human imagination in practices such as religion and art: "Imagination...evolved to mitigate that awareness, to discover offsetting information beyond the apparent horizon, to sense a more favorable reality, and thus, to make the emerging awareness of death more bearable, and to make the aware individual more fit" (2002, 5). We imagine an afterlife, we create artifacts or social structures that will survive us—all in an effort to transcend our mortal bodies. But we fail in the task of leaving our bodies behind; we fail because our imagination itself is keyed to the embodied, mortal, limited creatures that we are.

This is what a movement in the mind sciences known as "embodied cognition" teaches us. Embodied cognition provides the theoretical framework of this book; I will have more to say about it later in this introduction. For now, here is a thumbnail definition: embodied cognition holds that our psychological makeup is constrained by our bodily makeup, that our cognition is anchored to our bodies in fundamental ways. Perhaps the easiest way to grasp this claim is by imagining a counterfactual scenario: if our bodies were significantly different, if for instance we could fly or spend our lives underwater or reproduce asexually, then our minds would also be significantly different. Researchers working in this paradigm have shown how embodiment surfaces in human activities that have long been thought to be distant from the domain of sensory experience—including abstract ideas (Boroditsky and Prinz 2008) and mathematics (Lakoff and Núñez 2001). If this is correct, then we have good cause to think that the human imagination is *also* embodied; try as we might, our imagination can never be completely uncoupled from bodily experience, even as it seeks to move beyond this experience. That persistence of the body is the paradox that this book aims to explore. Psychologist James J. Gibson's notion of "intermediate world" can help me specify this idea. Gibson's work in the 1970s paved the way for the embodied cognition movement. Here is a passage lifted from Gibson's *The Senses Considered as Perceptual Systems*:

> The world can be analyzed at many levels, from atomic through terrestrial to cosmic. There is physical structure on the scale of

millimicrons at one extreme and on the scale of light years at another. But surely the appropriate scale for animals is the intermediate one of millimeters to kilometers, and it is appropriate because the world and the animal are then comparable.

(1983, 22)

Gibson refers to this human-scale slice of reality as the "intermediate world." I will call realities that transcend or elude this intermediate world "cosmic realities" (with an extension of the usual meaning of the word "cosmic"). Subatomic particles, DNA molecules, microbes, but also—with a leap to the astronomical scale—Mars, the Milky Way, a supernova millions of light-years away from us, and the universe as a whole are all cosmic realities. At first glance, these phenomena may seem to have little in common. But in fact they share two essential properties: (1) they are not part of our intermediate world, although they may impact it in significant ways; and (2) they are the object of scientific knowledge, which examines them by way of technological devices and statistical models. The thesis advanced by this book is simple: even as these cosmic realities seem to elude or resist ordinary modes of embodiment, the body still emerges in—and shapes—the ways in which we imagine them. I will concentrate on a specific imaginative practice, the reading of fictional narratives, and explore a set of novels and short stories written over the course of the twentieth century. These texts range from canonical literary texts, such as James Joyce's *Ulysses*, to Stanisław Lem's science fiction classic *Solaris*, from genre fiction of the 1920s (Ray Cummings's *The Girl in the Golden Atom*, 1923) to contemporary novels (Michel Faber's *Under the Skin*, 2000). This is a mixed bag, no doubt, and it is not meant to be exhaustive. But it is at least a representative sample of fiction engaging with the cosmos, and the diversity of the selection can only help my case: irrespective of differences in genre, historical context, and literary quality, the dialogue between science and the narrative imagination capitalizes on the embodied nature of mind.

Precisely because of the *distance* between cosmic realities and the intermediate world to which our bodies are attuned, imagining the cosmos puts pressure on our bodily experiences: cosmic narratives can distort everyday modes of embodiment, with surprising or even unsettling effects. Riffing on Viktor Shklovsky's (1991) influential discussion of defamiliarization or "ostranenie," I call this phenomenon "bodily defamiliarization": familiar patterns of bodily experience are triggered and at the same time "made strange" in a cosmic setting.[1] In watching a film like *Gravity* (2013), for instance, we have to readjust our understanding of bodily motion to a zero-gravity environment, which can prove quite disorienting at first. This is just a straightforward example of bodily defamiliarization, but as we'll see my case studies can put readers' embodiment to much more creative uses. There is bodily defamiliarization whenever readers' assumptions and expectations about embodied experience are challenged or modified in a significant way. Darko Suvin (1979) famously wrote about the "cognitive estrangement" that science fiction brings about by injecting an odd, defamiliarizing element (the "novum") into a recognizable reality.[2] My concept of bodily defamiliarization vis-à-vis the cosmos bears a close resemblance to Suvin's estrangement, but it is not limited to science fiction and it foregrounds the bodily dimension of readers' engagement with literature, in line with recent models of the reading experience. Cognitive estrangement, when successful, is not only a matter of recalibrating one's assumptions about what is possible and what isn't in a given world. The possibility of conceptual recalibration depends on more basic forms of imaginative and affective involvement, which are a primary dimension of narrative and embodied phenomena through and through. There can be no cognitive (in the sense of intellectual) estrangement if narrative, including science fiction narrative, doesn't develop strategies to pull us into its storyworlds and let us experience novel realities at close range.[3] Literary engagements with the cosmos are an excellent test bed to study this defamiliarizing dynamic.

In the remainder of this introduction, I will say more on how narrative may bring into play—and potentially defamiliarize—various dimensions of human embodiment. This will require surveying recent debates on embodiment in the mind sciences, with a particular focus on the so-called enactivist approach. I will also discuss the impact that these embodied models have had on cognitive literary studies and the related fields of cognitive poetics and cognitive narrative theory. Researchers in these areas build on conceptual models and empirical findings of the mind sciences to shed light on the workings of literary texts and readers' understanding thereof (Bernaerts et al. 2013; Herman 2013; Zunshine 2015). It should be noted that the cognitive study of literature is "cognitive" in a broad sense, in that it sees cognition as an umbrella term for human meaning-making. Scholars working within this paradigm do *not* typically consider cognition to be essentially distinct from emotion, because they are aware of how fundamental emotion is to our psychological makeup. Therefore, the word "cognitive" in my discussion is *not* interchangeable with "rational" or "inferential," as it can be in everyday usage.

After exploring the spectrum of embodied cognition, I will turn to discussions in other areas of the humanities, and more specifically discussions centering on the notion of the "nonhuman" (Grusin 2015b). Besides helping me contextualize my case studies, this section articulates the main theoretical ambition of this book—namely, opening a conversation between cognitive approaches to literature and areas of scholarship that have developed an interest in the many facets of the nonhuman (such as posthumanism and ecocriticism). I will thus attempt to dislodge cognitive literary scholarship from the fertile—but relatively isolated—niche that it has carved out for itself. The idea behind this move is that the embodiment hypothesis has ramifications well beyond the mind sciences, or cognitive literary studies—ramifications that should be explored in dialogue with other strands of contemporary thinking. This is what my emphasis on the cosmos allows me to do, due to the close alignment between the cosmic and the nonhuman. After bringing into focus what I mean by "cosmos," I will introduce the narratives I've chosen to analyze in this study and offer a synopsis of the chapters.

Mind, World, and Enactivist Philosophy

Language, and especially written language, has long been thought of as a disembodied medium in Western culture. This view of language goes hand in hand with dualistic distinctions between mind and body, and with a sense of human exceptionalism and superiority over nonverbal animals. David Bleich puts this point as follows in a book titled *The Materiality of Language*: "Because only humans have language, this linguistic capability must emanate from a divinely given soul, from a mind that is constituted differently—spiritually, incorporeally—in humans than in any other species" (2013, 61–62). This conception of language has shaped assumptions about literary reading—an activity that has been traditionally regarded as closer to moral and philosophical pursuits than other art forms (for instance, painting or sculpture). Clearly, words do not foreground their materiality in the same way as brush strokes and marble busts. But this does not mean that our understanding of language, including written language, can be uncoupled from our embodied experience of the world. Bleich questions this assumption from the vantage point of poststructuralist philosophy, such as Julia Kristeva's (1989) theory of language. Philosophically speaking, the embodied cognition hypothesis in the mind sciences has had limited conversation with poststructuralist thought, but it comes to surprisingly similar conclusions about the embodiment of language.

One of the earliest—and certainly one of the most influential—attempts to place the body center stage in the mind sciences was *The Embodied Mind* (1991), a book co-authored by two philosophers, Francisco Varela and Evan Thompson, and a psychologist, Eleanor Rosch. *The Embodied Mind* aimed to overthrow the notion that had until then held sway in cognitive psychology and related fields—namely, that human minds were computer-like in their operations. Artificial intelligence (AI) played a key role in the so-called "cognitive revolution" (George A. Miller 2003), and its premise was that, while our minds are physically realized in biological bodies, cognition can be achieved with nonbiological hardware as well. The embodied cognition movement questions this idea from multiple perspectives—through empirical routes (in cognitive psychology and psycholinguistics) and more speculative or evolutionary arguments (in the philosophy of mind). Here I will single out a strand of embodied cognitive science that directly grows out of Varela, Thompson, and Rosch's book—namely, enactivist philosophy.[4] From an enactivist perspective, the mind does not operate by constructing internal models or representations of reality, as AI-inspired cognitive science would have it. Instead, the mind and our sense of having a world arise from hands-on engagements that involve, simultaneously, our bodies and our evolutionary and cultural history. The interlocking of mind and world is what Varela, Thompson, and Rosch (1991, 151) call "structural coupling" with the environment. Patterns of interaction—with the physical milieu, material objects, and our fellow human beings—are the cornerstone of this enactivist account of the mind, which has been developed by researchers such as Alva Noë (2004), Daniel Hutto and Erik Myin (2012), and—in the domain of social cognition—Hanne De Jaegher and Ezequiel Di Paolo (2007).[5] Likewise, the works I will explore in this book utilize patterns at the level of narrative form to structure readers' experiences and shape their embodied imagination of cosmic realities.

In *The Experientiality of Narrative* (Caracciolo 2014d), I have argued that this embodied and enactivist view of the mind has direct implications for language comprehension, and particularly for the comprehension and interpretation of literary narratives: readers enact narrative just as they enact the world, through patterned engagements that draw on their past memories and bodily experiences. Enactivist philosophy foregrounds structural couplings with the world that are embodied, explorative, and nonrepresentational (i.e., do not employ internal representations of reality); likewise, adopting an enactivist approach to literature brings out the imaginative patterns that underlie readers' engagement with fiction. Many of my textual examples in this book resonate with this interest in patterns of embodied affect created through stylistic, narratological, and thematic means.

If literary reading implicates our bodies at such a fundamental level, why is it normally seen as a highly cerebral, conceptual, disembodied activity? The short answer is that we are often unaware of our own embodied involvement as we read. Only a small fraction of our mental processes is *conscious*—that is, results in experienced sensations and thoughts. Most of our cognitive activities take place below the threshold of our consciousness, in what Arthur Reber (1992) calls "the cognitive unconscious." When we traverse a city we know well, for instance, we do so effortlessly, without entertaining any conscious map-like representation of the space that we're negotiating. It would be impossible to move in this way without drawing on memories of previous embodied encounters with the city; these memories unconsciously guide us through this space. The same applies to language production or comprehension: even though handling language must involve a large number of psychological operations (retrieving the semantic meaning of words, for example, or working out what remains implicit), very few of these mental activities trickle down to consciousness. This is one of the reasons why it can be difficult to realize how indebted to embodied experience language comprehension really is.

Routes into Embodied Reading

In this book, I will explore four routes into the somatic basis of language comprehension, building on both experimental research in the mind sciences and concepts developed by cognitive literary scholars. These routes crisscross the distinction between unconscious and conscious cognition: put otherwise, the psychological processes they involve tend to remain unconscious; whether they rise to consciousness depends on a complex interaction between quantity and quality of textual triggers and readers' interests and predispositions. Arguably, this book's thematic focus on embodiment and the cosmos leads me to pay close attention to (and therefore become conscious of) responses that may never make it into most readers' awareness. But a potential for this awareness *is* there. In a sense, I want to use research in the mind sciences and mind-oriented literary scholarship to train my readers' sensitivity, putting them in a position to experience their own bodies as they are activated—and potentially defamiliarized—by the cosmic narratives I examine.

Here are, then, four routes into embodied reading:

1 DIEGETIC RE-ENACTMENT The representation of characters' physical actions and gestures can trigger a mechanism of motor resonance (Zwaan and Taylor 2006) or embodied simulation (Gallese 2005): readers re-enact a character's movements by drawing on their own past embodied interactions with the world.
2 METAPHORICAL MAPPINGS In the wake of George Lakoff and Mark Johnson's (1980) seminal *Metaphors We Live By*, scholars have shown that metaphorical language can create associations between embodied modes of engagement with the world and more abstract, conceptual structures. These associations lead to metaphorical mappings—a broad category that includes verbal metaphors and similes but also the evocation of perceptual patterns known as "image schemata" (more on this concept below).
3 AFFECTIVE INVOLVEMENT Narrative can trigger affect (sensations and emotional responses located in the body) either through the dynamics of its progression or through the explicit evaluations contained in literary style.
4 THEMATIC ENGAGEMENT A narrative may interrogate cultural assumptions and practices surrounding the body. When this happens, we can say that the body is "thematized." The cognitive-level responses that I listed as routes 1 through 3 are typically impacted by thematization.

These four routes span what I called elsewhere the "embodiment spectrum" (Caracciolo 2014b), which brings together basic (and largely automatic) responses to language and more culturally specific evaluations of the body. Why it is so important to address the cultural dimension of the body via thematic engagement will become clearer after examining the four routes in more detail.

Diegetic Re-Enactment

There is a growing body of empirical evidence suggesting that the comprehension of linguistically represented actions involves psychological mechanisms similar to those involved in performing *actual* actions. For instance, a study conducted by Glenberg and Kaschak (2002) asked participants to read sentences that contained verbs implying movement either *away from* or *toward* the body (e.g., respectively, "Close the drawer" and "Open the drawer"). The participants' task was to judge whether the sentences made sense or not; in order to do so, they had to press a button that was either closer to or farther from their body than the hand's resting position. Put more simply, participants responded to the experimental task by moving their hand in a way that was either similar to the verbally represented one (e.g., they read "Close the drawer" and had to move their hand away from the body) or opposite to it (e.g., they read "Close the drawer" and had to move their hand toward the body).

Glenberg and Kaschak found that response times were lower—that is, participants were faster at pressing the button—when the action they were asked to perform was consistent with the action they had just read about. This can be interpreted as an interference effect: "when the implied direction of the sentence contrasts with the actual response direction, there is interference" (2002, 561). What exactly is causing this interference? Glenberg and Kaschak's theory is that "language understanding taps into an action-based system" (2002, 561). The cognitive process activated by reading these sentences shares some of the neural underpinnings of the relevant actions (in this case, movement away from or movement toward the body). Hence, after a movement away from the body had been mentally triggered by the verbal stimulus, participants took a longer time to make the opposite movement because they had to switch from the "away" to the "toward" system. This finding ties in with neuroimaging evidence showing that when we read action verbs implying (for instance) hand motion the brain areas associated with *actual* hand motion light up (Hauk, Johnsrude, and Pulvermüller 2004).

Empirical evidence along these lines points to an embodied basis for language comprehension, and particularly for the understanding of verbally represented actions. The underlying psychological mechanism has been variously called "embodied simulation" (Gallese 2005) or "motor resonance" (Zwaan and Taylor 2006). The appeal of these concepts for literary and narrative scholars should be evident: they allow us to posit that, for instance, whenever we read about a character performing a certain bodily action, that diegetic action *resonates* in our own bodies—or, put otherwise, we *simulate* it internally, more or less as one can imagine performing a certain movement. Ellen Esrock (2004, 2007) was the first literary scholar to theorize about these simulative responses to fiction, usefully distinguishing them from the nonsimulative (but still embodied) responses that I will discuss below under the rubric of "affective involvement."

The term "simulation" is a tricky one.[6] It is important to keep in mind that the simulations involved in reading are usually *not* conscious ones. In Glenberg and Kaschak's case, the scientists went to great pains to conceal the purpose of the study from the participants, deflecting their conscious attention from the linguistic representation of bodily movement: "the participants were never instructed to consider the implied direction [of the movement]; their task was merely to judge sensibility" (2002, 559)—that is, whether the sentences they were reading made sense. The upshot is that, while the evidence points to an embodied basis for linguistic comprehension, it also suggests that this embodied basis will, for most readers and in most scenarios, pass completely unnoticed.

Several researchers, in both psycholinguistics and cognitive literary studies, have attempted to "scale up" the idea of embodied re-enactment, extending it from the representation of individual actions to that of spatial environments that can be apprehended by way of actions (such as body or eye movements). Rolf Zwaan's (2004) "immersed experiencer framework," for example, holds that in making sense of narrative texts we have to work out a perspective on the diegetic spaces—where perspective is defined as a "spatio-temporal relation between the experiencer and the situation" (2004, 43). This idea is consistent with previous work on mental models in language comprehension (van Dijk and Kintsch 1983), with the important difference that—for Zwaan—readers' mental modeling of narrative space is based on strategies derived from their embodied familiarity with real space.

Thus, building on Zwaan's model and David Herman's seminal work on narrative space (2002, Chap. 7), I suggested in two articles (Caracciolo 2011, 2013c) that readers' embodiment always shapes their understanding of the spatial references contained in narrative through the simulation of movement: in the so-called "body tour," for instance, we construct a mental model of the spatial environment by imagining moving through it with our bodies (and, whenever possible, by taking on the body of a character present on the scene). Again, I use terms such as "imagining" and "taking on" guardedly, because I don't imply that readers are necessarily *aware* of these activities. When they do become conscious of their embodied involvement at this level, they experience the feeling that is variously known as "transportation" (Gerrig 1993), "immersion" (Ryan 2001), and "presence" (Kuzmičová 2012). This feeling is a conscious experience of entering the narrated environment with one's body. Both immersion and re-enactment are diegetic phenomena insofar as they are prompted by textual cues at the level of narrative's subject-matter—characters' actions and the spatial domains constructed by stories. With the next section, we move to the stylistic level.

Metaphorical Mappings

The notion of embodied simulation has not only been invoked in connection to the verbal representation of actions. In a different research area, psychologists and cognitive linguists have hypothesized that metaphorical language is also understood through embodied simulation. In an article titled "Metaphor Interpretation as Embodied Simulation" (2006), for instance, Raymond Gibbs comments on a text that creates a set of metaphorical associations between the grief process and a journey. He explains:

> metaphorical references to getting over and through grief, needing directions, supplies, plans and support from others in dealing with grief, being lost in the dark tunnel of grief and moving forward to the other side, are all understood by simulating what it must be like to perform these specific activities, even though it is, strictly speaking, impossible to physically act on abstract entities like the emotion of grief.
>
> (2006, 435)

As we know, we should not see these "simulations" as involving consciousness: most of the time, they will only be unconscious responses to language. But Gibbs's claim points to another route through which readers' engagement with literary narrative can be said to be embodied: their understanding of creative metaphors and similes.[7]

To fully understand this point, we need to take a step backward and consider *why* metaphorical language has a close relationship with our bodies. In *Metaphors We Live By*, Lakoff and Johnson write that the "essence of metaphor is understanding and experiencing one kind of thing in terms of another" (1980, 5). This gesture is what Lakoff and Johnson, and researchers working in their wake, term a "mapping"—an association that allows language users to understand a semantic domain (for instance, the grief process) in terms of another (for instance, a journey). However, Lakoff and Johnson also draw attention to a bias in the direction of these associations: we tend to use metaphors to understand abstract concepts in terms of concrete scenarios of embodied interaction with the world (see Rohrer 2007, 28). This idea is one of the conceptual cornerstones of cognitive linguistics. We've seen that Gibbs comments on an article comparing grief to a journey; now consider the difference between the two terms of the comparison: dealing with grief is an emotional process that unfolds over time and may not follow a linear trajectory (there might be relapses in grief, for instance); a journey, by contrast, is a movement in space that has a clear "source-path-goal" structure. An intangible process is thus conceptualized in terms of a concrete scenario of physical motion. This is just an example, of course: embodied metaphors are ubiquitous in our understanding of time (Boroditsky 2000), emotion (Kövecses 2000), and even philosophical concepts (Lakoff and Johnson 1999).

The mapping between embodied scenarios and abstract concepts is often facilitated by schematic patterns derived from our bodily interactions with the world: cognitive linguists call them "image schemata" (see Hampe and Grady 2005). SOURCE-PATH-GOAL is an image schema, and so are UP-DOWN ("he has climbed the ladder," where UP stands for improved social or economic standing), BLOCKAGE ("there are a few bureaucratic hurdles," where bureaucracy acts as a physical obstacle), and so on.[8] Image schemata are important insofar as they serve as an intermediate step in the translation of abstract entities (such as social structures or administrative processes, in the case of my last two examples) into particularized embodied scenarios. On this view, metaphor is a form of understanding that applies embodied experience to more conceptual modes of thinking. We will have to bear this in mind, because metaphorical language (which includes similes and metaphors proper) plays a key role in achieving what I call "interconnectivity"—the process of bringing together everyday, embodied experience and more intangible cosmic realities.

Affective Involvement

As Ed Tan (1996) and, more recently, Patrick Colm Hogan (2011) have argued, the structure of narrative follows closely the structure of human emotional life: the major narrative genres (for instance, comedy) build on the dynamic of experiencing basic emotions (such as happiness). This is one of the reasons why stories are so effective at eliciting emotional responses in their audiences. Another reason has to do with emotional effects that can be found in *all* narratives, regardless of genre. Consider, for instance, Meir Sternberg's claim that narrative has three "universal…effects/interests/dynamics" (2001, 117)—namely, suspense, curiosity, and surprise. According to Sternberg, these universals depend on a fundamental feature of narrative, its double temporality: on the one hand, we have the temporality of the story, which is the inferred chronology of the events told by the narrative; on the other hand, we have the temporality of discourse, which is the order of presentation of those events (and may deviate significantly from the order in which the events happened).[9] The discrepancy between story and discourse time is responsible for Sternberg's emotional universals of narrative. In suspense, we wonder about the outcome of an action sequence that is located in the future of story time (e.g., will character X die?). In curiosity, we wonder about a piece of information that has been omitted by discourse but is located in the past of story time (character Y was killed, but who is the murderer?). Finally, in surprise, we are forced to revise our understanding of the story based on the delayed revelation of a fact or event (if character Z was already dead at the time of the murder, then he couldn't have killed Y). These are emotional effects, as Sternberg explicitly acknowledges. But because the body is the locus of emotions and affective experience, Sternberg's suspense, curiosity, and surprise must have bodily underpinnings, too.

Philosopher David Velleman describes narrative pattern in explicitly embodied terms: "The cadence that makes for a story is that of the arousal and resolution of affect, a pattern that is biologically programmed. Hence we understand stories viscerally, with our bodies" (2003, 13). As emotional effects, suspense, curiosity, and surprise can be inscribed within this affective arc ("cadence") of arousal and resolution.[10] More specifically, while surprise is likely to be tied to the passage or episode in which a surprising revelation occurs, suspense and curiosity are affective shifts in the audience's overall engagement with the story—except that the former is directed toward a future outcome, the latter toward a past situation. Thus, surprise, suspense, and curiosity display different "affective contours," to use the terminology introduced by Kimmel (2005, 224; see also 2009). If we could represent readers' affective responses to a narrative text in a graph, the affective contour would be the profile of the curve, how the intensity of our engagement with the story varies over time: surprise would be a sudden peak, suspense a more or less steep gradient, curiosity a steady, temporally extended rise. This pattern may follow an overall "rhythm," more or less as music does, depending on the pace of the story, or how quickly and dramatically the affective contour changes over time (see Caracciolo 2014c).

But the graph analogy is imperfect, because affective contour is a matter of experienced qualities as well as intensities, so we would need a multidimensional array to chart qualitative differences. The progression of our ideal curve may exhibit other qualities than surprise, suspense, and curiosity: Sternberg's categories are heuristically useful, but they are a relatively rough-grained means of capturing the ways in which narratives may offer variations on the general pattern of resolution and affect identified by Velleman. To arrive at a more fine-grained classification, Kimmel builds on the notion of image schema; he argues that image schemata may not only be evoked at a local level (through metaphors and similes, as discussed above) but may underlie readers' comprehension of an entire narrative:

> At this level, protagonist subgoals become LANDMARKS, and ultimate goals PATH END-POINTS. Temporal and hierarchical relations between scenes occur as PARTS AND WHOLES, embedded scenes as NESTING schemas, and episodic breakpoint [sic] as INTERVALS on the basic temporality PATH. The topmost level of image schemas holistically captures story evolution over time, a PATH, much like a melody or musical score, as variation in intensity. Such image schemas can be sensed by readers, often in their bodies, as an arc of FORCE tension or denouement as reinstated BALANCE schema.
>
> (2009, 172–73)

If Kimmel is right, narrative form activates and combines image schemata into an affective contour that guides narrative comprehension and may (or may not) rise to readers' consciousness. This is a process comparable to what Esrock calls the "vitalization" of the narrative, which "refers to the sense of aliveness or vitality we ascribe to the fictional world as the result of the reader's projection of her own bodily feeling into the literary work" (2004, 81). As Esrock points out, this embodied involvement is not merely the result of simulative re-enactments, but also depends on the reader's attunement to formal patterns in the text.

Consider "A Message from the Emperor," a paragraph-long story by Franz Kafka. This narrative was first published in Kafka's 1919 collection *A Country Doctor*; the text in Mark Harman's translation reads as follows:

> The emperor—it is said—sent to you, the one apart, the wretched subject, the tiny shadow that fled far, far from the imperial sun, precisely to you he sent a message from his deathbed. He bade the messenger kneel by his bed, and whispered the message in his ear. So greatly did he cherish it that he had him repeat it into his ear. With a nod of his head he confirmed the accuracy of the messenger's words. And before the entire spectatorship of his death—all obstructing walls have been torn down and the great figures of the empire stand in a ring upon the broad, soaring exterior stairways—before all these he dispatched the messenger. The messenger set out at once; a strong, an indefatigable man; thrusting forward now this arm, now the other, he cleared a path through the crowd; every time he meets resistance he points to his breast, which bears the sign of the sun; and he moves forward easily, like no other. But the crowds are so vast; their dwellings know no bounds. If open country stretched before him, how he would fly, and indeed you might soon hear the magnificent knocking of his fists on your door. But instead, how

uselessly he toils; he is still forcing his way through the chambers of the innermost palace; never will he overcome them; and were he to succeed at this, nothing would be gained: he would have to fight his way down the steps; and were he to succeed at this, nothing would be gained: he would have to cross the courtyard and, after the courtyard, the second enclosing outer palace, and again stairways and courtyards, and again a palace, and so on through thousands of years; and if he were to burst out at last through the outermost gate—but it can never, never happen—before him still lies the royal capital, the middle of the world, piled high in its sediment. Nobody reaches through here, least of all with a message from one who is dead. You, however, sit at your window and dream of the message when evening comes.

(Kafka 2011)

The narrative progression coincides with the messenger's physical motion in space, triggering the PATH image schema. But following this progression is far from being a purely conceptual activity. Through the dynamic of expectation, the narrative traces an affective contour that tinges readers' experience in bodily terms. We are encouraged to be hopeful at first, increasingly pessimistic as the likelihood of a positive outcome diminishes. Initially, our arousal is blended with the forward motion of the messenger, so that the perceived pace of the narrative is made to overlap with the character's: as we experience the speed and adroitness of his movements, we anticipate the successful delivery of the message. But our hopes for a quick resolution are fatally undermined when the text suddenly shifts its emphasis from the messenger's progress to the vastness of the crowds and the boundlessness of the abodes—a shift that activates the OBSTACLE image schema, because the messenger's movement appears to be obstructed. This results in an embodied feeling of faltering and stuttering as we move through this part of the piece. In short, the rhythm created by this story reflects a complex interaction between style and syntax, narrated events (in this case, a physical movement within the storyworld), and the overall teleology of the narrative. Readers are not always consciously aware of this rhythmicity, but once they pay close attention to it, they cannot miss its deeply embodied quality.

The affectivity of narrative can be modulated through means other than the progression of plot, of course: subject-matter and style play an important role in evoking emotional associations and feelings in reading.[11] These associations enrich the plot's contour and bring about bodily defamiliarization whenever the experienced feelings depart from expected or usual modes of embodiment. Thus, in Chapter 6, I will focus on how sublime affect triggered by the vast scale of the cosmos may impact readers in embodied, material terms and invite them to step outside the world of everyday experience. Affective feelings are also a key element of my analysis of how the cosmos can enter narratives centered on everyday life (Chapter 2) and inflect or guide sexual desire (Chapter 3). The takeaway is that narrative taps into bodily feelings at multiple levels, through the dynamics of its progression but also via the emotions triggered by the represented situations as well as literary style.

Thematic Engagement

In an article titled "What Makes a Body?" (2008, 164–66), philosopher Mark Johnson—the co-author, with George Lakoff, of *Metaphors We Live By*—distinguishes between five dimensions of embodiment: biological (the "body as organism" and its basic physiological routines), ecological (the body in its coupling with the physical environment), phenomenological (the lived experience of the body), social (the body in its relationship with social environments), and cultural (the practices and beliefs surrounding the body in human cultures). My discussion of embodiment in literary reading has focused on the first three dimensions so far. But part of the philosophy of this book is that cognitive-level processes can never be completely uncoupled from the social and cultural dimensions of embodiment. Phenomenologist Maurice Merleau-Ponty expresses this idea with great lucidity:

> Everything is both manufactured and natural in man, as it were, in the sense that there is not a word, not a form of behaviour which does not owe something to purely biological being—and which at the same time does not elude the simplicity of animal life, and cause forms of vital behaviour to deviate from their pre-ordained direction, through a sort of *leakage*.
>
> (2002, 170)

Biology seeps into culture, and conversely, human cultures can appropriate biological and cognitive patterns in substantially different ways, thanks to the fluidity of our cognitive makeup (see Slingerland 2008a, 151).

This is why this book, despite taking a cognitive approach, does not steer away from the social and cultural dimensions of the body. In many of my case studies, the body is thematized in the sense that it becomes entangled with beliefs and assumptions regarding the position of humankind vis-à-vis cosmic realities. These cultural meanings are central to several of my close readings, especially in the second half of the book (Chapters 3–6). I will interrogate them by pursuing what Daniel Punday calls a "corporeal hermeneutics—a theory of how the text can be meaningfully articulated through the body" (2003, 5). Unlike Punday, and following in the footsteps of cognitive literary scholars such as Ellen Spolsky (2001) or Guillemette Bolens (2012), I move beyond a purely thematic or hermeneutic approach to the body: I focus on how the embodiment of human cognition acts as a *constraint* on cultural representations of the cosmos (remember the discussion of biological limitations at the beginning of this introduction). In turn, I show how the narrative imagination of cosmic realities can build upon, and defamiliarize, cognitive-level processes. I am interested, in other words, in the creative interchange between biological (in a broad sense) and sociocultural dimensions of the body.[12]

My approach to cosmic fictions aims to illustrate this interaction. In several chapters, for instance, my discussion overlaps with issues of gender and sexuality, showing how social norms are always bound up with both the phenomenology of the body and scientific knowledge. In other chapters major historical events come to the fore, bringing along culturally specific traumas and anxieties: for example, the Holocaust in Primo Levi's "Carbon" (Chapter 2), the Cold War in J. G. Ballard's "The Terminal Beach" (Chapter 4), or large-scale exploitation of nonhuman animals in Michel Faber's *Under the Skin* (Chapter 5). Even more central to my project is the cross-fertilization of cognitive science and contemporary thinking developing in the wake of poststructuralist philosophy. Cosmic narratives are an ideal focus for this conversation, because—as we will see—they raise questions that encompass physical realities as well as mental ones, the farthest reaches of the universe as well as social structures and cultural assumptions here on Earth. So far, I have elaborated on the cognitive side of the equation. In the following sections, I turn to theorizations of the nonhuman, explaining how this notion can be situated vis-à-vis my emphasis on cosmic realities.

Narrative Turning Nonhuman

In the introduction to a landmark volume titled *The Nonhuman Turn*, Richard Grusin writes that "humans must now be understood as climatological or geological forces on the planet that operate just as nonhumans would, independent of human will, belief, or desires" (2015a, vii). Grusin's project is to bring together, under the heading of the "nonhuman," a complex and highly diverse array of approaches, ranging from animal studies to affect theory and Bruno Latour's (2005) actor-network theory. What is the common denominator of these approaches? In order to begin explaining what the "nonhuman" is we must clear up a possible misunderstanding of the prefix non-: scholars working within this paradigm do not intend to oppose the human to an alleged nonhuman "other," which would only reify and strengthen the idea of the human; on the contrary, these scholars are interested in showing that the human, at least in a certain sense of the word, never existed in the first place, because our own species falls on a continuum with a wide range of realities, including the "climatological or geological forces" mentioned by Grusin.

Consider, for example, the idea of the "Anthropocene"—a term coined by chemist Paul Crutzen (Crutzen and Stoermer 2000) to refer to the current geological epoch: the Anthropocene is the era in which humankind becomes a quasi-geological agent due to the lasting effects of large-scale industrialization. Human activity has already left a mark on our planet—and its consequences are bound to become even more significant in the future (with climate change, rising sea levels, and so on). In the Anthropocene, as argued by Dipesh Chakrabarty (2014) in an influential article, three different temporalities collide: the geological history of our planet, the evolutionary history of life on Earth (including our own species), and the history of (largely Western) civilization, which led to large-scale industrialization and a global capitalist economy—two major factors in the current ecological crisis. From the vantage point of the Anthropocene, the boundaries that have long been thought to de-marcate human society from biology and geology become blurry.

Ultimately, the main goal of the nonhuman turn is to challenge as-sumptions regarding the historical and metaphysical *autonomy* of the human, and in doing so pull the rug from under the feet of human exceptionalism. Hence the politically engaged side of this movement: researchers affiliated with the nonhuman question notions of human ex-ceptionality and superiority over a wide gamut of nonhuman realities (from animals to the environment)—notions that have repeatedly served as an excuse for vast exploitation and, in many cases, destruction.[13]

The Anthropocene and climate change raise a major challenge for hu-mankind. As philosopher Dale Jamieson writes, "climate change can be seen as presenting us with the largest collective action problem that humanity has ever faced, one that has both intra- and inter-generational dimensions" (2014, 61). Closer to our focus in this book, but not un-relatedly, nonhuman realities also pose a challenge for storytelling, in-cluding the literary forms of storytelling I will examine in the following chapters. We have already encountered Gibson's concept of "intermedi-ate world"—the world of human-scale objects and interactions. Narra-tive is at home in this world: it exhibits an "anthropomorphic bias," as Monika Fludernik puts it in *Towards a "Natural" Narratology* (1996, 9). Compare, for example, the sentences: "John and Rosie fell in love" and "A star exploded in a distant galaxy." Both sentences relate events—i.e., things that happened. Yet the former has much more potential from a narrative perspective, because the event it relates is, in most contexts, inherently more tellable—or worthy of being told (see Baroni 2013)—in that it ties in with the interests and concerns of social animals like us.

In fact, the link between narrative and human social interaction runs deep. "Stories model and abstract the human social world," write psy-chologists Raymond Mar and Keith Oatley (2008, 173). Philosopher Daniel Hutto (2008) goes even farther, seeing in narrative a building block of so-called folk psychology, which is the set of skills we use to ascribe mental states, particularly beliefs and desires, to other subjects: we understand the reasons for other people's actions by telling a narrative about them, a narrative that links their external behavior with inner, mental states. Thus, narrative's bias toward the intermediate world is not an accident but a direct result of the function stories play in human societies. Virtually every feature of storytelling is geared toward human-scale reality: the characters exhibit a human or human-like embodied subjectivity, the temporalities involved are commensurate with the human lifespan, plots tend to be structured teleologically, with characters' intentionality—their beliefs and desires—driving their progression.[14]

All this goes a long way toward explaining why nonhuman realities resist narrative representation. The nonhuman escapes our everyday experience; it calls into question dichotomies between human agents and inanimate processes, such as the climate or natural evolution. But these dichotomies are part and parcel of the intermediate world to which narrative is keyed. This is not to say that narrative cannot overcome its bias toward the human scale; it can, but it must develop creative solutions to do so. Because the nonhuman puts pressure on the conventional structures of narrative, the only way to convey or at least gesture toward nonhuman realities is to move *beyond* these conventions. Not all my case studies in this book are successful in this experimentation with narrative form; but they all acknowledge, explicitly or implicitly, the challenge that the nonhuman represents for narrative.

This book is part of an ongoing attempt—spearheaded by Nancy Easterlin (2012), David Herman (2014, 2018), Erin James (2015), and Alexa Weik von Mossner (2017)—to unsettle the human-scale bias not just of narrative but of narrative *theory*: these writers have started thinking about the modes of narrative's engagement with nonhuman realities, such as animals (for Herman) and the environment (for Easterlin, James, and Weik von Mossner). Both animals and the environment fall within the broad scope of what Grusin and his colleagues call the nonhuman; but they are still, to a large extent, part of the world of everyday experience. Indeed, in Gibson's (1986) ecological psychology human perception is *defined* by our interaction with an external environment that may include nonhuman animals. This book seeks to take narrative theory more decidedly beyond the intermediate world; it confronts the nonhuman in its most radical and unsettling form, because it concentrates on narratives that capture and convey *cosmic* realities. My claim is that bodily defamiliarization—the process whereby human embodiment is evoked, and at the same time imaginatively reconfigured—is part of the solution my texts offer to the problem of coming to grips with the nonhuman. In the hands of a skilled storyteller, the embodiment of our narrative imagination is no longer a cognitive limitation or liability; on the contrary, it affords thrilling opportunities for connecting with the cosmos.

Narrowing Down the Cosmic

At this point, my reader will be wondering: what do I really mean by "cosmic"? This is not a trivial question, because this book is based on an intentionally broad understanding of the cosmos. The term may evoke associations with the outer reaches of the universe. But, as anyone familiar with the etymology of "cosmos" in ancient Greek will know, the word implies more than spatial distance from our planet: cosmos is the opposite of chaos in that it refers to the universe considered as a well-ordered system.[15] The cosmos is a principle of organization, a law—or set of laws—that brings reality together into a coherent whole. An example of a cosmic principle in this sense is the idea of the "great chain of being" or "scala naturae." This notion has its roots in Greek (and particularly Aristotelean) philosophy but underpins the bulk of Western thought through the eighteenth century, as Arthur Lovejoy (2001) has shown in an influential study. The great chain of being embraces the whole of creation, from angels to humans, from trees to rocks. The implication is that existence is a continuum, there are no clear-cut boundaries between forms of being. Referring to Leibniz's dictum "natura non facit saltum" ("nature does not make leaps"), Lovejoy writes: "there are no sudden 'leaps' in nature; infinitely various as things are, they form an absolutely smooth sequence, in which no break appears, to baffle the craving of our reason for continuity everywhere" (2001, 327). A second important implication of the great chain of being is that this cosmic unity emanates from God himself; it is hierarchically ordered from beings closer to Him (angels and humans) to simpler life forms and, finally, mere inanimate matter.

In the nineteenth century, scientific thinking came to question this hierarchical conception of nature and, eventually, surpassed it completely. As Lovejoy argues, Darwin's theory of evolution by natural selection suggests that simpler life forms *preceded* more complex ones, thus undercutting the idea of a God-sanctioned hierarchy. Even the principle of continuity has come into question with the emergence of modern science: as Allen Thiher puts it in a book on the dialogue between literature and science, "a putative cosmic unity went asunder when Galileo, Descartes, and Newton undertook the objectifying of nature by reducing it to abstract, quantified relations" (2005, 12). Fast-forward to our times, and continuity remains problematic: physicists are still looking for a "theory of everything" that would span the gap between quantum phenomena (which take place on infinitesimally small scales of matter) and the physics of macroscopic objects, which is explained by Einstein's general relativity (see, e.g., Deutsch 1997).

In this book, I focus my attention on the rift between these theories and Gibson's intermediate world of human-scale objects. Most present-day humans in the Western world accept the existence of protons and neutrinos, or exoplanets and black holes—entities that they will never be able to perceive without an astoundingly long chain of mediations, which involve sophisticated technologies, scientific models and theories, and the popularization of science. Because evolution moves much more slowly than human culture, we share the bodily makeup and perceptual world of our ancestors, who lived thousands of years ago. But, conceptually, our universe is several orders of magnitude larger in space and older in time. The upshot is that our view of the universe is fraught with tensions and gaps—between perception and scientific knowledge, but also between the spatio-temporal scales investigated by different sciences. Thus we continue yearning for a cosmic principle, a perspective from which the universe would make sense as a whole, including the history of our species. Literary scholar Kathryn Hume expresses this cosmic anxiety as follows: "We must augment the revelations of science if our view of the universe and of ourselves is to give us a sense of meaning. We need to experience the cosmos imaginatively as well as analytically" (1982, 47–48).

In the twentieth century, literary fiction has repeatedly attempted to fill in the gaps left by science. The aspiration was to give readers an illusion of continuity between the social and perceptual world toward which narrative, as we have seen, is geared and the realities explored by scientists. These realities are fundamentally, and irreducibly, nonhuman, in that they escape—and at least potentially challenge—human agency and subjectivity. Seen in this light, the cosmos becomes the ultimate test bed for literary narratives confronting the nonhuman. Any formal solution to this problem of narrativizing the nonhuman has to start where human cognition starts—namely, from the human body. The narratives I will consider in the following chapters take advantage of the four routes into embodied reading discussed in the first section of this introduction. Through different strategies and to different degrees, these novels and short stories combine bodily defamiliarization with what I call "cosmic perspective-taking": readers are detached from the intermediate world and brought closer to nonhuman realities—an imaginative process that encourages them to envision the cosmos in its totality and continuity.

The Corpus

Needless to say, I am not the first scholar to develop an interest in literature's engagement with cosmic questions. In *Fictions of the Cosmos* (2011), Frédérique Aït-Touati discusses the impact of new cosmologies on French literature of the seventeenth century. In *The Starry Sky Within* (2014), Anna Henchman explores the multiple intersections between the history of astronomy and Victorian literature and culture. My investigation turns to the twentieth century, which was marked by dramatic shifts in our understanding of the cosmos and the scales it involves, to the extent that historian of science Malcolm Longair (2013) calls it a "cosmic century." At one end of the spectrum, physics has offered an increasingly detailed picture of the minuscule particles and invisible forces that make up reality. At the opposite end, advances in astronomy have brought to light the universe's unimaginably large proportions. Thanks to groundbreaking work by Georges Lemaître and Edwin Hubble in the 1920s, we discovered that the universe is *expanding*, and therefore that it must have originated at a specific point in time (the so-called Big Bang).[16] Arguably, these revolutionary insights prompted literary writers to engage with cosmic questions with renewed energy. Those questions, and the scientific discoveries that fueled them, serve as a backdrop to the fictional texts I will scrutinize in this book.

My case studies are based on a sampling of twentieth-century narratives dealing with cosmic realities. This is a representative selection, but it is by no means exhaustive. Each of my six chapters takes a particular angle on the enmeshment of the cosmos and the human body; in each of these chapters, I offer close readings of three different—but thematically related—narratives. The goal of this juxtaposition is twofold: on the one hand, I probe continuities and discontinuities in narrative solutions to the problem of representing nonhuman realities; on the other hand, I aim to expose the levels of embodiment these solutions tap into. The case studies follow a trajectory of increasing spatio-temporal scale, from the subatomic microcosm of Chapter 1 to the totality of the universe in Chapter 6.

In Chapter 1, I start off by analyzing Italo Calvino's short story "All at One Point" (in the collection *Cosmicomics*, 1965).[17] I then move on to two other narratives that deal with microscopic spatial scales, Ray Cummings's *The Girl in the Golden Atom* (1923) and Richard Matheson's *The Shrinking Man* (1956). Chapter 2 offers close readings of texts that, in different ways, attempt to embed the cosmic in everyday contexts and situations: the "Ithaca" chapter in James Joyce's *Ulysses* (1922); Pamela Zoline's science fiction short story "Heat Death of the Universe" (1967); and "Carbon," the last chapter of Primo Levi's autobiographical book *The Periodic Table* (1975). Chapter 3 takes another perspective on the embedding of the cosmic in the everyday, looking at how the body qua the locus of sexual desire and feelings may become a vehicle of cosmic anxieties in three novels: John Updike's *Roger's Version* (1986), Jeanette Winterson's *Gut Symmetries* (1997), and Michel Houellebecq's *The Elementary Particles* (1998). In Chapter 4, I explore narratives that foreground large-scale temporalities in order to gain purchase on the so-called "hard problem" of consciousness— namely, the problem of how physical, inanimate matter can give rise to psychological states. These narratives are two short stories, Jorge Luis Borges's "The Immortal" (1947) and J. G. Ballard's "The Terminal Beach" (1964), and Kurt Vonnegut's novel *Galápagos* (1985).

Chapter 5 transitions back to the question of *spatial* scale, with its case studies attempting to come to grips with alien bodies that originate from (or are encountered in) outer space: they are H. P. Lovecraft's *The Shadow Out of Time* (1936), Stanisław Lem's *Solaris* (1961), and Michel Faber's *Under the Skin* (2000). Finally, the narratives examined in Chapter 6 take on the challenge of representing the cosmos in its unconceivable *distance* from the intermediate world: Olaf Stapledon's *Star Maker* (1937), Vladimir Nabokov's "Lance" (1952), and Arthur C. Clarke's *2001: A Space Odyssey* (1968) attempt to envision the cosmos in its sublime vastness.

As my reader will have noticed, these narratives are quite diverse in literary-historical context and geographical provenance. Moreover, a few case studies belong to science fiction, others are canonical literary novels and short stories; yet others blur the distinction between science fiction and literary modes of writing, as often in the second half of the twentieth century (see Gerald Alva Miller 2012, 6). To observe the coming together of embodied cognition, cultural conceptualizations of the body, and cosmological questions we need to cast our net as wide as possible, adopting a comparative rather than strictly historiographical method. The historicity of human meaning-making practices cannot and should not be sidelined, of course, as the book's focus on the twentieth century shows. But, in general, this book should be primarily read as a contribution to cognitive literary theory as the study of how cognitive constraints on meaning-making (including our embodiment) impact literary and narrative form. My close engagement with cosmic fictions seeks to demonstrate the continuing relevance of a formalist method as we explore narrative pathways for understanding human-nonhuman interactions. It is not a coincidence that the idea of *pattern* plays such a central role in my textual readings: cosmic fictions create and front-load formal templates for understanding our position vis-à-vis nonhuman realities; as we will see, style and narrative form are particularly well suited to overcome the representational limitations of our imagination. In turn, only sustained textual analysis can fully bring out the intersection of literary form, themes, and embodied cognitive strategies.

The concept of form here, as in recent work in the area of so-called New Formalism (see, e.g., Levine 2015), is not limited to *textual* form: on the contrary, one of my guiding assumptions is that the form of the text is closely related to the affective patterning of the text's reception—what I call its "affective contour."[18] Moreover, formal choices are always in dialogue with socio-cultural issues and dynamics. Some of the formal solutions developed by the authors I will discuss are particularly innovative in their dialogue with their contexts, others are more in line with the values and expectations of modernity (for instance, surrounding science as mastery over the nonhuman world). Yet it seems to me that all these strategies point up a set of problems and possibilities that are, fundamentally, transhistorical. What are the implications of acknowledging the mediocrity of the human vis-à-vis cosmic realities? Is this realization of our cosmic insignificance bound to nihilistically distance us from socially and politically meaningful action? Or, on the contrary, can it deepen our sense of belonging to human and more-than-human (planetary) communities? Those key questions will be taken up in the final chapter. Impatient readers may want to skip to that coda and then work backward to the textual encounters staged in the body of this book.

Notes

1 See Berlina (2015) for a comprehensive history of Shklovsky's concept and its multiple English translations (defamiliarization, estrangement, making strange, etc.)
2 Suvin's "cognitive estrangement" has been the subject of much discussion in science fiction studies. Vint (2014, Chap. 3) and Csicsery-Ronay (2008, Chap. 2) offer a useful point of entry into these debates.
3 In the terminology introduced by Herman, "storyworlds" are spatial "models built up on the basis of cues contained in narrative discourse" (2002, 20). For discussion of this concept from an embodied, enactivist standpoint, see Caracciolo (2019).
4 I will not offer a comprehensive survey of embodied cognitive science in this introduction; other researchers have already reviewed this work in great detail (Lakoff and Johnson 1999; Anderson 2003; Gibbs 2005).
5 This focus on sensorimotor patterns allows enactivist philosophy to avoid the dangers of ableism—that is, an essentialist conception of the body that uncritically endorses the socio-cultural norms defining "able" bodies. Sensorimotor patterns underlie the structural coupling with the world of all bodies, regardless of their perceptual or cognitive limitations. For further discussion, see Söffner (2017).
6 See also Caracciolo (2013b) on the difficulties surrounding the concept of simulation.
7 Such creative metaphors and similes are particularly frequent in literary texts, as Goatly (2011, 333–40) has demonstrated in an empirical analysis.
8 I here follow the cognitive-linguistic convention of printing image schemata in small capitals. For a more complete inventory of image schemata, see Evans and Green (2006, 190).
9 The distinction between story and discourse time is an essential element of structuralist theories of narrative (see, e.g., Chatman 1978).
10 Work in so-called affect theory (see, e.g., Massumi 2002) has driven a wedge between emotions and affect, arguing that emotions are individualized responses with a distinct object (e.g., being afraid of flying), while affects are vague bodily feelings that precede cognitive processing. My discussion follows Leys's (2011) critique of that dichotomy: emotions and affect fall on a continuum, and should not be separated categorically.
11 See Keith Oatley's discussion in Chapter 5 of *Such Stuff as Dreams* (2011).
12 More on this interchange between biology, cognition, and culture in Caracciolo (2014b).
13 Eileen Crist (2013) offers an insightful critique of scientific discourse on the climate crisis, including the label "Anthropocene" itself. Scientific language, Crist claims, papers over the violence that has led to the current ecological predicament.

14 Fludernik's (1996) notion of "experientiality," which is central to her definition of narrativity, consists precisely in this assumption of human or human-
   like subjectivity. On plot and its basis in characters' mental states, see Ryan
   (1991).
15 The word "cosmos" may also bring to mind a monumental nineteenth-
   century treatise by German naturalist Alexander von Humboldt and a
   widely read science book by astronomer Carl Sagan (1980), later expanded
   into a television series. Both are titled *Cosmos* (or *Kosmos* in the German
   of Humboldt's original title), both achieved tremendous popularity in their
   times, and both are attempts at defining humankind's position in an over-
   arching order. On Humboldt's *Kosmos*, see the discussion in Andrea Wulf's
   The Invention of Nature (2016), particularly Chapter 18.
16 This discovery—and its implications for contemporary cosmology—are
   chronicled by Marcia Bartusiak in her compelling *The Day We Found the
   Universe* (2009).
17 In this paragraph, I give these texts' original publication dates, not the dates
   of the editions I'll be using in the book. Likewise, the order in which I list
   the case studies is chronological, and doesn't always reflect the order of their
   treatment in the chapters.
18 Karin Kukkonen (2013) offers an interesting discussion of the relevance of
   cognitive poetics to New Formalism. See also Stockwell (2009) for an excellent demonstration of this approach.

1　Strange Spaces

Our exploration begins with three narratives where space takes center stage: the dimensionless void occupied by the narrator of Italo Calvino's "All at One Point," one of the stories collected in the volume *Cosmicomics* and first published in 1965; the atomic terra incognita charted by Ray Cummings's *The Girl in the Gold Atom* (a classic science fiction story from the 1920s, belonging to the subgenre of "space romance"); and the diminutive world of the protagonist of Richard Matheson's *The Shrinking Man* (originally published in 1956). I choose these narratives as the focus of this first chapter because, already in Gibson's formulation (discussed in the introduction), spatial scale is the most straightforward illustration of cosmic realities—that is, realities that elude the intermediate world.

As Brian Stableford and David Langford (2019) write in *The Encyclopedia of Science Fiction*, one "of the commonest fantastic devices in literature and legend is the alteration of scale." Whether the protagonist encounters extraordinarily short or tall people (as in Jonathan Swift's *Gulliver's Travels* [1726]), or whether the protagonist him- or herself undergoes an alteration in size (as in Lewis Carroll's *Alice's Adventures in Wonderland* [1865]), the question of scale has fascinated writers well before the twentieth century. This fascination is partly explained by the emotional and cultural connotations of "small" or "large"—two basic concepts that tend to be bound up with value in human societies. Thus, for instance, Lakoff and Johnson (1980, 50) identify the conceptual metaphor "significant is big," which straightforwardly maps size onto importance and is at the root of many linguistic expressions. Shifts in scale are more than a matter of physical size: they are conducive to a form of *conceptual* perspective-taking whereby what we normally regard as irrelevant or insignificant rises to prominence—or, conversely, the importance of our human-scale world is quite literally downsized. In the *Divine Comedy*, for instance, Dante has a vision of the Earth from "space" (in Dante's astronomy, the sphere of the fixed stars) and compares it to an "aiuola" or "little patch of earth":

> L'aiuola che ci fa tanto feroci,
>   volgendom' io con li etterni Gemelli
>   tutta m'apparve da' colli a le foci.

> The little patch of earth that makes us here so fierce,
> from hills to rivermouths, I saw it all,
> while I was being wheeled with the eternal Twins.
>
> ("Paradise" XXII, 151–53)[1]

The metaphor shrinks the Earth to something small and trivial, and in so doing conveys a celestial perspective on human struggles. The same conceptual mechanism underlies Swift's satire of human society, or Carroll's fantasy world—even though the cultural meanings and frames of reference brought into play by these works are significantly different. In my guiding texts for this chapter, it is *science*—not Dante's theology or Swift's human nature—that inspires a shift in scale. While this interest in the infinitesimally small is a common theme in twentieth-century science fiction, I have chosen to focus on three narratives that offer vastly different, and complementary, variations on this theme. These stories by Calvino, Cummings, and Matheson take place on scales ranging from an ideal zero—the dimensionless space of Calvino's short story—to the infinitesimal but still material space of *The Girl in the Golden Atom*, ending with the macroscopic, but rapidly diminishing, world experienced by the protagonist of *The Shrinking Man*. The question of spatial scale is foregrounded through a dialog with scientific cosmologies, or an imaginative version thereof: the theory of the Big Bang (in Calvino) and the physics of the extremely small (in Cummings and Matheson).

Scale has been discussed extensively in recent debates on literature's engagement with the Anthropocene: climate change brings into view significant discontinuities between everyday experience and planetary phenomena such as global warming (Woods 2014; T. Clark 2015). These discontinuities are perhaps best illustrated by our lack of phenomenological *awareness* of how our choices contribute to climate change, which highlights a gap between embodied actions (such as regularly driving a car to work) and conceptual knowledge of those actions' environmental impact. The intermediate world and the Earth system function on scales that are not only profoundly different but also, in significant ways, incommensurable. The goal of my discussion is to show how literary narrative may bridge this gap by projecting our experience of physical environments onto scalar levels that *resist* human phenomenology, because it is this kind of cognitive leap that is required to understand the multiscalar complexity of the climate crisis. Indeed, Calvino, Cummings, and Matheson challenge readers' familiarity with the intermediate world even as they appeal to bodily patterns typical of this world. Their challenges are not equally radical, as we will see, but a degree of bodily defamiliarization is present in each text. In this way, this chapter begins illustrating and deploying in close readings the categories proposed in the introduction; it thus constitutes a conceptual laboratory for the book as a whole, and will float a number of ideas that are to be developed and systematized in the following chapters.

In the Beginning

In the beginning was a feeling of being packed like sardines—or this, at least, is the simile that captures the situation before the Big Bang in one of Calvino's *Cosmicomics*, "All at One Point":

> Naturally, we were all there—*old Qfwfq said*—where else could we have been? Nobody knew then that there could be space. Or time either: what use did we have for time, packed in there like sardines?
>
> I say "packed like sardines," using a literary image: in reality there wasn't even space to pack us into. Every point of each of us coincided with every point of each of the others in a single point, which was where we all were. In fact, we didn't even bother one another, except for personality differences, because when space doesn't exist, having somebody unpleasant like Mr Pber^t Pber^d underfoot all the time is the most irritating thing.
>
> (2009, 62; emphasis in the original)

This passage illustrates many of the conceptual tensions underlying Calvino's "cosmic" narratives. *Pace* the narrator, the simile "packed like sardines" is emphatically *not* a "literary image." It—and its equivalent in the Italian original, "pigiati come acciughe" (1984, 157)—are extremely common, perhaps even clichéd expressions that have little to do with literary inventiveness. Yet, by displacing this phrase to a situation that is anything but mundane, this short story manages to infuse the simile with new life. This process closely resembles what linguist Guy Cook (1994) calls "schema refreshment"—namely, how certain linguistic constructs can afford new perspective on stereotypical knowledge. Note also how the narrator comments on his choice of terms, increasing the simile's salience in readers' experience of the text. It thus becomes more difficult to consider this expression as a mere linguistic device; we are invited to take the characters' feeling (and the situation evoked to convey that feeling) at face value, imagining what it must be like to be tightly packed in this way. Recent work in psycholinguistics gives us reason to think that the comprehension of similes like Calvino's may foster a specifically embodied mode of reading.

In an intriguing experiment on embodied responses to metaphorical language, psychologist Raymond Gibbs (2013) asked two groups of blindfolded participants to walk toward a marker in front of them. The 128 participants had previously seen the marker, and they had to mentally estimate their distance from it. Before starting to walk, one group heard a short narrative of around 70 words containing an embodied metaphor for a romantic relationship: "Your relationship was moving along in a good direction" (2013, 364). "Moving along" is an embodied metaphor because it maps a relatively abstract state of affairs (two people being romantically involved for a certain time) onto a much more concrete scenario of physical movement along a path. The second group heard exactly the same narrative, with the words above replaced by the nonmetaphorical statement "your relationship was very important to you" (2013, 366). Each group was divided into two subgroups: one heard a story with a positive ending (with the relationship continuing to move "along in a good direction"), while the other heard the story with a negative ending (with the relationship eventually failing).

The results were complex but showed a significant interaction between the ending of the story and the time and distance walked by the participants: if the story included an embodied metaphor and had a positive ending, the participants reliably walked for a longer time and distance than when they listened to a story that did *not* include the metaphorical statement (despite having a positive ending). By contrast, if the story had a *negative* ending, the participants walked consistently for a shorter distance if they heard the metaphorical statement than if they didn't. This interaction suggests, according to Gibbs, that participants tended to mentally re-enact the metaphor, drawing on the same neural resources that are involved in actual walking. This phenomenon is known as "embodied simulation" (Gallese 2005) or, more specifically, as "motor resonance" (Zwaan and Taylor 2006). Put simply, the idea is that re-enacting the metaphor prompted participants to walk in ways congruent with the story's ending: the simulation, Gibbs suggests, led them to walk for a longer distance if the relationship also continued moving (metaphorically), whereas if the relationship came to a halt, participants tended to cover a shorter distance. The study shows—along with many other convergent studies in psycholinguistics (see Introduction)—that linguistic comprehension, and particularly the comprehension of metaphorical language, relies on schemata drawn from the domain of embodied experience.

Could this apply to Calvino's "packed like sardines" as well? Linguistically, this is a simile and not a metaphor—as we've seen—but the underlying conceptual mechanism is fundamentally the same: the simile maps an abstract, and almost unimaginable, state of affairs (how there was no space and time prior to the Big Bang) onto a household object (the sardine can) that evokes a sense of firmness and compactness.[2] The difference is that the simile, as an *explicit* comparison (introduced by words such as "like"), is even more likely to call readers' attention to its own embodied qualities—an effect doubled by the narrator's self-conscious comment about the "literary image" he or she is using.[3] This strategy has an interesting consequence. In Gibbs's study, embodied simulation in response to the "moving along in a good direction" metaphor remained unconscious—a fleeting pattern of brain activation that had behavioral effects (people walking for a longer or shorter distance) but probably did not emerge in the participants' consciousness. By contrast, in Calvino's short story the simile may well give rise to a consciously embodied experience as a result of schema refreshment. Esrock (2004) has already offered a perceptive account of sensorimotor patterns and readers' involvement in another story collected in Calvino's *Cosmicomics*, "The Form of Space." What my analysis of "All at One Point" adds to Esrock's discussion is an appreciation of how embodied responses to Calvino's language push readers out of their anthropocentric comfort zone: they get a sense of what it is like to be "packed in there like sardines" through paradoxical identification with a nonhuman object.

Seemingly, we are in the vicinity of what Ian Bogost (2012) calls "alien phenomenology." Bogost's work is part of a larger movement known as object-oriented ontology, which is part of the nonhuman turn discussed in the introduction. Bogost's 2012 book explores the provocative thesis that things—like a can of sardines—should be given serious attention in philosophy, because there is a sense in which we can think "with" objects and even take their perspective on the world. Bogost's phenomenology is not just alien because it deals with things but alienating because it challenges an ontological landscape—our own—based on the dichotomy between (human) subjects and (nonhuman) objects—with the latter being seen as inert and passive. Calvino's image of the can of sardines in this primordial situation works along lines similar to Bogost's alien phenomenology: it invites readers to empathize with a thing, which is used as an equivalent for a certain feeling of being "all at one point" in time and space. Several commentators have toyed with this posthumanist reading of Calvino. Serenella Iovino, for one, writes that in the *Cosmicomics*

> Calvino expresses at the same time the contingency of the human as a cosmic agent and the vast, a-subjective and an-individual [sic, "a-individuale" in the Italian original] narrativity of things considered in their evolutionary becoming, from atoms to planetary forces.
>
> (2014, 131; my translation)

Iovino further acknowledges that this strategy is fundamentally anthropomorphizing. In Calvino's stories, cosmic phenomena are given recognizably human faces and voices: they gossip and bicker like nosy neighbors; they have personalities and all-too-human flaws.

The strangeness of Calvino's operation cannot go unnoticed: in order to decenter the human and open up imaginative perspectives on the "alien" world of matter, his narratives inject a human element into nonhuman realities. Isn't this a counterintuitive move? Why should the *flight* from anthropocentrism be accompanied by the projection of human traits and features onto nonhuman entities? Jane Bennett argues as follows: "We need to cultivate a bit of anthropomorphism—the idea that human agency has some echoes in nonhuman nature—to counter the narcissism of humans in charge of the world" (2010, xvi). Anthropomorphization comes so naturally to us because we are limited beings, and imagining what is beyond us necessarily involves building on familiar frames of reference. When coupled with cosmic phenomena, the human can function along the lines of a contrast agent in medical imaging, with reversed roles: in order to reveal certain areas of the (human) body in X-ray photography, we need to ingest or inject chemicals such as iodine or barium. Conversely, to approximate nonhuman phenomena in our imagination, we need to infuse them with human qualities. This is what Calvino does in the *Cosmicomics*. But the medical analogy is not coincidental—for the human body itself is key in this process. Indeed, anthropomorphization is more than a generic appeal to readers' familiarity with cultural practices and expectations regarding human societies: it employs patterns arising from somatic experience, and at least potentially it employs readers' bodily experience itself.

The simile "packed like sardines" fulfills precisely this function: this enigmatic point in time/space before the Big Bang is conceptualized by way of a sardine can. However, the so-called "ground" of the simile (the actual similarity involved) is a *feeling* that we can only imagine through prior experiences of having our bodies pushed against other bodies, or objects, in a confined space. This feeling builds on a cognitive mechanism, as we've seen, known as embodied simulation. Thus, anthropomorphization in Calvino's *Cosmicomics* is not just a projection of conceptual features; it consists in a projection of bodily schemata and feelings that put us in touch with cosmic realities, resulting in a form of cosmic perspective-taking. ("In touch" is, of course, *another* relatively conventionalized embodied metaphor.) Because these realities are incompatible with human embodiment (how can bodies exist without time and space?), the embodied ground of the simile is completely incongruous—an incongruity from which Calvino's stories derive their distinctive irony.

This incongruity underlies the whole story, which offers a series of variations on the same, paradoxical, motif: bodies and objects existing in the absence of time and space. First, some character-like entities are singled out (typically with unpronounceable names), but their exact number remains indeterminate due to the spatial compression:

> How many of us were there? Oh, I was never able to figure that out, not even approximately. To make a count, we would have had to move apart, at least a little, and instead we all occupied that same point.
>
> (2009, 62)

Imagining this kind of embodied cohabitation is already tricky, insofar as the idea of spatial extension is inextricable from the notion of "body." Thus, Calvino's story appeals to our embodiment (through the initial simile and the feelings it may evoke) even as it undermines the very

possibility of embodiment. This effect is typical of bodily defamiliarization: patterns of somatic experience are drawn upon *and* challenged
in the same breath. But the text soon raises the ante as we realize that
this dimensionless point contains not only an indefinite number of anthropomorphic characters but also the building blocks of what will later
become *the entire universe*:

> You have to add all the stuff we had to keep piled up in there: all
> the material that was to serve afterwards to form the universe, now
> dismantled and concentrated in such a way that you weren't able
> to tell what was later to become part of astronomy (like the nebula
> of Andromeda) from what was assigned to geography (the Vosges,
> for example) or to chemistry (like certain beryllium isotopes). And
> on top of that, we were always bumping against the Z'zu family's
> household goods: camp beds, mattresses, baskets.
>
> (2009, 62–63)

The "stuff" of the universe is here shown in its raw, undifferentiated
form, before human knowledge forces it into neat conceptual and disci-
plinary pigeonholes (astronomy, geography, chemistry)—even before the
basic distinction between natural and human-made realities comes into
effect. This situation is deeply perplexing, but the simile of the packed
sardines, with its intense yet displaced familiarity, does manage to make
it more imaginable. How exactly does this happen? First, through the initial involvement of bodily feelings of compactness and tightness, which
elicit empathy for a nonhuman object. Second, through the suggestion of
an *alternative* conceptual scenario: the coexistence of the universe "all
at one point" is mapped onto the human togetherness of a small family
or group, with all that it implies (petty disputes, jealousies, sexual attraction, etc.). For instance, Calvino uses the physical impossibility—or
at least unimaginability—of this place to voice a mind-bending sexual
fantasy:

> the happiness I derived from [Mrs. $Ph(i)Nk_0$] was the joy of being
> concealed, punctiform, in her, and of protecting her, punctiform,
> in me; it was at the same time vicious contemplation (thanks to the
> promiscuity of the punctiform convergence of us all in her) and also
> chastity (given her punctiform impenetrability). In short: what more
> could I ask?
>
> (2009, 65)

We'll see many more instances of this blending of cosmic phenomena
and sexuality in Chapter 3.

At one level, the simile of the packed sardines and these sexual con-
tortions point in opposite directions: the former is object-oriented, the

latter is organic. But at another level they converge on a sense of every-day intimacy: just as the expression "packed like sardines" is a perfectly common one, the narrator's sexual desire is a familiar way of wanting to be close to, and perhaps even one with, another body. These models of togetherness—the object-oriented and the intersubjective—go hand in hand in modulating our imagination of this primordial situation. The interpersonal relations among the characters extend the embodied feelings hinted at by the initial simile—while anchoring them further to Gibson's intermediate world at the level of readers' imagination. The narrator's informal tone ties in with this sense of human-scale familiarity even as we are invited to mentally entertain a reality that challenges all our assumptions regarding time and space.

With these considerations in mind we can turn to the conclusion of the short story. Just as Lucretius's *De rerum natura* opens with an invocation of Venus—the goddess of love and fertility, and the driving force for all life forms on Earth—Calvino's story ends with an explosion of gendered love. But here, of course, the ending is also a beginning, for it ushers in the Big Bang—and with it time and space as we know them. This long passage is worth quoting in full:

> It was enough for [Mrs. Ph(i)Nk$_o$] to say, at a certain moment: "Oh, if I only had some room, how I'd like to make some tagliatelle for you boys!" And in that moment we all thought of the space that her round arms would occupy, moving backwards and forwards with the rolling pin over the dough, her bosom leaning over the great mound of flour and eggs which cluttered the wide board while her arms kneaded and kneaded, white and shiny with oil up to the elbows; we thought of the space that the flour would occupy, and the wheat for the flour, and the fields to raise the wheat, and the mountains from which the water would flow to irrigate the fields, and the grazing lands for the herds of calves that would give their meat for the sauce; of the space it would take for the Sun to arrive with its rays, to ripen the wheat; of the space for the Sun to condense from the clouds of stellar gases and burn; of the quantities of stars and galaxies and galactic masses in flight through space which would be needed to hold suspended every galaxy, every nebula, every sun, every planet, and at the same time we thought of it, this space was inevitably being formed, at the same time that Mrs Ph(i)Nk$_o$ was uttering those words: "...ah, what tagliatelle, boys!" the point that contained her and all of us was expanding in a halo of distance in light-years and light-centuries and billions of light-millennia, and we were being hurled to the four corners of the universe (Mr Pber^t Pber^d all the way to Pavia), and she, dissolved into I don't know what kind of energy-light-heat, she, Mrs Ph(i)Nk$_o$, she who in the midst of our closed, petty world had been capable of a generous impulse,

"Boys, the tagliatelle I would make for you!", a true outburst of general love, initiating at the same moment the concept of space and, properly speaking, space itself, and time, and universal gravitation, and the gravitating universe, making possible billions and billions of suns, and of planets, and fields of wheat.

(2009, 65–66)

Curiously, and ironically, it is Mrs. Ph(i)Nk$_0$'s sudden desire to make tagliatelle that causes the Big Bang. As mentioned in the introduction, the discovery that the universe is expanding, and hence that it must have originated at a specific time, created quite a few headaches in the second half of the twentieth century, bringing in questions such as: What was before the Big Bang? What caused it? And, of course, why is there a universe rather than nothing (Holt 2013, 27)? These metaphysical anxieties were less salient for scientists who—like most until the 1930s—believed the universe to be stable and immutable (whether it had been created by God or just happened to exist). Calvino's playful answer to these questions puts the mental processes of his characters before everything else: the universe as we know it was created by the characters' imagining what it would take to realize Mrs. Ph(i)Nk$_0$'s "generous impulse."

This thinking process unfolds in an exceptionally long sentence, which starts with the words "And in that moment" and continues until the end of the passage (and the short story). This sentence has a telescopic quality, zooming out from the detailed description of Mrs. Ph(i)-Nk$_0$ making tagliatelle to the final vision of "billions and billions of suns, and of planets." The logic of this list is strictly causal, insofar as every object requires the next one in the sequence for its existence or possibility. Yet, despite the cosmic scope and significance of Mrs. Ph(i)-Nk$_0$'s gesture, the point of departure is again the human body, not only because tagliatelle (like sardines) are nourishment for the body but also because our attention is drawn to Mrs. Ph(i)Nk$_0$'s "round arms" and "bosom," and to her skillful kneading of the dough. Like the simile at the beginning of the short story, these expressions—and especially the motion verbs "moving backwards and forwards with the rolling pin"—will trigger an embodied simulation in readers: they will activate brain areas related to motion (Pulvermüller 2005), and they may evoke the relevant sensations in readers' imagination. In turn, this sense of heightened embodiment may extend to readers' understanding of the whole sentence: after all, the narrator's list derives its vividness from a syncopated rhythm (notice the play of commas and semicolons) that can easily be seen in terms of periodic "movements" from one scene or object to another. Put otherwise, Mrs. Ph(i)Nk$_0$'s bodily actions set the pace for the following description, as if her rhythmic kneading of the dough tinged the syntax (along with the meaning) of the narrator's sentence. From implicit, this motion becomes actual in the second half of the sentence, where—after the reprise of Mrs. Ph(i)Nk$_0$'s initial prompt—the narrator suddenly realizes that he and the other characters are "being hurled to the four corners of the universe."

The most striking feature of this passage is that, while the entities referred to by the narrator gradually distance us from the intermediate world, a sense of kinesthetic involvement propels us along, fusing the direct representation of embodied actions (kneading, being hurled) with the stylistic rhythm and affective contour of Calvino's prose. The enactive school of embodied cognition, I pointed out in the introduction, foregrounds patterns of sensorimotor interaction with the world: it is this kind of embodied and affective patterning that drives the reader's engagement with Calvino's language. At the same time, this long sentence crisscrosses the boundary between quotidian and cosmic realities (here exemplified by the incongruous juxtaposition of tagliatelle and the Big Bang). Like the simile "packed like sardines," the sentence conveys a sense of joyful—if ironic—togetherness, fusing household objects and bodily patterns with the history of the universe itself. The blending of human and nonhuman phenomena reflects the suggestion that the universe was somehow made necessary by the generosity of Mrs. Ph(i)Nk$_0$'s offer.[4] Calvino translates this notion into an imaginative experience readers go through with their bodies, following the somatic pathways laid out by the text in ways that prove, at the same time, recognizably human and ironically alien. Whether the alienness prevails over the anthropomorphic features rests, ultimately, on each reader's sensitivity. But the challenge Calvino raises should be clear: it has to do with imagining a space that is not really a space, because it precedes the birth of space itself. In the following sections we'll turn to two science fiction novels that represent spaces that also resist the reader's imagination. In these texts the integration of cosmic perspective-taking and bodily defamiliarization is less smooth than in Calvino's short story. Instead of the telescopic (and kinesthetically continuous) effect of Calvino's virtuoso syntax, we encounter a number of unsettling hesitations and discontinuities—a symptom of the inevitable scalar gaps involved in moving from an anthropocentric mindset to cosmic realities. There is value in embracing such experiential ruptures, particularly in times when the disconnect between the intermediate world and planetary phenomena such as climate change is becoming impossible to ignore.

Into the Atom

Ray Cummings was a prolific science fiction writer who returned to the miniaturization motif throughout his oeuvre; as Gary Wolfe writes, he "popularized the worlds-within-worlds theme that later became a staple of pulp stories (most of them, it sometimes seems, written by Cummings himself)" (2006, 528). The plot of *The Girl in the Golden Atom* borrows heavily from H. G. Wells's *The Time Machine* (1895).[5] The main difference is that the romantic subplot of Cummings's novel (the love story between the protagonist, the Chemist, and the titular girl) is absent from Well's earlier, and more famous, book. In fact, *The Girl in the Golden Atom* starts with the Chemist lecturing on how "things can be infinitely small just as well as they can be infinitely large" (Cummings 2005, 1), but the plot only takes off when—in testing this abstract idea—he examines a golden ring with the aid of a powerful microscope and discovers a beautiful girl living in it. The account of what the Chemist sees when he looks at the ring through the lens of the microscope deserves some attention, because of how it anticipates some crucial conceptual tensions that will emerge later on in the novel. The Chemist's narrative contains the first of the novel's many extended spatial descriptions, and it is prepared by a number of strategic (but somewhat formulaic) expressions of excitement and surprise—for instance, "I was about to see into another world, to behold what no man had ever looked on before" (2005, 3) and "what I saw staggered even my own imagination" (2005, 3). Yet the description that follows does have some interesting aspects:

> I seemed to be inside an immense cave. One side, near at hand, I could now make out quite clearly. The walls were extraordinarily rough and indented, with a peculiar phosphorescent light on the projections and blackness in the hollows. I say phosphorescent light, for that is the nearest word I can find to describe it—a curious radiation, quite different from the reflected light to which we are accustomed.
>
> I said that the hollows inside of the cave were blackness. But not blackness—the absence of light—as we know it. It was a blackness that seemed also to radiate light, if you can imagine such a condition; a blackness that seemed not empty, but merely withholding its contents just beyond my vision…
>
> Another curious thing was the outlines of all the shapes in view. I noticed that no outline held steady when I looked at it directly; it seemed to quiver. You see something like it when looking at an object through water—only, of course, there was no distortion. It was also like looking at something with the radiation of heat between.
>
> (2005, 4–5)

The first surprising aspect of this description is that, in David Herman's words, it constructs a "projective location" (2002, 280)—one in which the representation of space is seemingly mediated by an observer positioned *inside* this space. This is quite literally what the opening sentence suggests ("I seemed to be inside an immense cave"), and it questions assumptions about the flatness and two-dimensionality of images obtained through a microscope. Put otherwise, this strategy problematizes readers' imaginative access to this space. In an article titled "The Reader's Virtual Body" (Caracciolo 2011), I suggested that readers can take various stances in decoding spatial references in narrative: they can adopt an external perspective, they can experience the storyworld as if they were in it but still distant from the action, or they can project themselves into a character's body. In reading this descriptive passage, this imaginative stance-taking becomes particularly problematic. The Chemist states that he is inside a microscopic cave, and his highly detailed description is consistent with that sense of presence within the cave. But on the other hand we know that the Chemist is only looking through a microscope: his body occupies the intermediate world, not the allegedly "atomic" world that the microscope is disclosing.[6] The character's uncertain positioning on an internal/external axis makes it difficult for us to know where we stand as we read these lines and imagine the space they describe. This gives rise to an imaginative hesitation, of which the visual "quivering" mentioned at the end of the quotation is perhaps a textual correlative.

Note also how the description lingers on the strange lighting of the scene: both the cave's phosphorescence and its patches of blackness are unlike anything that the Chemist has ever seen in the intermediate world. This feature ties in with an idea put forward by Elaine Scarry—namely, that it is much easier to form mental images of vague substances than of solid ones. Take fog, for instance: "we might say that in fog the physical universe approaches the condition of the imagination" (Scarry 2001, 23). Likewise, these textual references to unusual patterns of light and darkness serve as stage-setting devices: they ease readers' imagination of the cave, because the vagueness of their mental imagery overlaps with the visual vagueness of the cave itself. In turn, this effect compounds the problem of knowing where we stand with respect to the imagery. This problem is inextricable from the question of embodiment: it has to do with how, even in our imagination, we can't leave our bodies behind, insofar as mental imagery is structured by the same patterns that accompany perceptual experience—a point made repeatedly by philosophers of mind working within the enactivist paradigm (Thompson 2007a; Thomas 2014) and by cognitive literary scholars building on their insights (Troscianko 2010; Caracciolo 2013a). By making it difficult for readers to determine whether they stand outside of the ring world (with the Chemist's body) or inside it (as the perspective of the description logically implies), the passage accomplishes something akin to bodily defamiliarization.

It is telling that, even after the Chemist comes to physically inhabit the space of the ring, the spatial references continue to pose a challenge. Externality is no longer an issue, of course, because the Chemist is *inside* the ring, but Cummings's text still manages to problematize the reader's imaginative access to this space. By looking at the ring through the lens of the super-microscope, the Chemist comes to realize that reality—and life itself—are "scalable" in the sense that they exist at multiple levels of analysis; he states:

> I believe that every particle of matter in our universe contains within it an equally complex and complete a [sic] universe, which to its inhabitants seems as large as ours. I think, also that the whole realm of our interplanetary space, our solar system and all the remote stars of the heavens are contained within the atom of some other universe as gigantic to us as we are to the universe in that ring.
>
> (2005, 7–8)

This passage reads almost as a profession of faith in the structural equivalence between the microcosm, the intermediate world, and astronomical realities: not only do other worlds exist beyond the reach of human perception (in the infinitesimally small or in the extremely distant), but they largely mirror our own, intermediate world. Philosophers would describe this situation as one of "infinite regress": namely, worlds contain other worlds, which in turn contain other worlds, and so on without ever reaching a bottom (or a ceiling) of indivisible reality—an infinite Chinese box universe.[7]

For Cummings, the universe of the ring is still "to scale" with ours, it is governed by the same physical laws, and therefore it can be experienced through a body more or less analogous to ours—provided, of course, that the observer has the right size:

> I saw then but one obstacle standing between me and this other world—the discrepancy of size...In my present size it is only a few feet from here to the ring on that plate. But to an inhabitant of that other world, we are as remote as the faintest stars of the heavens, diminished a thousand times.
>
> (2005, 12)

This is a powerful idea, but Cummings is no Borges (or Calvino), and his novel only rarely manages to give readers the vertigo of this realization. The main exception is the peculiar spatial hesitation created by some of the descriptions. Let us take a closer look at what happens when the Chemist enters the world of the ring.

The Chemist starts looking for a substance that can make his body smaller without altering its physiology or proportions. The conscious mind is presented as an obstacle to this transformation: "I could not act upon the cells separately, so long as they were under control of the mind" (2005, 12). In the subsequent experiments, the Chemist soon realizes that body size can be drastically reduced only by temporarily suspending consciousness, in a state similar to a coma—an idea that explains the distortions of consciousness reported by the characters whenever they take the miniaturizing pill. In his first journey into the world of the ring, for example, the Chemist loses consciousness and experiences "a horrible sensation of sliding headlong for what seemed like hours. I felt that I was sliding or falling downward. I tried to rouse but could not" (2005, 30).

I will have more to say about these sensations in a moment; for now, let us consider what the Chemist finds in the world of the ring: not only does he meet the girl seen through the microscope, but he discovers that she belongs to a whole people (the Oroids). Taking advantage of his ability to change size at will, the Chemist helps the Oroids defeat their sworn enemies, the Marites. This storyline—which unfolds in an embedded narrative, with the Chemist addressing his friends at the Club—is rather uninspiring, and becomes even more conventional in the novel's second part (originally published as a sequel, under the title *The People of the Golden Atom*; see Bleiler 1990, 172). But the interest of some of Cummings's spatial descriptions does partly make up for his flawed storytelling. At first sight, the environment in which the Chemist finds himself resembles a familiar natural landscape, with valleys and rivers and craggy mountains. Yet Cummings subtly calls into question this sense of familiarity. Halfway through the account of his first expedition, the Chemist interrupts his narrative to offer the following comment:

> Perhaps I am giving you a picture of our own world. I do not mean to do so. You must remember that above me there was no sky, just blackness. And yet so much light illuminated the scene that I could not believe it was other than what we would call daytime.
>
> (2005, 32)

While addressed to the Chemist's diegetic narratees, this statement reaches the readers as well: it is an explicit invitation to "update" their mental imagery to reflect the specificity of this world—which may look like ours, in terms of its proportions and natural elements, but is still to some extent an alien or "weird" world (as the Chemist explicitly remarks later on; see Cummings 2005, 55). The difference between the world of the ring and our world is rendered through a series of contrasts in color or lighting (remember the phosphorescent light described in the passage quoted above), which can easily "tinge" our mental imagery of the storyworld. While simple, this device is quite effective at reminding us that—despite the appearances—the universe that the Chemist is exploring is not our everyday, intermediate world.

An even more powerful effect is produced by the sequences describing the reshuffling topography of the universe within the ring as the Chemist changes in size. Under the effect of the miniaturizing drug or its antidote (which allows traveling "up" in scale), the Chemist experiences outward sensations of motion in addition to inner, vertigo-like feelings: "the ground seemed to open up before me as I advanced, changing its contour so constantly that I was never at a loss for an easy downward path" (2005, 28); "I saw the hills beyond the river and forest coming towards me, yet dwindling away beneath my feet as they approached. The incline seemed folding up upon itself, like a telescope" (2005, 64). We'll find a much more detailed exploration of the phenomenology of scale in *The Shrinking Man*, but even these passing references are sufficient to evoke in readers an experiential equivalent of the distance *in scale* traveled by the Chemist. As in our microscope view of the ring, this experience of a shifting landscape creates a peculiar tension between ease of imaginability and difficulty of fully accepting the consequences of what we are asked to imagine. We have seen that, according to Elaine Scarry, the textual representation of fluid or impalpable objects can foster mental imagery. Another scholar working from a cognitive perspective, Anežka Kuzmičová (2012), has suggested something similar for passages focusing on characters' motion: because perception is closely bound up with bodily movements (of the body, head, or eyes), representing a character's movements can encourage readers to take his or her embodied perspective on the storyworld. This produces an overlap between our mental imagery and the perceptions that we are attributing to the character— an example of the reading strategy that I have labeled "consciousness enactment" (Caracciolo 2014d, Chap. 5). In Cummings's novel, kinetic references underlie all spatial descriptions, whether it is the protagonist who is moving through the environment or the environment that seems to morph under his gaze.

The upshot of this descriptive technique is twofold. On the one hand, readers, or at least those who are willing to read Cummings's extended spatial description with undivided attention, will develop an illusion of bodily presence in the atomic world. This illusion is based on readers' familiarity with patterns of embodied interaction with the world; readers may be dimly aware of the difference in scale between the ring and our own universe, but this awareness is unlikely to matter because the former seems to mirror the latter in its physical configuration (and in the bodily movements required to engage with it). We are thus encouraged to enact the Chemist's consciousness as he negotiates his way through the space of the ring. On the other hand, the sequences describing shifts in scale or differences in color and lighting (and their respective effects on the character's perceptions) will disrupt this sense of imaginative closeness to the world of the ring: as readers, we are invited to consider multiple spatial scales at the same time, and we're thus faced with the difficulty of imagining how a forest could "fit" in the atomic structure of the ring. Put otherwise, the universe of the ring is *both* easily imaginable (when we abstract from its scale) and paradoxical (when we consider it in relation to our own world). This tension problematizes the notion of an exact structural equivalence between intermediate and atomic universes, pointing toward scalar discontinuities and thus calling for bodily defamiliarization. Even though Cummings does not deploy this strategy to the fullest, his lingering on the Chemist's altered consciousness as he changes size plants at least the suggestion that our usual bodily patterns may have to be drastically revised as we imagine worlds beyond the human scale.

Matheson's *The Shrinking Man* also harnesses bodily defamiliarization to cosmic perspective-taking, as we'll see—despite the fact that this novel focuses on a space that is, in principle, much closer to the intermediate world than Cummings's atomic realities. What enriches the picture in *The Shrinking Man* is the already mentioned association between physical size and importance (or value). In *The Girl in the Golden Atom*, the space of the ring is associated with a familiar rhetoric of scientific domestication of the unknown, where the belittling connotations of the "small" do not really count (based on the assumption that size is always a relative matter in the infinite Chinese box of reality); the Chemist himself puts this point quite clearly at the beginning of the novel: smiling, he remarks that the "existence of no individual, no nation, no world, nor any one universe is of the least importance" (2005, 8). This sweeping statement is also a missed opportunity, because—aside from the limited defamiliarization at work in the spatial descriptions—the plot falls short of dramatizing the cosmological questions raised by the Chemist's dry exposition. In *The Shrinking Man*, by distinct contrast, the protagonist's shrinking takes on emotional and ethical meanings as he realizes his increasing irrelevance to his family. In turn, this unsettling realization makes cosmological concerns more central to the narrative—and also, I will argue, to the reading experience.

Shrinking with Scott

The plot of *The Shrinking Man* can be summarized in a few sentences: the protagonist, Scott Carey, a middle-aged white-collar worker, is exposed to a cloud of radioactive insect repellent. This radioactive spray wreaks havoc on Scott's metabolism, causing his body to shrink by about 1/7 of an inch per day. Scott's personal and family life is gradually affected by this condition: alienated from his wife—who starts treating him like a boy—and increasingly incapable of dealing with the tasks of everyday life, Scott loses his job and is condemned to live in a doll house. Eventually, his own cat attacks him and forces him to take shelter in the cellar. His wife's desperate attempts to locate him prove unsuccessful, because his stature and feeble voice make him virtually invisible to normal human beings. Presumed dead, Scott is left on his own, struggling to find food and water while battling against a (to him) giant spider that also lives in the cellar.

While the film adaptation—Jack Arnold's *The Incredible Shrinking Man*—follows this summary in a linear fashion, Matheson's novel features a more sophisticated narrative structure, with two interlaced temporal planes. Most of the chapters relate—in a third-person narrative with internal focalization—Scott's experiences in the cellar. Only occasional flashbacks reveal how he ended up there: readers thus have to piece together the plot from these retrospective sections, which can take up a few paragraphs or an entire chapter. In most cases, these temporal shifts are diegetically motivated—that is, they are triggered by Scott himself as he reminisces about his past life. For instance, about halfway through the novel Scott has just missed a rare opportunity to escape from the cellar. Famished and dejected, he reflects that it "was the lowest point, the nadir of his existence in the cellar. It made him think of another lowest point, in the other life he had once led" (Matheson 2012, 662). The section that follows is a flashback to an earlier scene, in which Scott, sickened by the turn his family life has taken, decides to venture outside of his house—only to be violently beaten by a band of youngsters.

The effect of these temporal shifts is that the reader's understanding of the story is firmly grounded in the character's perspective: the flashbacks trace the way in which, on the brink of complete obliteration, Scott looks back on his past life and miseries. Further, the flashbacks serve to slow down the narrative's progression, heightening readers' interest in its final outcome: because Scott is convinced that he will die as soon as his height reaches zero inches, the plot is oriented toward this future endpoint, with the flashbacks going against the grain of this teleological orientation. However, Scott is wrong: the morning after the day of his supposed death he wakes up, even shorter but miraculously alive. He thus realizes that "to nature there was no zero. Existence went on in endless cycles. It seemed so simple now. He would never disappear, because there was no point of non-existence in the universe" (2012, 774). With this realization, the cosmological undercurrent of the novel rises to the surface of the protagonist's thoughts. The novel also comes full circle, because the cosmic force that had caused Scott's condition (the radiation to which he is exposed in the first chapter) is finally acknowledged as such by the character. We'll see that this acknowledgment leads to an insight into the nature of reality similar to the Chemist's Chinese box theory in *The Girl in the Golden Atom*. Here, however, the cosmic insight has a completely different flavor, because it is not an abstract principle but something that Scott—and at least potentially the reader—have *experienced* through Scott's daily struggles with a shrinking body. In order to fully understand that cosmic vision we will thus have to take a closer look at how the novel dramatizes Scott's experiences.

That dramatization takes two distinct but ultimately converging paths, both of which result in a sense of the character's inadequacy when faced with the intermediate world. The first path is more external: it shows how Scott's environment changes as a consequence of his shrinking size. This strategy is similar to the morphing landscape of *The Girl in the Golden Atom*, but it is adopted much more systematically—and to a more interesting effect. I've already introduced James J. Gibson as one of the forerunners of the embodied cognition movement. Matheson's spatial descriptions throw into sharp relief the psychological phenomenon that Gibson studies under the heading of "affordance." Here is the definition of affordance, as found in Gibson's seminal *The Ecological Approach to Visual Perception*:

> The *affordances* of the environment are what it offers the animal, what it *provides* or *furnishes*, either for good or ill. The verb to *afford* is found in the dictionary, but the noun *affordance* is not. I have made it up. I mean by it something that refers to both the environment and the animal in a way that no existing term does. It implies the complementarity of the animal and the environment.
>
> (1986, 127; emphasis in the original)

In Gibson's example, an area of flat and solid terrain is an affordance for a land animal, because it "affords support." A swamp, by contrast, affords support to a water bug but not to a heavy land animal. This simple observation suggests that affordances are not just a matter of physical properties; rather, affordances are possibilities of interaction with the environment that reflect *both* the physical properties of space and the organism's size, weight, and bodily makeup.

This is precisely what Matheson's novel reveals by focusing on how Scott's world changes in tandem with his body. To some, the long descriptions of Scott's actions in the chapters set in the cellar may prove exasperating. Undoubtedly, at times these pages read like a humorless account of a gameplay session in a "platform" videogame, with Scott constantly moving around the environment and interacting with small objects in an effort to secure food and water.[8] But the protracted focus on the protagonist's physical actions serves a clear purpose: it offers readers the chance to develop a sort of "double vision," where the same scene is imagined *both* from the viewpoint of our intermediate world and from Scott's perspective—with each of them involving a specific set of affordances. Consider, for example, the following spatial description:

> He ran to the [log] pile. It rose above him like a hill of boulders and giant logs, some as high as houses. Could he hope to drag some of them to the base of the step, at least enough to prop the straw on and make up five of those eight to ten feet? The rest of the footage he could chance with an upward spring, as he had done in climbing to the tabletop. But you almost fell from the tabletop, he reminded himself. If it hadn't been for that paint-can handle...He ignored

the recollection. This was beyond argument. Every action since his plunge into the cellar had been dedicated to the hope of getting up those steps. In the beginning, he'd been up and down them a hundred times, always stopped by the closed door. When he thought of how easily he'd been able to mount the steps then, it made him sick. It was cruel that now, when the door was finally opened, the steps should no longer be walls to him, but cliffs.

(2012, 653–54)

Superficially, this passage bears a resemblance to Cummings's description of the ring world in *The Girl in the Golden Atom*. However, in that novel, the forests and mountains explored by the Chemist are described so factually that we tend to forget that they exist on an object as small as a ring (the only exception being the morphing landscape as the Chemist gains or loses height). Here, by contrast, three factors ensure that readers never lose track of the "real" nature of this environment (i.e., its dimensions as they would appear to an average human being within the intermediate world). First, the household entities described, such as the tabletop, paint-can handle, or steps, are so familiar that it would be difficult to ignore their normal affordances—for instance, how we could easily place an object on the tabletop or walk up the steps. Second, Matheson's skillful use of metaphors and similes constantly juxtaposes the intermediate world with Scott's diminutive perspective on that environment. Already in the second quoted sentence, the log pile has become "a hill of boulders and giant logs"; later on the steps are compared to "cliffs." Figurative language of this kind is pervasive in the novel, forging connections (but at the same time underscoring the divide) between Scott's reality and objects that appear large and insurmountable to normal human beings. Third, the character's recollections explicitly contrast the affordances of his current environment with those of the intermediate world he knew before he started shrinking. In a later passage, Scott finds some water inside a water hose; as he drinks,

there crossed his mind a brief vision of himself holding a hose much like this one, carrying it outside, connecting it to the faucet, playing a glittering stream of water across the lawn. Now, in a similar hose, he crouched, less than one fifth of its width, a mote man sipping dribblets of water from a hand no bigger than a grain of salt.

(2012, 709)

The final simile helps the reader imagine the size of Scott's body, and thus the very different affordances of the hose compared to his life before the shrinking started.

These strategies accomplish systematically what the descriptions of the shifting landscape accomplish occasionally in *The Girl in the*

Golden Atom: they present readers with an experiential equivalent of the scalar discontinuity between Scott's reality and our everyday reality. This process is complicated by the fact that, as in Cummings's novel, the close attention devoted to the character's physical actions—along with the internal focalization—encourage readers to approximate Scott's perspective in their mental imagery. At the same time, however, Matheson's style and the character's own awareness of his previous affordances disrupt this perspective-taking. In imagining the space of the cellar, we hover between taking on the character's miniature body and distancing ourselves from it on the basis of our everyday reality (which is also the reality Scott was used to before the shrinking started). This double vision is a form of bodily defamiliarization: the affordances that accompany our normal interactions with the world are *both* implicated by the text and relentlessly called into question by Scott's experience. The net result is that we draw closer to Scott's predicament, and we are given the chance to experience his distress and desperation vicariously through an empathetic mechanism.[9] Differences in scale are therefore problematized far more systematically than in the Chemist's dry exposition, because they coalesce into an *experience* readers may go through imaginatively.

Empathy for Scott is made easier—and more likely—by the sheer abundance of information about the character's emotional and somatic states. This is the second path taken by Matheson to involve readers in Scott's lot—and interestingly, just like the first path, it capitalizes on figurative language. Matheson's style is rich in what I have called elsewhere "phenomenological metaphors" (see Caracciolo 2013d)—metaphors and similes that attempt to convey the exact qualities of Scott's emotional states by way of comparisons with other experiences or states of affairs. This, for instance, is the moment when Scott first realizes that his shrinking could go on forever:

> He didn't know at what precise second the question came to him. But suddenly it was terribly there and he was staring fixedly at his upheld, spread-fingered hands, his heart throbbing and swollen in an icy trap.
> How long could he go on shrinking?
>
> (2012, 596)

The metaphorical description of the "heart…swollen in an icy trap" is not a particularly original or sophisticated way of describing this feeling, but it gets the job done. In other cases, the metaphors and similes point to a far more interesting analogy between bodily feelings and nonhuman objects. This comparison goes in the same direction as the alien phenomenology of Calvino's "packed like sardines." Here are a few examples: "There was a painful tension through his back and groin that loosened very slowly, as if the muscles had been twisted *like wrung-out cloths*"

(2012, 656–57; emphasis mine here and in the following quotations); "his hands uncurled *like flowers dying*" (2012, 659); his "tongue stirred *like a piece of thick dry cloth* in his mouth" (2012, 676); "him, his feet and legs were running into the floor *like candle wax*" (2012, 689). The italicized similes are effective at conveying Scott's phenomenology because they underscore the "alienness" of his diminutive body—an alienness that is, first of all, subjectively perceived by the character himself. Matheson's language repeatedly blurs the boundary between what is internal to the body and what is external to it, subjectivity and nonhuman objects, so as to convey Scott's unsettling experience to the reader.

Note how the objects that serve as a vehicle for the similes are household items of little value: cloths, wilted flowers, candle wax. The objectification of the protagonist's body clearly suggests how his shrinking correlates with a diminution in value: Scott is implicitly compared with worthless things that—like him—could be easily forgotten in a cellar. Again, this comparison should be interpreted psychologically, since it conveys the humiliation experienced by Scott. His bodily size does not just affect his physical affordances, but also his intersubjective relations with others (particularly his wife and daughter). Inadvertently, Scott's wife starts addressing him as she would address a boy. In a passage that is particularly uncomfortable to read, Scott's sexual advances are received with the attitude of an embarrassed but compliant mother. What is even more intriguing, the novel strongly implies that Scott's social relations change not just as a result of others' perception of his stature, but also because of internal psychological shifts. For example, in the following passage the infantilizing attitude of Scott's wife creeps into the character's own mental processes:

> He began to cry. It was not a man's crying, not a man's despairing sobs. It was a little boy sitting there in the cold, wet darkness, hurt and frightened and crying because there was no hope for him in the world; he was beaten and lost in a strange, unloving place.
>
> (2012, 675)

Should this be read as a narratorial, and possibly ironic, judgment of the character? I doubt it, because the narrator is fairly unobtrusive in this internally focalized novel. Rather, it is Scott himself who feels like "a little boy sitting there in the cold," his shrinking having undermined his adult self-confidence.

Thanks to its careful spatial descriptions and psychological characterization, Matheson's novel explores how the protagonist's shrinking is also a descent into irrelevance (from the perspective of the outside world) and desperation (for the character himself). The narrative structure, with its systematic juxtaposition of Scott's struggle for survival in the cellar and past humiliations, fuels readers' interest in the character's existential predicament. The novel thus renders the problems raised by physical size and spatial scale in strongly experiential terms—through the disjointed "double vision" of readers' mental imagery and through a sense of empathetic closeness to Scott's emotions.

The cosmic ending of the novel should be read in light of readers' involvement in Scott's life trajectory. In the penultimate chapter, Scott finally finds a way to escape from the cellar. This freedom—along with his victory over the spider a few pages earlier—rekindles the character's sense of heroic manliness. Scott can thus spend outside the cellar what he believes to be his last night on Earth (remember that he is expecting to die as soon as his height reaches zero inches):

> He bellowed at the universe. "I've fought a good fight!" And under his breath he added, "God damn it to hell." It made him laugh. His laughter was the faintest icy sprinkling of sound against the vast, dark earth. It felt good to laugh, and good to sleep, under the stars.
>
> (2012, 773)

Here, uncharacteristically, the metaphor ("the faintest icy sprinkling of sound") does *not* underscore the protagonist's littleness but rather the boldness of his laughter and well-being *in face of* this littleness. When he wakes up the following morning and discovers that he is still alive, the stars seen during the night seem to linger in his thoughts:

> The idea came. Last night he'd looked up at the universe without. Then there must be a universe within, too. Maybe universes.
>
> He stood again. Why had he never thought of it; of the microscopic and the submicroscopic worlds? That they existed he had always known. Yet never had he made the obvious connection. He'd always thought in terms of man's own world and man's own limited dimensions. He had presumed upon nature. For the inch was man's concept, not nature's. To a man, zero inches meant nothing. Zero meant nothing.
>
> But to nature there was no zero. Existence went on in endless cycles. It seemed so simple now. He would never disappear, because there was no point of non-existence in the universe.
>
> It frightened him at first. The idea of going on endlessly through one level of dimension after another was alien.
>
> Then he thought: If nature existed on endless levels, so also might intelligence.
>
> (2012, 774)

This realization is, no doubt, a form of cosmic perspective-taking. It links up with the beginning of the novel, as we've seen—for the radioactive cloud that had caused Scott's shrinking is a manifestation of the "microscopic and the submicroscopic worlds" that he discovers here. This link is even clearer in the film adaptation of the novel, where Scott's voiceover narrative asks: "If there were other bursts of radiation, other clouds drifting across other seas and continents, would other beings follow me into this brave new world?" (see Rosenheim 1995, 19). The rhetoric, in both the film and the novel (though perhaps more pointedly in the former), is a familiar one, of exploration and domestication of the unknown. The radiation is now perceived not as the cause of Scott's misfortunes but as a cosmic force disclosing a realm of possibilities—also in the sense of physical affordances—that were previously unheard-of, and may even put Scott in touch with other life forms. In this sense, the plot of *The Shrinking Man* does seem to converge with Cummings's novel and the Chinese box cosmology it outlines. But what was, for the Chemist, a merely theoretical point of departure is for Scott the end of a process, and a hard-won realization. Ultimately, Scott can take a step back from the intermediate world ("He'd always thought in terms of man's own world") and see how the environment offers different—but no less exhilarating—affordances to a being of his size ("the inch was man's concept, not nature's"). This cosmic "conversion" redeems the pains and miseries that readers have witnessed—and may have experienced vicariously—while following the character's life narrative. Unlike Calvino's radical inventiveness in "All at One Point," the redemption narrative of *The Shrinking Man* is still fairly conventional. But by reinterpreting—or giving us the chance to reinterpret—the protagonist's desperate struggle for survival, this ending does successfully bring together his experiences of altered embodiment with a specific conception of the universe. Through its form and focus on the character's phenomenology, the novel suggests that cosmic insight can be found even in the infinitesimally small—where the "small" is defined in terms both of spatial scale (Scott's diminutive size and its affordances) and psychological detail (the fine-grained texture of Scott's experiences as portrayed by the novel).

***

When we think about the cosmos, our imagination is typically drawn to very large things—planets, galaxies, and the sheer grandeur of the universe that surrounds us. We will come to these large-scale realities at the end of this book. This chapter has taken a different tack, focusing on the very small and showing how even tiny realities can raise cosmological questions and evoke anxieties about humankind's position in the universe. In fact, as discussed in the introduction, the cosmos is best conceptualized not as a specific level of reality (be it infinitely large or infinitesimally small) but as the set of laws and relations existing *across* levels of reality.

The three narratives I have analyzed in this chapter use space, and more specifically spatial *scale*, to probe this cosmic principle. Space has long been a neglected area of research in narrative theory, but it has attracted increasing interest in recent years (Herman 2002, Chap. 7; Caracciolo 2013c; Gomel 2014; Ryan, Foote, and Azaryahu 2016), partly following the rise of cognitive approaches to narrative. Stories, it has been argued, can evoke a sense of spatial "presence" in readers' minds; mental imagery—the spontaneous emergence of quasi-perceptual sensations—plays a significant role in fleshing out the spatiality of stories. Recent work that explores narrative's engagement with the nonhuman— econarratology, in Erin James's (2015) terminology—has consistently pointed to the spatial imagination as a privileged site for that encounter. Alexa Weik von Mossner's *Affective Ecologies* (2017), in particular, argues for the centrality of an embodied, affective sense of space in understanding and experiencing the effects of environmental narrative.

Work in this vein has tended to foreground embodied *immersion* as a primary response to the narrative figuration of nonhuman spaces. My discussion shows that spatial immersion is often the result of a defamiliarizing process, whereby narrative taps into our everyday, embodied strategies for apprehending the world—but also asks us to revise such strategies in significant ways. In order to really "reshape individual and collective environmental imaginations," to quote from James's *The Storyworld Accord* (2015, 39), narrative has to produce immersion by *challenging* established ways of thinking about the human body in relation to the nonhuman environment. This is why bodily defamiliarization, as I theorize it in this book, should be a key concern of econarratology. As I argued in the introduction, our bodies are the result of our species' evolutionary history, which in turn reflects the features and constraints of the terrestrial environmental in which we evolved. We are beings geared toward intermediate-level realities, but we only have a tenuous perceptual grip on realities that exist below or above this intermediate world. Even technology—with its promise of augmenting perception and extending cognition—cannot completely eliminate this divide. Nonhuman realities may be accessible through scientific models and technological tools, but phenomenologically, they are still at a remove from the embodied dynamics of our everyday perception and social interaction. In many cases, they even raise a challenge to our embodied being: consider the difficulty of long-term survival in environments even marginally different from Earth or how the invisible world of bacteria and viruses poses a constant threat to our health.

These considerations explain why the narrative representation of spaces beyond the intermediate world can activate two conflicting frames: on the one hand, it draws on readers' familiarity with space and the bodily schemata that enable its apprehension; on the other hand, it confronts readers with realities that potentially resist or reject normal patterns of human embodiment. The dimensionless (Calvino), atomic (Cummings), or microscopic (Matheson) spaces examined in this chapter are a case in point. All these spaces are inspired by scientific hypotheses (about the Big Bang, atomic physics, the effects of radioactivity, and so on); yet they are imaginable only to the extent that their representation builds on our everyday experience. This underlying tension puts pressure on readers' embodiment, leading to forms of bodily defamiliarization: the human can be compared to the nonhuman (in Matheson's "objectifying" phenomenological descriptions) or the nonhuman to the human (Calvino's anthropomorphic characters), or spaces can be described in ways that directly face us with discontinuities in scale (in Cummings's morphing landscape and Matheson's "double vision").

As I pointed out in my analysis, these narratives are not equally effective at defamiliarizing readers' embodiment. Extending the enactivist notion of structural coupling between an organism and its environment (see Introduction), we may think of this conceptual dynamic as a "coupling" between cosmic perspective-taking and bodily defamiliarization. The coupling may be more or less loose—depending on the degree to which cosmological questions are tied to the surprising or challenging use of bodily experiences. It is quite loose in Cummings's novel, where the world of the ring is presented as a mirror of our own intermediate world and apprehendable through similar perceptual patterns. There are some exceptions, as we've seen, in the form of scalar gaps and ruptures, but they remain peripheral to Cummings's narrative. *The Girl in the Golden Atom* thematizes cosmological questions through the Chemist's exposition, but it mostly stops short of turning these questions into an experience that readers may go through imaginatively. Bodily defamiliarization has a more central role in Matheson's *The Shrinking Man*, where we are asked to follow the protagonist's psychological trajectory as he comes to distance himself from the affordances of the intermediate world. Both mental imagery and emotional empathy contribute to readers' involvement in the character's predicament—and to their sharing his cosmic "conversion" in the last chapter. Finally, bodily defamiliarization and cosmic perspective-taking are strongly coupled in Calvino's ironic narrative, which anthropomorphizes nonhuman entities and encourages readers to identify with them in order to offer a playful explanation for the birth of the universe. These differences in coupling show that, while a certain degree of tension between embodiment and nonhuman realities is present in all narratives dealing with the cosmos, it can be exploited to various degrees, depending on the storyteller's stylistic and narrative choices (and also, to some extent, on readers' interpretive interests and predispositions). Such literary engagements with spatial scale have particular relevance today, as climate change confronts us with the phenomenological gap between everyday actions and their planetary repercussions. Bodily defamiliarization helps reduce this gap by bending and augmenting the reader's body through metaphorical language and syntax (in Calvino's short story), or by highlighting profound ruptures in the audience's imaginative experience (as is the case in Cummings's and Matheson's works). Among my case studies in this chapter, *The Shrinking Man* is the closest to the intermediate world, even as it dramatizes the protagonist's progressive exclusion from this world. Matheson's novel thus paves the way for the next chapter, where we turn to texts that directly conflate cosmological concerns with mundane, intermediate realities.

Notes

1 The text of the *Divine Comedy*, in both the original and Robert and Jean Hollander's English translation, is available on the website of the Princeton Dante Project: http://etcweb.princeton.edu/dante/pdp/.

2 On the shared cognitive workings of metaphor and simile, see Michael, Harding, and Tobin (2005).

3 For more on the distinctiveness of literary similes and their effects on the reader, see Harding (2017, 37):

> all types [of similes] are much more *visible* than metaphors, making their presence in literary texts consequential in different ways from metaphor. In particular, similes may make readers more aware of the creativity involved in the author's composition of the text.

4 The primacy of generosity in Calvino's short story anticipates John Leslie's (2001) speculative cosmology. Leslie, a contemporary philosopher, argues that the idea of "goodness" can explain why there is something rather than nothing: the universe exists because the drive toward ethical value could *not* have gone unfulfilled (despite being imperfectly realized in the universe as we know it).

5 See R. D. Mullen (1999, 295–96) on the similarities between the two novels.

6 Though Cummings's novel is set inside a single atom, I prefer the term "atomic" over "subatomic" here because of the latter's association with particle physics, which developed only after the publication of the novel.

7 This notion should be distinguished from the idea of parallel universes, which is also a staple of science fiction. In Cummings's Chinese box universe, different worlds are nested vertically, not juxtaposed horizontally as alternative "versions" of reality. For more on parallel universes in cosmology see Tegmark (2004); for the intersections between this idea and narrative theory see Ryan (2006).

8 For an example of this language, see this passage: "The second stone teetered a little on the first, he discovered. He had to cram pieces of torn cardboard into the gaps between the two facing surfaces. That done, he climbed up on top of it and jumped up and down. So far, his little platform was secure" (2012, 654).

9 For more on empathy for fictional characters, see at least Coplan (2004) and my account in Caracciolo (2014d, Chap. 5).

2 The Cosmology of Everyday Life

[Stephen Dedalus] turned to the flyleaf of the geography and read what he had written there: himself, his name and where he was.

Stephen Dedalus
Class of Elements
Clongowes Wood College
Sallins
County Kildare
Ireland
Europe
The World
The Universe

(Joyce 1992, Chap. 1)

This list from James Joyce's *A Portrait of the Artist as a Young Man* connects the individual—here a young Stephen Dedalus, taking his first steps at school—with the universal. Symbolically, the passage reflects the child's expanding consciousness as he comes to understand his position vis-à-vis the geographical, political, cultural, and astronomical realities that surround him. The list is, thus, a formal device that mirrors—in an abridged, tentative form—the cosmos as a system of relations across levels of reality. The *Portrait* was published in 1916; only a few years later, in 1922, Joyce made another, more ambitious attempt at figuring that systemic interrelation. That attempt is "Ithaca," the penultimate chapter of *Ulysses*—a chapter that, through its unique question and answer format, obstinately asks how to bring together human-scale realities and scientific knowledge, the fleetingness of our bodies and the vastness of the cosmos. I use the term "interconnectivity" to refer to the problem of creating linkage between domains that we normally think of as distinct and impermeable to one another: recognizable objects and bodies that afford direct interaction within the world of day-to-day experience, on the one hand, and phenomena that escape this intermediate world while being the object of scientific knowledge, on the other hand.

Interconnectivity has to do with the strategies through which narrative can graft cosmological questions onto what Michel de Certeau (1984) has influentially termed the "practice of everyday life."

"Ithaca" is my first case study in this chapter. I will read it alongside two narratives that are similarly concerned with the cosmology of everyday life: Pamela Zoline's science fiction short story "The Heat Death of the Universe" (first published in 1967) and "Carbon," the last chapter of Primo Levi's *The Periodic Table* (originally published in Italian in 1975). These texts revolve around scientific theories that, in their abstraction, put extreme pressure on human-scale embodiment; but the body is still part of these narratives' solution to the problem of interconnectivity. While, in the case studies of the previous chapter, the body was shrunk (or reduced to one dimensionless point) at the diegetic level, the texts discussed here draw on embodiment through a more indirect—but no less thought-provoking—combination of formal strategies: they employ schematic patterns of movement (Joyce and Zoline), a concrete object (Zoline), and the writer's own embodied self (Levi) as "interconnectivity anchors"—that is, material stand-ins for the interdependency of human and nonhuman realities. I start from Joyce's chapter, which contains a particularly radical attempt to defamiliarize the body at the level of style and narrative representation; but by foregrounding vectors of physical movement, Joyce still manages to evoke the possibility of linkage between its human characters' (and by extension the readers') body and scientific models of cosmos. Such interconnectivity anchors can prove helpful to bridge the gap, imaginatively and affectively, between the abstract revelations of nonhuman-oriented philosophy and the practice of everyday life. This chapter, then, explores the heuristic value of literary storytelling as a means of embedding a sense of humannonhuman interconnectedness within the intermediate world.[1] As I will discuss below, the imagination of movement tends to play a central role in bringing together these realities.

Schema and Skeleton

We know from Frank Budgen's memoir *James Joyce and the Making of* Ulysses (1972, 21) that Joyce once called *Ulysses* an "epic of the human body." Not only does Joyce's novel thematize the body in ways that proved scandalous to some of its early readers, by unashamedly showing characters masturbating or defecating, but it incorporates the body into its own style and narrative form. At the stylistic level, to quote Maud Ellmann, Joyce uses language that "enacts organic processes, miming the activities of nerves and organs, such as peristalsis in 'Lestrygonians,' orgasm in 'Nausicaa,' seizures in 'Circe'" (2008, 54). Joyce's style thus wrestles with physiological processes, serving as a verbal bridge toward the nonverbal. The novel's various episodes also have different somatic "dominants" (i.e., tone-setting bodily parts), which Joyce outlined in two famous schemata: he discussed the first in a letter to his friend Carlo Linati in 1920, whereas the second was sent to the French poet Valéry Larbaud a year later and published in 1930 in Stuart Gilbert's *James Joyce's* Ulysses (hence, this is known as the "Gilbert schema").[2] At least in Joyce's conception, then, the body informs the novel all the way down to the level of narrative structure and organization.

The Linati and Gilbert schemata, which assign an organ to each chapter, are partly dissimilar: one of the discrepancies concerns our chapter, "Ithaca," which is first compared to "juices" (Linati) and later to the novel's "skeleton" (Gilbert). The difference is significant: while juices are shapeless as they flow through the body, the skeleton provides structure and tends to survive the body's soft, fleshy parts. This discrepancy captures the strange duality of the chapter, which combines a rigid structure (the Q&A format that we will examine in more detail) with long lists and enumerations that flow with juice-like ease. In turn, the stylistic tension between structuration and messy fluidity reflects the way in which the chapter integrates scientific knowledge about the cosmos into the characters' everyday lives and obsessions.

First of all, however, we should contextualize the chapter within the novel as a whole. Positioned just before Molly Bloom's monologue, "Ithaca" narrates the homecoming of Leopold Bloom—the modern Ulysses—and Stephen Dedalus, the young artist who is also the protagonist of Joyce's *Portrait*. Having met, at last, after a day during which their paths through Dublin intersected twice, Bloom and Stephen walk to Bloom's house. Bloom discovers that he has forgotten to take the key with him and has to jump over the fence in order to open the door for Stephen. The two characters talk over a cup of hot chocolate, while Bloom is immersed in his fantasy of having found a son in Stephen (a surrogate of Rudy, his son who died shortly after birth—hence the identification between Stephen and Telemachus). Bloom offers Stephen hospitality for the night, but Stephen declines, and the characters part ways after having urinated together in the garden. Finally, Bloom joins his wife, Molly, in bed (where the thought of Molly's adulterous habits haunts him). This is the chapter's narrative in a nutshell: the setting as well as the subject-matter are clearly quotidian. Yet what we read in the novel has a completely different flavor, because "Ithaca" is based on the questions and answers of an anonymous, and impersonal, narrator. For example, this is Bloom preparing to boil the water for the hot chocolate:

> What did Bloom see on the range?
> On the right (smaller) hob a blue enamelled saucepan: on the left (larger) hob a black iron kettle.
> What did Bloom do at the range?

He removed the saucepan to the left hob, rose and carried the iron kettle to the sink in order to tap the current by turning the faucet to let it flow.

(Joyce 2008, 623)

This Q&A style rich in factual—and apparently irrelevant—details is sustained through the chapter; though most of the answers are much longer than the ones we see here (in fact, "Ithaca" is the second-longest chapter of the novel). Where does this unusual strategy come from? Joyce himself provides a clue in the Gilbert schema: the chapter's technique, he argues, is that of "Catechism (impersonal)." No doubt, the narrator's firm and impassive tone has something of the doctrinal single-mindedness of Catholic catechism; but—thanks to the repeated references to science and technology—it is also reminiscent of a science textbook, as noted by Fleishman in a seminal article:

A further characteristic of the catechism form has a more precise relevance to scientific activity. The form by its very nature is a discontinuous one: the questions divide up reality into segments and the responses give only the requisite data.

(1967, 381)

The impersonality of the catechism could be, then, scientific just as well as religious in inspiration.

If we look at the *content* of these exchanges, however, science clearly has the upper hand—in the sense that many of the answers either engage with scientific themes or display scientific precision (consider, for instance, the methodical but ultimately pointless description of Bloom tapping "the current by turning the faucet to let it flow" in the passage quoted above). Many Joyce critics have explored this aspect of the chapter: Perlis (1982), to name just one scholar, argues that "Ithaca" is a reductio ad absurdum of Newton's mechanistic worldview (a "Newtonian nightmare," as Perlis puts it) where human beings are seen as cogwheels in a cosmic machine, entities devoid of agency or subjectivity. This reading is encouraged by a famous comment made by Joyce in a letter to Budgen. It is worth quoting here because of how it resonates with my own concerns in this chapter:

All events are resolved into their cosmic, physical, psychical etc. equivalents, e.g. Bloom jumping down the area, drawing water from the tap, the micturating in the garden, the cone of incense, lighted candle and statue so that the reader know everything and know it in the baldest and coldest way, but Bloom and Stephen thereby become heavenly bodies, wanderers like the stars at which they gaze.

(February 1921; Gilbert 1957, 159–60)

According to the Oxford English Dictionary, the expression "heavenly bodies" is well attested in English, dating back to at least the fifteenth century. Technically, it implies a metaphorical comparison between astronomical objects and living bodies, but its relative conventionality—at least in a certain kind of philosophical discourse—tends to conceal the metaphorical link with biological embodiment. Its use in this context, however, should not pass unnoticed. If *Ulysses* is an epic of the human body, and if "Ithaca" is predicated (as Joyce hints and Perlis argues) on the equation between human beings and nonhuman objects, what role does embodiment play in this equation? The question is complicated by the fact that, at first sight, this reads like a very disembodied chapter. The language of science and the narrator's impassive voice evacuate the sensory texture of Stephen's and Bloom's experiences—that same texture that is so carefully explored in some of the previous chapters. Yet it is precisely because the prose of "Ithaca" strikes us as cerebral and abstract that its few, but strategically positioned, embodied cues take on special significance. My analysis of "Ithaca" thus focuses on what is in many respects a limit case, one in which the body *almost* does not seem to matter—until we dig deeper into the embodied basis of Joyce's language.

To explicate this point, I suggest going back to what I said in the introduction about the embodied nature of language comprehension. The idea, as the reader will remember, was that some linguistic strategies tend to activate a mechanism of embodied simulation or motor resonance, whereby language is understood by drawing on traces of past sensorimotor interactions with the world. Prototypical cases are verbal representations of movement or somatic experience, or figurative language mapping relatively abstract concepts onto physical ones. But of course not all language is equally likely to trigger these embodied responses. Especially when reading abstract texts devoid of references to specific objects or experiences, the involvement of embodied schemata will seem to be extremely limited. Consider the following exchange from "Ithaca":

> What various advantages would or might have resulted from a prolungation [sic] of such extemporisation?
>
> For the guest: security of domicile and seclusion of study. For the host: rejuvenation of intelligence, vicarious satisfaction. For the hostess: disintegration of obsession, acquisition of correct Italian pronunciation.
>
> (Joyce 2008, 648)

The "prolungation of such extemporisation" refers to Bloom's suggestion that Stephen ("the guest") spend the night in Bloom's house. Note how the rapid accumulation of nouns, most of them abstract, dissolves the concrete scenario hinted at by this passage into a list of "advantages" that is particularly difficult to understand in embodied terms. Our processing efforts are mostly inferential in nature: we need to identify the referents of "guest" and "host," figure out why Stephen's staying for the night would result in a "rejuvenation of [Bloom's] intelligence," and so on. Cognitive scientist Benjamin Bergen acknowledges this possibility when he argues that "language [sometimes] activates the appropriate inferences. This might be faster and more efficient than performing an embodied simulation of the whole described scene" (2012, 281). In "Ithaca," embodied simulation is made less likely by a host of stylistic strategies that transform everyday reality into a gratuitous enumeration or mathematical abstraction.

To explain these cases in which conceptual and inferential comprehension prevails over embodied mechanisms, we need to build some flexibility into the notion of embodied simulation. Put otherwise, we need to account for the idea that language can accommodate various degrees of embodied involvement. Linguist David Ritchie's (2009) distinction between three levels of "depth of processing" is helpful here. Language particularly rich in embodied cues will result in conscious somatic feelings: in reading or listening to narrative, we may empathize with a character's pain or mentally enact his or her gestures in fully conscious ways. In other cases embodied simulation may be a "subpersonal" phenomenon—i.e., one that can be detected through objective measurements (response times or neural imaging) but does not emerge in readers' consciousness.[3] Finally, in comprehending the abstract language that we may find in a scientific textbook or technical description the implication of bodily feelings and past sensorimotor experiences will be minimal. This degree zero of embodiment corresponds to what Louwerse and Jeuniaux (2008) call "shallow processing."

Of course, it is an oversimplification to ascribe these differences only to linguistic devices: the kind of attention invested by the reader or listener and the context in which the reading or listening takes place are equally important. Even accounting for these individual differences, however, the prose of Joyce's "Ithaca" seems to tilt the balance toward a shallow mode of understanding—one in which readers do not (or do not fully) access their embodied resources in modeling the situations described in the chapter. Should we conclude that Joyce's "epic of the human body" is put on hold in "Ithaca," before being resumed—in "Penelope," the last chapter—by Molly Bloom's sensuous monologue? The hypothesis I will discuss in this section is that even in this apparently incorporeal chapter the body does not cease to matter. In the Gilbert schema "Ithaca" is seen as the novel's skeleton, and the skeleton is embodiment reduced to a bare minimum of mineral structure. By the same logic, in these pages the reader's embodied involvement is not completely eliminated but rather stripped down to its schematic components.[4] The result is that, while

shallow processing is the dominant mode of understanding, bodily schemata still emerge from time to time in "Ithaca," and they often take
a strategic position—just like the skeleton is normally hidden but fulfills an essential function in the body of vertebrates. One could even
argue that these embodied cues become all the more important because
of their rarity, since readers will be particularly receptive to the few experientially derived patterns that can help them model the storyworld.
Whenever this happens, readers will be suddenly thrust from shallow
processing to a fully embodied mode of understanding. Consider the
chapter's beginning:

> What parallel courses did Bloom and Stephen follow returning?
>
> Starting united both at normal walking pace from Beresford Place
> they followed in the order named Lower and Middle Gardiner streets
> and Mountjoy square, west: then, at reduced pace, each bearing left,
> Gardiner's place by an inadvertence as far as the farther corner of
> Temple street, north: then, at reduced pace with interruptions of
> halt, bearing right, Temple street, north, as far as Hardwicke place.
> Approaching, disparate, at relaxed walking pace they crossed both
> the circus before George's church diametrically, the chord in any
> circle being less than the arc which it subtends.
>
> (2008, 619)

Note how the characters' nocturnal trip through Dublin is reduced to
a vector-like path, with the narrator describing changes in pace and direction as a series of differential steps. For all its apparent abstraction,
this geometrical description actually captures the schematic structure of
the characters' walk. I said that the passage is "abstract," but it is useful
to keep in mind the polysemy of the word "abstraction," which can
denote the generalizing impulse of scientific thinking (with its interest
in general laws and regularities) as well as the paring away of sensory
details. Typically, these meanings go together, but scientific abstraction
is not the only mental activity that requires reducing sensory input to
its skeletal (schematic) structure—for perception itself can be said to
work in this way. In his seminal *Visual Thinking* (1969), for example,
Rudolf Arnheim examines how abstract patterns underlie perception
and mental imagery. These patterns have a lot in common with what
cognitive linguists working in the wake of Lakoff and Johnson (1980,
1999) have called "image schemata." As discussed in the introduction,
image schemata are basic forms—or Gestalten, to use a more technical
term—that structure our perception. To mention an example close to
Joyce's passage, perceiving a billiard ball's movement involves comput-
ing what we may think of as its schematic trajectory: we extrapolate
from the sensory details in order to make a prediction about where the
ball will end.

Another key idea advanced by cognitive linguists—and anticipated in some respects by Arnheim—is that even conceptual thinking makes use of image schemata: whenever we think about our life as a journey from one place to another, for example, or of two ideas being in opposition, we are applying image schemata such as "path" and "counterforce" (see Evans and Green 2006, sec. 6.1). These and similar expressions, which are ubiquitous and universal in human cultures, are often cited as evidence for the embodiment of our conceptual and linguistic apparatus: even in modeling relatively abstract ideas we appeal to patterns derived from our perceptual experience, and therefore embodied.

Image schemata emerge constantly in Joyce's chapter. For instance, one page after the passage quoted above the narrator asks the following questions: "Were their views on some points divergent?...Was there one point on which their views were equal and negative?" (2008, 620). The wording may seem unremarkable at first sight, but it is quite interesting in that it presents the characters' views as if they were material objects that can point in different directions ("divergent") or counterbalance one another ("equal and negative"). Surely, this language is in keeping with the scientific inspiration of Joyce's style throughout the chapter. But looking at these expressions from the perspective of visual thinking and image schemata does invite us to reconsider the apparent disembodiedness of this chapter: embodiment is not so much denied as reduced to its schematic components, which are at the same time perceptual and conceptual. This reduction constitutes the bodily defamiliarization at work in "Ithaca": Joyce's style evokes image schemata and thereby implicates their link with embodied experience, but at the same time places them in a context that deeply unsettles our familiarity with the body. These skeletal components play here a particularly important role, because they anchor and structure readers' understanding of what is in all other respects a very intangible storyworld.

Image-schematic references to motion are especially prominent in "Ithaca." The repeated use of these references is what I call an interconnectivity anchor, a textual device that connects multiple levels of reality. The chapter itself begins under the sign of motion, as we've seen, with Joyce tracing his characters' "parallel courses." Under a veneer of scientific distance, what is conveyed here is the deeply embodied schema of a movement that is discontinuous in speed and direction. But there is more. Consider how, in the already mentioned letter to Budgen, Joyce suggested that Bloom and Stephen become not just "heavenly bodies" but "wanderers like the stars at which they gaze." The word "wandering" crisscrosses the boundary between human and nonhuman realities: normally used for animate motion, it characterizes the motion of the stars, which are in turn compared to animate subjects like Bloom and Stephen. Put otherwise: the embodied schema of motion underpins the parallel between astronomical objects and human subjects, bringing together cosmic and human-scale phenomena. Another remarkable example of this blending can be found in a passage that describes how Bloom, having discovered himself keyless, decides to enter his house by climbing over the railing:

> Resting his feet on the dwarf wall, he climbed over the area railings, compressed his hat on his head, grasped two points at the lower union of rails and stiles, lowered his body gradually by its length of five feet nine inches and a half to within two feet ten inches of the area pavement, and allowed his body to move freely in space by separating himself from the railings and crouching in preparation for the impact of the fall.
>
> (2008, 621)

As usual in "Ithaca," this description offers much more detail than we actually need to make sense of Bloom's actions. The narrator overspecifies the character's bodily gestures, even those that would normally be glossed over in a more standard narrative: compressing the hat, grasping the rails, lowering the body, allowing it "to move freely in space," crouching, etc. The effect of this descriptive strategy is comparable to a psychological phenomenon known as "verbal overshadowing"—a well-known interference between verbal description and visual recognition. In a classic paper by Schooler and Engstler-Schooler (1990), a series of experiments showed that verbally describing a human face from memory impaired a subsequent face recognition task involving visual stimuli: participants were less accurate in recognizing a face after being asked to describe it in words.[5] Something similar happens in Joyce's account of Bloom's jump, except that the interference in this case is between verbal description and mental imagery. Because the text overspecifies Bloom's action, it becomes more difficult to form a smooth and coherent image of how it unfolds: we are too busy mentally processing the details. However, the disruption of our mental imagery has an interesting consequence: we pay more attention to the individual components of Bloom's movement, especially the basic embodied schemata that underlie his actions (such as compressing, grasping, etc.). Recall Fleishman's (1967) emphasis on the discontinuity of Joyce's prose: the text here works toward breaking down movement into its perceptual building blocks. The next exchange puts this technique into a broader perspective:

> Did he [Bloom] fall?
>
> By his body's known weight of eleven stone and four pounds in avoirdupois measure, as certified by the graduated machine for periodical selfweighing in the premises of Francis Frœdman, pharmaceutical chemist of 19 Frederick street, north, on the last feast of the Ascension, to wit, the twelfth day of May of the bissextile year one thousand nine hundred and four of the christian era (Jewish era five thousand six hundred and sixtyfour, mohammadan era one

thousand three hundred and twentytwo), golden number 5, epact 13, solar cycle 9, dominical letters C B, Roman indication 2, Julian period 6617, MXMIV.

(2008, 621–22)

At one level, this passage satirizes scientific precision and its flourish of unnecessary data. But there is more: what the narrator does, effectively, is position Bloom's fall—and the gravity causing it—vis-à-vis a set of technological and scientific frames of reference that gradually shift the focus from Bloom's human-scale fall to nonhuman realities. Bloom's fall is a function of his weight, which is caused by the joint action of his mass and the Earth's gravitational pull. We are told that Bloom last measured his weight on a particular day; the narrator attempts to specify (or, again, overspecify) the date of that measurement by reference to the calendar systems developed by various civilizations (Roman, Christian, Jewish, and Islamic). Finally, the last sentence, with its mention of the "solar cycle" and "epact," hints at the astronomical phenomena that guide the human measurement of time.[6] In the space of two Q&A exchanges, Joyce's account of Bloom's fall bridges the divide between the image schemata underlying human motion and astronomical objects which are themselves in motion (the cycles of sun and moon as the basis for human time measurement, and the Earth itself as the determinant of gravity). This is a first, tentative suggestion of how movement underlies the parallel between human and celestial bodies in "Ithaca"; but it will be developed more explicitly later on in the chapter.

As the two characters sit down in Bloom's kitchen, the narrator begins probing—through the repeated questions and answers—Bloom's beliefs about the "generic conditions imposed by natural, as distinct from human law, as integral parts of the human whole" (2008, 650). Bloom's worldview is shown to be secular, materialistic, and particularly sensitive to the fragility of human existence. In Allen Thiher's (2005) account of the chapter, these ideas resonate with Blaise Pascal's anxieties about the position of the human vis-à-vis physical and cosmic realities:

On a starry night, Odysseus and Telemachus [i.e., Bloom and Stephen] recognize that they seek knowledge in the framework of the Pascalian universe in which the description of the eternal silence of infinite space is also an answer to some of their questions.

(2005, 178)

These concerns are voiced over the course of the chapter's first protracted foray into cosmic territory (a passage worth quoting in full):

What spectacle confronted them [Bloom and Stephen] when they, first the host, then the guest, emerged silently, doubly dark, from obscurity by a passage from the rere [sic] of the house into the penumbra of the garden?

The heaventree of stars hung with humid nightblue fruit.

With what meditations did Bloom accompany his demonstration to his companion of various constellation?

Meditations of evolution increasingly vaster: of the moon invisible in incipient lunation, approaching perigee: of the infinite lattiginous scintillating uncondensed milky way, discernible by daylight by an observer placed at the lower end of a cylindrical vertical shaft 5000 ft deep sunk from the surface towards the centre of the earth: of Sirius (alpha in Canis Maior) 10 lightyears (57,000,000,000,000 miles) distant and in volume 900 times the dimension of our planet: of Arcturus: of the precession of equinoxes: of Orion with belt and sextuple sun theta and nebula in which 100 of our solar systems could be contained: of moribund and of nascent new stars such as Nova in 1901: of our system plunging towards the constellation of Hercules: of the parallax or parallactic drift of socalled fixed stars, in reality evermoving from immeasurably remote eons to infinitely remote futures in comparison with which the years, threescore and ten, of allotted human life formed a parenthesis of infinitesimal brevity.

Were there obverse meditations of involution increasingly less vast?

Of the eons of geological periods recorded in the stratifications of the earth: of the myriad minute entomological organic existences concealed in cavities of the earth, beneath removable stones, in hives and mounds, of microbes, germs, bacteria, bacilli, spermatozoa: of the incalculable trillions of billions of millions of imperceptible molecules contained by cohesion of molecular affinity in a single pinhead: of the universe of human serum constellated with red and white bodies, themselves universes of void space constellated with other bodies, each, in continuity, its universe of divisible component bodies of which each was again divisible in divisions of redivisible component bodies, dividends and divisors ever diminishing without actual division till, if the progress were carried far enough, nought nowhere was never reached.

(2008, 651–52)

The passage opens with a vision of the "heaventree of stars hung with humid nightblue fruit," a poetic metaphor that (as noted by Karen Lawrence [1980, 562]) is likely to stand out in this chapter dominated by dry, nonmetaphorical language. This image is so striking because it plays on—and reverses—the normal perception of a starry sky, where stars are seen as emerging from a background of darkness. In the terms of Gestalt psychology, the stars and the constellations they trace are typically the figure (the object on which we focus), the black sky is the ground. By contrast, Joyce's metaphor shifts the emphasis from the stars—viewed as a branch-like ground in the first part of the phrase—to the blackness of the night sky itself, which is turned into a figure: dark fruits hanging from a backdrop of stellar branches. This perceptual "spectacle" has clear implications from a conceptual viewpoint, in that it begins to distance the reader from the human-drawn constellations of the "heaventree" to the unsettling darkness of outer space.

The flight from the human-scale world continues more forcefully with the two following exchanges. Here the perceptual—and image-schematic—nature of humans' imagination of the nonhuman is thrown into even sharper relief, for the two questions and answers center on the concepts of (respectively) "evolution" and "involution" in their etymological sense: a movement of outward unfolding and inward folding. The first paragraph encompasses cosmic visions of increasingly vast scale, from the moon to the motion of so-called fixed stars (in Aristotelian astronomy)—until the final sentence plunges readers back into the "infinitesimal brevity" of human existence. The second paragraph executes an "equal and negative" movement toward the infinitesimally small, from bacteria to blood cells to molecules—a movement that, in principle, could go on forever (as suggested by the three negations of the last clause, "nought nowhere was never reached"). We've already encountered this parallel between micro- and macrocosm in the previous chapter. Joyce's syntax is able to enfold these nonhuman realities into an image-schematic pattern in two steps: a spiral-like expansion ("evolution") followed by a contraction ("involution"). In this way, a perceptual schema similar to those that underlie the description of Bloom's fall—and equally grounded in the human body and in our interaction with the human-scale world—is adopted to conceptualize realities far beyond the human scale.

The bodily defamiliarization performed by Joyce's *Ulysses* has two components: it sees the cosmic in terms of image schemata deriving from embodied experience, and it trims down the characters' everyday experiences to image schemata so distant from concrete sensory details that the quotidian become almost unrecognizable as such. This two-pronged strategy foregrounds pattern, and particularly the pattern of motion, as an interconnectivity anchor capable of bringing together human and nonhuman realities, terrestrial and celestial bodies. Movement, as Maxine Sheets-Johnston (2011) has shown, is the signature of all animate beings: to be animate means to move one's body, and consciousness itself cannot be extricated from motion. But movement is also inscribed in the universe through physical forces like gravity: even the fixed stars, we learn, are "in reality evermoving."

Yet the chapter does not end with a cosmic vision. After the spectacle of the "heaventree," Bloom and Stephen part ways, and Bloom prepares to sleep next to Molly, his wife. This last third of the chapter is more limited in scale: the grand references to the human condition become sparser, with Bloom's own personal life looming larger. But the cosmic anxieties stirred by the narrator do not disappear entirely. The parallel between bodies and astronomical objects emerges again, in a passage where Bloom is playfully considering the possibility of giving up his life in Dublin and moving to another country—also as a way to escape his (justified) concerns about Molly's marital fidelity:

> Would the departed never nowhere nohow reappear?
>
> Ever he would wander, selfcompelled, to the extreme limit of his cometary orbit, beyond the fixed stars and variable suns and tele-scopic planets, astronomical waifs and strays, to the extreme bound-ary of space, passing from land to land, among peoples, amid events. Somewhere imperceptibly he would hear and somehow reluctantly, suncompelled, obey the summons of recall. Whence, disappearing from the constellation of the Northern Crown he would somehow reappear reborn above delta in the constellation of Cassiopeia and after incalculable eons of peregrination return an estranged avenger, a wreaker of justice on malefactors, a dark crusader, a sleeper awak-ened, with financial resources (by supposition) surpassing those of Rothschild or the silver king.
>
> (2008, 680)

The passage is perhaps an echo of Dante's Ulysses, who, after his return to Ithaca and the apparent end of his journey, cannot resist the impulse to travel onward. He decides to sail past the pillars of Hercules and ven-ture into the terra incognita, where he meets his death in a shipwreck (*Divine Comedy*, "Inferno" XXVI). Dante's image of human hubris is turned here into a story of interstellar travel and success, for in this fantasy Bloom would return to Earth (and his home) "with financial resources (by supposition) surpassing those of Rothschild or the silver king." The mention of material realities is not a coincidence: this is, after all, a chapter obsessed with the enumeration of material things (e.g., the books on Bloom's bookshelf) and possessions (e.g., Bloom's expenses on that day). These lists are now shown to be implicated in a larger, cosmic order: they descend from the same categorizing urge that inspires the narrator's account of the macro- and microcosm, and they imply the same sense of interdependency of human and nonhu-man realities. In this way, "Ithaca" interweaves the everyday and the cosmic, household objects and planets, human and nonhuman realities, by leveraging image schemata as an interconnectivity anchor. Human embodiment may be made unrecognizable and defamiliarized in that interweaving gesture, but it is still there, operating beyond the scientific façade of Joyce's style, as a skeleton of perceptual patterns—including, of course, the perceptually derived notion of "interwovenness" itself. Even in a text that calls for shallow processing, embodiment is thus not completely evacuated: its skeletal traces demonstrate how we cannot do without the body in imagining the cosmic.

Entropic Housekeeping

After engaging with one of the most influential works of twentieth-century literature, we turn to a less canonical short story that never-theless raises very similar questions about the cosmology of everyday life. The story is Pamela Zoline's "The Heat Death of the Universe," originally published in 1967 in the British science fiction magazine *New Worlds*. Science fiction readers and scholars will be familiar with this periodical, and possibly with Zoline's short story itself, as it is often in-cluded in anthologies of science fiction from the 1960s. In 1964 Michael Moorcock became the editor of *New Worlds*, and he steered the mag-azine away from conventional science fiction, toward more experimen-tal and even avant-garde narratives.[7] Under Moorcock's direction *New Worlds* had a lasting influence on the history of the genre: the magazine published work by writers associated with so-called "new wave" sci-ence fiction, including—to name just two of the most famous authors— J. G. Ballard and Brian Aldiss. (I'll turn to one of Ballard's short stories, also published in *New Worlds*, in Chapter 4.) As Peter Nicholls (2015) puts it, "New-Wave sf [science or speculative fiction] did more than any other kind of sf to break down the barriers between sf and mainstream fiction." Zoline's "Heat Death" was published in *New Worlds* and fully embraces the journal's innovative agenda and ambition to break with the conventions of genre fiction.[8] In fact, some commentators (see Hewitt 1994) question whether "Heat Death" should be regarded as science fiction at all, because it does not share the setting and themes that are usually seen as distinctive of the genre. However we categorize the nar-rative, its experimental style runs together the protagonist's everyday life and cosmological questions, with often surprising results.

"Heat Death" is the story of Sarah Boyle, a housewife living in Los Angeles. Sarah is a Californian Mrs. Dalloway on the verge of a nervous breakdown. Like Virginia Woolf's high modernist novel, the narrative focuses on a day in Sarah's life, from breakfast time to the preparations for the birthday party of one of her children (which involve cleaning the house and buying the cake at a grocery store), to the party itself and Sarah's final mental collapse when the children are in bed. This linear plot is punctuated by seven paragraph-long "inserts" dealing with apparently extraneous themes; each of them carries a heading in small caps: "entropy," "heat death of the universe," "on light," "dada," "love," "Weiner on entropy," and "turtles." Both these inserts and the other paragraphs of the short story are numbered from 1 to 54, and the whole text reads like a glossary, with explicit definitions, key terms in capitals, and cross-references to the inserts. This is evident from the very beginning of the short story: "1. ONTOLOGY: That branch of metaphysics which concerns itself with the problems of the nature of existence or being" (Zoline 1988, 13). This beginning sets the tone for the narrative, where ontological and cosmological questions are embedded within the protagonist's housekeeping routine.

Let us focus on the formal features for now. The numbered paragraphs—like the Q&A format in Joyce's "Ithaca"—are meant to reflect a particular attitude toward the story's subject-matter. In Joyce, Bloom's own scientific interests may play into that stylistic choice to some extent, but ultimately the questions and answers are more likely to be attributed to an anonymous, and impersonal, narrative figure. In Zoline, by contrast, there is a clear association between the reference book format and the protagonist's obsession with catalogues and lists:

> Sometimes [Sarah] numbers or letters the things in a room, writing the assigned character on each object. There are 819 separate moveable objects in the living room, counting books...She is passionately fond of children's dictionaries, encyclopedias, ABCs and all reference books, transfixed and comforted at their simulacra of a complete listing and ordering.
>
> (1988, 17)

The narrative form thus latches onto the protagonist's need for order and systematicity, potentially bringing the reader close to Sarah's viewpoint through an empathetic route.

What jeopardizes Sarah's desired order is a phenomenon known in physics as "entropy." This concept was introduced by German physicist Rudolf Clausius in 1865, in an early formulation of the so-called second law of thermodynamics. Over the course of the twentieth century entropy has been conceptualized in substantially different ways, and has been applied to fields beyond physics itself (particularly information theory). Here we need to take on board only the scientific insights that are necessary to understand Zoline's story. Entropy can be seen as a measure of disorder within an isolated system; more specifically, in the context of thermodynamics, entropy depends on the availability of energy within a system: if the energy is in a disordered, dispersed state, it will become unusable. Clausius's proposition was that "in all natural processes the total entropy of everything involved in the process can never decrease: it can remain unchanged in certain idealized processes, but in all real changes, the entropy will always increase" (Goldstein and Goldstein 1995, 6).

A classic illustration of entropy in popular science is that of a lump of sugar dissolved in a coffee cup: once the sugar has melted, reverting to the original—and more orderly—state (one cup of unsweetened coffee, one lump of sugar) seems impossible. This is an intuitive example of how entropy tends to increase over time. Indeed, entropy is commonly associated with the idea of time's irreversibility: once we have dissolved the sugar, there is no way (or at least no straightforward way) to reverse the process and magically extract a lump of sugar from sweetened coffee. This idea has implications for cosmology: as Grandy puts it,

> our cosmological outlook has changed considerably in a hundred years [i.e., after pioneering work by Clausius and others], but both philosophers…and scientists…continue to proffer an explanation for the Second Law [of thermodynamics] in terms of time asymmetry in the universe, or vice versa. In this modern scenario, the universe is thought to have begun in a uniform state of very low entropy.
>
> (Grandy 2012, 151)

If entropy in the universe itself is increasing, at some point in the future there will be no available energy to harness: this final state is the heat death of the universe that inspires the title of Zoline's story—an idea that goes back to scientific theories advanced by Lord Kelvin and Hermann von Helmholtz in the late nineteenth century (see Holton and Brush 2001, 259–61).

None of this is cutting-edge physics, not even by the standards of 1967 (when Zoline's short story was first published). The notion of heat death predates key discoveries in physics and astronomy, which altered substantially our understanding of cosmology in the first part of the twentieth century. It is doubtful whether the idea of entropy can even be meaningfully applied to a universe that has been found to be expanding:

> It is rather presumptuous to speak of the entropy of a universe about which we still understand so little, and we wonder how one might define thermodynamic entropy for a universe and its major constituents that have never been in equilibrium in their entire existence.
>
> (Grandy 2012, 151)

The narrator of Zoline's story acknowledges this point: "The total entropy of the Universe therefore is increasing, tending toward a maximum, corresponding to complete disorder of the particles in it (*assuming that it may be regarded as an isolated system*)" (Zoline 1988, 16; italics added). The parenthetical remark warns the reader that the universe as a whole may not behave as an isolated system (a precondition for the increase in entropy posited by Clausius), and thus that the laws of thermodynamics may not apply to the universe in the usual way.

Nevertheless, entropy and the heat death are particularly effective as literary devices because of how they dovetail with everyday concepts of energy, order, and disorder—concepts whose understanding is grounded in our bodies and in our physical interactions with objects. Energy is closely related to what psychologist Daniel Stern (2010) has called "forms of vitality"—the dynamic qualities of human action and motion. Take, for example, activities as different as watching a dance performance, listening to a piece of music or a speech at a political rally, or running a half marathon. Whether we perform these activities ourselves or experience them as spectators, we can perceive them as "forceful," "swelling," "tense," "fading," and many other qualities (Stern 2010, 7). These are all examples of vitality forms. While energy as a thermodynamic notion has, in principle, little to do with these experiences, in practice it is very difficult to disentangle them—because, if mind scientists are right (see Introduction), our own bodily experience is the intuitive starting point for understanding abstract concepts. Likewise, our comprehension of order and disorder depends on our ability to interact with human-scale objects in order to change their spatial position and arrangement.

Zoline's short story not only builds on this parallel between scientific concepts and the protagonist's human-scale world but also reveals that this parallel is inevitable *because of our cognitive predispositions*. To explicate this idea, let us turn to the following paragraph:

> 11. Cleaning up the house. One.
> Cleaning up the kitchen. Sarah Boyle puts the bowls, plates, glasses and silverware into the sink. She scrubs at the stickiness on the yellow-marbled formica table with a blue synthetic sponge, a special blue which we shall see again. There are marks of children's hands in various sizes printed with sugar and grime on all the table's surfaces. The marks catch the light, they appear and disappear according to the position of the observing eye. The floor sweepings include a triangular half of toast spread with grape jelly, bobby pins, a green band-aid, flakes, a doll's eye, dust, dog's hair and a button.
> (Zoline 1988, 15)

As we know from the previous chapters, the straightforwardly embodied language of the first sentences ("puts the bowls...into the sink," "scrubs at the stickiness") will trigger an embodied simulation mechanism in readers, inviting them to mentally enact the character's actions. In the following sentences embodiment is less salient, but it is still present in inchoate form, such as when the text refers to the marks of children's hands or to "the position of the observing eye" (which implies the possibility of the observer's motion). The mention of "floor sweepings" is another embodied trace, since the noun "sweepings" derives from, and therefore presupposes, the action of sweeping the floor. The final enumeration depicts an assemblage of disparate objects which fall into different conceptual categories and yet all somehow converge on the body, human (food, clothes, band-aid, etc.) or nonhuman (a doll's eye, dog's hair). As we read the passage, we are thus led through different stages, starting from an intention to "[clean] up the kitchen" and the attendant bodily gestures to the identification of past embodied actions and their traces (as reflected in the children's "marks") to a list of random objects that are still thematically relevant to the body. This progression has two dimensions: on the one hand, it connects a subjective state (Sarah's desire to clean the kitchen) with material objects; on the other hand, it moves from the direct representation of bodily action to the more abstract and conceptual realm of objects associated with the body.

The text thus distances itself from the intermediate world of human interaction. This trend continues in the next paragraph, where the narrator comments on cultural patterns in a globalized world: "can we any more postulate a separate culture? Viewing the metastasis of Western Culture, it seems progressively less likely" (Zoline 1988, 15). Here the text goes even further in its treatment of the body: the logic of thematic association that underlies the list discussed above is replaced by a *metaphorical* association (Western culture as a metastasis). This metaphorization of the body continues in the next sentence, where geography and body modification are run together: "Sarah Boyle imagines a whole world which has become like California, all topographical imperfections sanded away with the sweet-smelling burr of the plastic surgeon's cosmetic polisher" (Zoline 1988, 15). In this image and in the previous metastasis metaphor, the body is mapped onto vast abstract entities (the whole world and Western culture).

Finally, the following paragraph contains the first definition of entropy, couched in unmistakably scientific and abstract language: "ENTROPY: A quantity introduced in the first place to facilitate the calculations, and to give clear expressions to the results of thermodynamics" (Zoline 1988, 16). This insert completes the flight from bodily action initiated by the previous paragraphs: for a moment, we get the impression that the somatic has been completely evacuated, even in metaphorical terms. Yet, as soon as the narrator returns to Sarah Boyle's housekeeping duties in the next paragraph, this apparently disembodied notion of entropy is placed in an intimate relationship with the body. The beginning of this section reads: "14. CLEANING UP THE HOUSE. Two. Washing the baby's diapers" (Zoline 1988, 15). The transition from the scientific language of the insert to baby's diapers is more than an ironic device. For the text continues:

> On the fluted and flowered white plastic lid of the diaper bin she has written in Blushing Pink Nitetime lipstick a phrase to ward off fumey ammoniac despair: "The nitrogen cycle is the vital round of organic and inorganic exchange on earth. The sweet breath of the Universe."
>
> (Zoline 1988, 15)

We can see this diaper bin as a mixed material/symbolic object whose function is to bring together the multiple levels of reality articulated by the previous paragraphs: first, the diaper bin is a human-scale object that has certain affordances—in Gibson's term—or possibilities of interaction (including being written upon in lipstick); second, it is meant to contain objects, the diapers, that are semantically associated with the body; third, the unpleasant odor given off by the diapers is metaphorically compared to the "sweet breath of the Universe"; fourth, the "nitrogen cycle" ties in with entropy insofar as any energy transaction is subject to the second law of thermodynamics—i.e., there is inevitable loss in the "organic and inorganic exchange" between the diapers and the atmosphere. The diaper bin thus becomes an interconnectivity anchor—a material stand-in for the conceptual link between the intermediate world of embodied experience and nonhuman or cosmic phenomena. In this process, entropy itself is extended beyond the strictly scientific worldview of the previous paragraph, grounded in the protagonist's everyday reality, and revealed as the principle that governs not just the cosmos ("the sweet breath of the Universe") but the human-scale world as well (the disorder in Sarah's home as symbolized by the diapers). The concept of disorder is thus shown to be intrinsically connected to the body and humans' interaction with physical objects in space. The same conceptual blend—to use the term introduced by Fauconnier and Turner (2002)—underlies another striking passage, where Sarah "imagines, in her mind's eye, cleaning and ordering the whole world, even the Universe. Filling the great spaces of Space with a marvelous sweet smelling, deep cleansing foam. Deodorizing rank caves and volcanoes. Scrubbing rocks" (Zoline 1988, 26).[9] The universe itself is seen here as a human-scale environment that can be scrubbed clean in the same way as Sarah's untidy home.

The metaphor of the "fumey ammoniac despair" in the diaper bin passage brings in another important element, since the entropic disorder explored by this short story is emotional as well as material in character. Sarah Boyle is in a state of emotional disarray, which depends largely—or so the story implies—on her struggle to reconcile personal aspirations and societal demands:

> On the wall by the washing machine are Yin and Yang signs, mandalas and the words, "Many young wives feel trapped. It is a contemporary sociological phenomenon which may be explained in part by a gap between changing living patterns and the accommodation of social services to these patterns." Over the stove she had written "Help, Help, Help, Help, Help."
>
> (Zoline 1988, 16)

This feminist undercurrent reflects yet another level of reality brought into play by Zoline's story (namely, social dynamics), enriching the parallel between Sarah's messy household and the entropic fate of the universe: material disorder, emotional struggles, social patterns, and of course the general increase in cosmic entropy all conspire against the protagonist.

In her reading of the short story, Hewitt writes: "By juxtaposing entropy with housewifery, Zoline disrupts a model that would make either 'science' or 'sociology' metaphor for the other" (1994, 292). I would go even further: by exploring the protagonist's existential predicament, the story suggests how individual human experience, society, and the cosmos itself effectively obey the same entropic principle. The linkage between these levels of realities is nonmetaphorical (in the sense of "actual"), even as metaphors and other analogical devices (including the diaper bin passage) can bring that deep interconnectedness to the fore.

In Joyce's "Ithaca," the integration of human and celestial bodies set in motion a number of image schemata stripped down to their abstract Gestalten, as we've seen. In Zoline's story, image schemata still play a role—for instance, when we are told that the heat death of the universe corresponds to its "unwinding" itself, "no energy being available for use" (1988, 28). This final fate of the cosmos is seen, through a mechanical analogy, as a toy that unwinds itself into stasis—a notion that we understand on the basis of our familiarity with image schemata having to do with force (and the exhaustion thereof).[10] Mostly, however, the work of interconnectivity is carried out not by abstract image-schematic language but by careful exploration of the protagonist's phenomenology— that is, perceptual and affective sensations that put her in touch with the cosmos. While Joyce reduces embodiment to a skeletal core, Zoline moves in the opposite direction, overemphasizing the texture of bodily experience instead of erasing it. Accordingly, Sarah tastes the heat death of the universe while drinking a can of ice-cold soda:

> Sarah Boyle pours out a Coke from the refrigerator and lights a cigarette. The coldness and sweetness of the thick brown liquid make her throat ache and her teeth sting briefly, sweet juice of my youth, her eyes glass with the carbonation, she thinks of the Heat Death of the Universe.
>
> (1988, 18)

This direct conflation of bodily experience and cosmic phenomena has an even more spectacular epiphany in the short story's conclusion. In these final sentences we see Sarah "enacting" the heat death in what appears as a nervous breakdown:

> She begins to break glasses and dishes, she throws cups and cooking pots and jars of food which shatter and break and spread over the kitchen. The sand keeps falling, very quietly, in the egg timer. The old man and woman in the barometer never catch each other. She

picks up eggs and throws them into the air. She begins to cry. She opens her mouth. The eggs arch slowly through the kitchen, like a baseball, hit high against the spring sky, seen from far away. They go higher and higher in the stillness, hesitate at the zenith, then begin to fall away slowly, slowly, through the fine, clear air.

(1988, 28)

Sarah realizes the futility of her attempts at housekeeping and suddenly decides to embrace the entropy: she starts *creating* chaos instead of resisting it. Remember Stern's notion of "vitality forms," the dynamic qualities implicit in human action: through its motion verbs, the first sentence is associated with forcefulness and agitation, and may evoke analogous feelings in readers. From the second sentence, however, the dynamic contour of the narrative suddenly changes: time seems to slow down, and Sarah's tense movements are contrasted with the quietness of the falling sand and the immobility of the "old man and woman in the barometer." In the final, slow-motion sequence Sarah is seen opening her mouth without ever closing it and throwing eggs that follow a ballistic path without ever touching the ground (the story ends with the words "fine, clear air"). The eggs' drawn-out rise and fall reflect how in the absence of available energy—that is, when the universe meets its heat death—time itself ceases to matter. We thus experience the heat death of the universe through a carefully orchestrated series of perceptual and kinetic sensations, which culminate in a sense of suspended stillness. These experienced qualities are grounded in the body—the one we attribute to the protagonist but also to our own body, which we use to understand the narrative's rhythm and affective contour.

In this final burst of energy, Sarah's desperation at her social condition fuses with the motion of household objects (dishes, eggs, etc.), and blends into the fate of the cosmos itself. Like the diaper bin in the passage discussed above, but in an even more explicitly embodied fashion, the objects' slowing motion functions as an interconnectivity anchor: it is a kinetic pattern causally related to psychological and social factors (Sarah's burnout, her frustration over gender roles in society), and at the same time it indicates that the universe has reached a state of maximum entropy. Human subjectivity and nonhuman objects are caught as if immortalized in their interrelation, yet this final revelation also negates the possibility of any further exchange between them: the cosmology of everyday life comes to a standstill.

The Life of a Carbon Atom

Originally published in Italian in 1975, Primo Levi's *Il sistema periodico* (*The Periodic Table*) is an autobiography in 21 chapters, each bearing the name of—and revolving around—a chemical element. Levi, who was born in Turin to Jewish parents, is a major figure in Holocaust literature and is well known for his testimonial works narrating his confinement in the Nazi concentration camp of Auschwitz (*If This Is a Man*, 1947) and his difficult return to Italy in the aftermath of World War II (*The Truce*, 1963). Yet Levi was also a trained chemist and continued practicing this profession throughout his life: reconciling his experiences as a Holocaust survivor, writer, and scientist was always one of the focal points of Levi's thinking, and it emerges repeatedly in interviews, essays, and in Levi's literary works.

Il sistema periodico is a particularly striking demonstration of this complex dialogue, since chemical elements—and Levi's work as a chemist before, during, and after Auschwitz—structure his autobiographical narrative. In Levi's imaginative recreation of Mendeleev's periodic table, each element is associated with an episode of his life: for instance, the chapter entitled "Hydrogen" tells the story of his first scientific experiment while studying chemistry in Turin, "Gold" reconstructs his arrest at the hands of the Fascist Party, whereas "Vanadium" centers on Levi's postwar correspondence with a German chemist who turns out to be an old Auschwitz acquaintance. *Il sistema periodico* has been construed as an intervention in the "two cultures" debate, that is, the view, famously advanced by C. P. Snow in 1959, that "the intellectual life of the whole of western society is increasingly being split into two polar groups" (Snow 1990, 169): the humanists and the scientists. It is this dangerous polarization that Levi addresses, indirectly, in this hybrid book—part autobiographical memoir, part science book with an implicit didactic agenda. Yet Levi was also keenly aware of the tension between the two cultures and always spoke of literary writing and chemistry as occasionally converging but ultimately distinct trades.[11]

Il sistema periodico negotiates this tension by embedding chemical elements and the science behind them in Levi's everyday life, and by demonstrating the deep interrelation of human-scale events and invisible happenings—hence the interest of this book for my discussion. Also relevant is Levi's characteristic conception of science work: as Pierpaolo Antonello explains, "Levi's preference was never for so-called big science, but rather for the small-scale lab science he had practised as a young man, before and after the Lager" (2007, 91). Crucially for our purposes, "for Levi, the homo faber does not operate through abstract mental schemes, but mainly through direct, sometimes painful, contact with matter, which engenders a form of cognitive response that is channelled through the body and through the senses" (2007, 98). As we've seen in the introduction, modern science has gradually distanced itself from the intermediate world; Levi's attempt at bridging the two cultures resists this trend, seeking to reinstate the role of embodied experience and observation as a meeting point for human-scale and nonhuman realities. This project can be understood in light of Levi's unflinching commitment to humanism: throughout his work, Levi shows faith in science and technology as human activities that can serve worthwhile ends if used wisely and ethically. As has been noted multiple times, Levi's own writing embraces the principles of clarity and rationality delineated during the Enlightenment era. This position is particularly remarkable coming from a Holocaust survivor who experienced first-hand a totalitarian regime that originated—according to Horkheimer and Adorno's (2002) influential account—from a grotesque overextension of Enlightenment values.[12] Scholars have paid particular attention to the uneasy tensions and contradictions in this aspect of Levi's thought: Françoise Carasso, for example, writes that "his humanism is that of a twentieth-century man, a troubled humanism that has been violently affected and deeply marked by the experience of Fascism and Nazism" (2009, 8–9; my translation).

This "troubled humanism" emerges with extraordinary intensity in the last chapter of *Il sistema periodico*, "Carbon," and the body—human and nonhuman—is central to its articulation. Playing on the title of Calvino's *Cosmicomics*, Marco Belpoliti (1998, 159) has called "Carbon" a "cosmichimica"—literally a "cosmichemistry." Undoubtedly, there are many overlaps with Calvino's collection. The most striking of these overlaps is the use of a nonhuman protagonist—a carbon atom in Levi's case. Yet the first seed of the story told in this chapter precedes Calvino's *Cosmicomics* (originally published in 1965) by two decades, since it was conceived during Levi's time at Auschwitz, as the narrator states: "To carbon, the element of life, my first literary dream was turned, insistently dreamed in an hour and a place when my life was not worth much: yes, I wanted to tell the story of an atom of carbon" (1984, 225). Levi's narrator follows the vicissitudes of a carbon atom through a series of steps: a miner first dislodges this atom from the rock that enclosed it for thousands of years; released in the form of carbon dioxide, the atom is breathed by a falcon; later, it is trapped in a vine leaf and transformed into a grape's glucose; it is then used to make wine, ingested by a man and released again into the atmosphere; absorbed by the trunk of a cedar tree as cellulose, it is eaten by a wood worm and finally reappears in a glass of milk—which the author himself is drinking as he prepares to complete *Il sistema periodico*.

To elaborate on the parallel between Levi's chapter and Calvino's *Cosmicomics*: I discussed in Chapter 1 the sheer inventiveness of one of Calvino's stories, which anthropomorphize cosmic entities and place them in surprising and usually humorous situations. Only a minimal degree of anthropomorphization is present in Levi's chapter. For instance, we read at the beginning that for the atom,

> time does not exist, or exists only in the form of sluggish variations
> in temperature, daily or seasonal...Its existence, whose monotony

cannot be thought of without horror, is a pitiless alternation of hots and colds, that is, of oscillations (always of equal frequency) a trifle more restricted and a trifle more ample: an imprisonment, for this potentially living personage, worthy of the Catholic Hell.

(1984, 225–26)

Whenever the narrator's language involves or implies anthropomorphization, it becomes remarkably cautious: the monotony of the atom's existence "cannot be thought of without horror," but this very comment—in the passive voice in English, in the impersonal form in the original ("non si può pensare senza orrore"; Levi 1982, 230)—distances the thought from the atom, which is emphatically *not* the thinking subject. Likewise, the metaphor of the atom's existence as "imprisonment" (and the attendant reference to the Catholic Hell) are downplayed by the remark that it is a "potentially [i.e., not actually] living" being. This is quite different from Calvino's flamboyant anthropomorphization, which often results in naturally or physically impossible situations (such as the characters existing "all at one point" before the Big Bang). In fact, there is very little in this chapter that *could not* plausibly happen to a carbon atom. This story is invented, but it is also absolutely naturalistic. The narrator himself makes this point in a key passage:

It is possible to demonstrate that this completely arbitrary story is nevertheless true. I could tell innumerable other stories, and they would all be true: all literally true, in the nature of the transitions, in their order and data. The number of atoms is so great that one could always be found whose story coincides with any capriciously invented story. I could recount an endless number of stories about carbon atoms that become colors or perfumes in flowers; of others which, from tiny algae to small crustaceans to fish, gradually return as carbon dioxide to the waters of the sea, in a perpetual, frightening round-dance of life and death, in which every devourer is immediately devoured; of others which instead attain a decorous semi-eternity in the yellowed pages of some archival document, or the canvas of a famous painter; or those to which fell the privilege of forming part of a grain of pollen and left their fossil imprint in the rocks for our curiosity; of others still that descended to become part of the mysterious shape-messengers of the human seed, and participated in the subtle process of division, duplication, and fusion from which each of us is born. Instead, I will tell just one more story, the most secret, and I will tell it with the humility and restraint of him who knows from the start that his theme is desperate, his means feeble, and the trade of clothing facts in words is bound by its very nature to fail.

(1984, 232)

The passage opens with a dizzying realization: there are so many carbon atoms on Earth that *any* story, no matter how "capriciously invented," is or was true at some point. Nature is thus presented as a virtually inexhaustible narrative repertoire, which the narrator begins to unravel as he tells the stories—again, invented but plausible—of other carbon atoms. The subtext is clear: the limitations of human creativity are such that it will never be able to compete with nature's own boundless productivity. This realization leads to the narrator's declaration, at the end of the quoted passage, that this story can only be told with a sense of "humility," "restraint," and awareness of one's feebleness. Further, the carbon atom may be negligible, but it can achieve something no human being is capable of: while continually changing, it continues existing. When the wood worm that had eaten the carbon atom dies, it becomes "a slough, a 'thing,'" but the death of atoms, unlike ours, is never irrevocable" (1984, 231). In fact, before being extracted from a rock, the atom already had what the narrator calls a "very long cosmic history" (1984, 225) that he is forced to ignore, because it would be a tale far too long for any human being to narrate or comprehend. Carasso sees this idea as potentially consoling: the carbon atom, "unlike us humans, unlike the other living beings of which it is temporarily part, never dies" (Carasso 2009, 114; my translation). But here, consolation and sense of vulnerability go hand in hand because the "round-dance of life and death" is a frightening reminder of our mortality just as it is a soothing image of nonhuman constancy: life on Earth could not exist without "long stable chains" of carbon atoms (1984, 226), and yet these insentient and apparently insignificant atoms far surpass the limits of our human imagination and existence.

Our means are feeble, but they are not completely powerless. And our means, for Levi, are deeply steeped in our embodied history of interaction with the world. For what is the "round-dance of life and death" itself, other than a metaphor lifted from bodily experience? The body is everywhere in the infinite permutations of the carbon atom, in subject-matter and theme but also—more importantly—in language and style. The carbon atom is breathed by a falcon, drunk as wine, swallowed by a wood worm, and—in its last embodiment in a glass of milk—ingested by the narrator. We are told that the carbon atom lingered in the wine drinker's liver for a week, "well curled up and tranquil, as a reserve aliment for a sudden effort; an effort that he was forced to make the following Sunday, pursuing a bolting horse" (1984, 229). This micro-history is, we realize, the daily business of life. It is "micro" in scale *and* in scope, for each of the countless atoms in our body has analogous—but wonderfully different—stories to tell. Thematically, we are thus reminded that our corporeality is always already transcorporeal, to borrow Stacy Alaimo's (2010) term, insofar as our bodies are not just open to the nonhuman world—they are *constituted* by it in ways that blur distinctions between the inner and the outer, the human and the nonhuman. This is where the cracks in Levi's humanism begin to show: his belief in the possibility of scientific understanding—which underlies this story—is accompanied, and to some extent undermined, by a keen awareness of our own cognitive limitations.

Because of these limitations, the nonhuman can be properly—if partially—understood only in its dynamic relation with the quotidian. Hence, even as Levi's language carefully avoids anthropomorphizing the carbon atom, patterns derived from bodily experience—image schemata—cannot but slip through. Consider, for instance, this passage:

> [The carbon atom] was caught by the wind, flung down on the earth, lifted ten kilometers high. It was breathed in by a falcon, descending into its precipitous lungs, but did not penetrate its rich blood and was expelled. It dissolved three times in the water of the sea, once in the water of a cascading torrent, and again was expelled. It traveled with the wind for eight years: now high, now low, on the sea and among the clouds, over forests, deserts, and limitless expanses of ice; then it stumbled into capture and the organic adventure.
>
> (1984, 226)

If one pays attention to kinetic patterns, this passage reads like a roller-coaster ride: almost one out of five words is a motion verb ("flung down," "lifted," "breathed in," etc.) or otherwise implies spatial relations such as "high" and "low." This concentration of kinetic cues serves to involve readers—and their bodies—in the carbon atom's adventure: it is as if readers were given the chance to enact nature's "round-dance of life and death" through a mechanism of motor resonance. The atom's invisible transmutations are thus translated into a stylistic rhythm that is also, at least potentially, an embodied happening. While in Zoline's short story the embodied experience of the protagonist serves as a bridge toward the nonhuman, "Carbon" eschews a human (or even a sentient) protagonist, using subtle but insistent hints of embodiment to help us connect with a nonhuman entity. At the same time, Levi's strategy departs from Joyce's use of image schemata in "Ithaca," where embodiment itself is reduced to barely recognizable units: here, by contrast, we follow an atom's trajectory with an ease that turns into wonder as soon as we realize how far we are from the intermediate world—and yet how this world *depends* on the transformations we witness in these pages. No doubt, this sense of spontaneity is made possible by the clarity and flow of Levi's prose, which is so different from the staccato rhythm of Joyce's questions and answers.

The conclusion of "Carbon" raises the stakes of this engagement with the cosmos. It begins innocently enough, with the carbon atom dissolved in a glass of milk and being drunk by an as yet unspecified character.

It "crosses the intestinal threshold and enters the bloodstream: it migrates, knocks at the door of a nerve cell, enters, and supplants the carbon which was part of it" (1984, 232). And then, unexpectedly in a chapter that had taken a step back from the book's autobiographical material, the writer comes on stage:

> This cell belongs to a brain, and it is my brain, the brain of the *me* who is writing; and the cell in question, and within it the atom in question, is in charge of my writing, in a gigantic minuscule game which nobody has yet described.
>
> (1984, 232)

The carbon atom was not just inside a human body, but inside the *writer's* body, which is all of a sudden drawn into the text (and into the reader's awareness). Finally, we are told that the carbon atom, along with the neuron of which it is part, make

> my hand run along a certain path on the paper, mark it with these volutes that are signs: a double snap, up and down, between two levels of energy, guides this hand of mine to impress on the paper this dot, here, this one.
>
> (1984, 232–33)

Writing itself is depicted as a performative gesture, an embodied event where the hand is controlled by "a double snap" or more literally "twitch" (the Italian original has the word "scatto") "between two levels of energy" inside the writer's brain. Not only does life depend on the kinetic transformations of a carbon atom, but the very basic processes of mind are shaped by a carbon atom's movement.

Despite the characteristic restraint of its presentation, this idea is quite radical: it does away with a whole tradition that sees mind and matter as fundamentally distinct substances (Descartes's "res cogitans" and "res extensa"), effectively implying that mind is just what happens to matter when arranged in sufficiently complex ways (this is the "gigantic minuscule game which nobody has yet described").[13] Further, this materialist view extends into the act of writing itself, which is not a purely intellectual pursuit but a physical activity that involves moving hands and flickering synapses. The author's creativity—and the book that we're holding in our hands, along with the autobiographical episodes told therein—thus become part of a material history that started when a carbon atom was freed from a rock by a miner's pickaxe. This final revelation is an ontological metalepsis, to use a narratological term (see Pier 2010), insofar as it runs together what we thought of as essentially separate narrative levels—namely, the carbon atom's invented (but naturalistic) story and the narrator's own autobiography. The sudden failure of this narrative divide corresponds to another important collapse of conceptual boundaries: the human, of which writing is a powerful symbol, is reabsorbed into the cosmic, with the writer's own body becoming a living reminder of this merger—an interconnectivity anchor. As readers, we are invited to reenact the writer's gesture in the same embodied way as we followed the carbon atom's ups-and-downs in the previous pages. This is how Levi's "troubled humanism" is conveyed to the reader: the positive value of science and human knowledge is affirmed, even as the bodily patterns evoked in the attempt to translate science into experience problematize the very notion and autonomy of human subjectivity. In this way, "Carbon" throws into sharp relief the interrelatedness of a carbon atom and a writer's day-to-day (but by no means ordinary) life.

* * *

In a seminal contribution to the field of embodied cognition, psychologist Lawrence Barsalou (2003) argued that our comprehension of concepts is always "situated," that is, shaped by concrete contexts of action and interaction. Take "car," for example: for Barsalou, this concept does not operate as a list of abstract features (such as "is a vehicle," "has four wheels," "is powered by a combustion engine," etc.), but rather serves as the trigger of a mental simulation that reflects past experiences of cars. In Barsalou's words,

> the situated simulation view assumes that conceptual representations are contextualised and dynamical. A concept is not a single abstracted representation for a category, but is instead a skill for constructing idiosyncratic representations tailored to the current needs of situated action.
>
> (2003, 521)

This theory has clear implications for pedagogy: if we want to hone this "skill for constructing idiosyncratic representations," and therefore learn to apply concepts with precision, we need to encounter them in situations that are as specific and experientially rich as possible. Scholars working in education had made a similar move a decade before Barsalou's article, also under the heading of "situated cognition": as Brown, Collins, and Duguid argue in a seminal article, situated cognition "suggests that activity and perception are importantly and epistemologically prior—at a nonconceptual level—to conceptualization" (1989, 41). In an essay co-authored with Karin Kukkonen (Kukkonen and Caracciolo 2014, 265–66), we made the case that such situated conceptualizations are central to how literary narrative works, because of its remarkable ability to bring together the abstract and symbolic and the concrete and embodied.

Thus, the three narratives examined in this chapter are so effective at staging cosmic questions because they capitalize on the situated nature of our thinking: in order to convey the abstract notion of human-nonhuman interrelation, my case studies embed the cosmic in everyday situations, making use of lists and enumerations that populate the storyworld with a wide gamut of familiar objects. We read about a late-night conversation in a house in Dublin, a housewife shopping for a child's birthday party while trying to keep up with her domestic chores, a writer drinking a glass of milk as he prepares to finish his manuscript. While these are all familiar scenarios, literary style and narrative work toward defamiliarizing them: everyday events are juxtaposed or even fused with processes that would not normally fall within the scope of the intermediate world. Thus, in Joyce's "Ithaca," the human bodies of Bloom and Stephen are treated as astronomical objects, their actions and words transfigured into remote cosmic events that can be captured only through the lens of impersonal questions and answers. In Zoline's short story, a housewife's experience is merged with the thermodynamic concept of entropy, so that her final nervous breakdown prefigures the moment when the universe itself will run out of energy and suffer a heat death. Levi's "Carbon" reconstructs the encounters between life (human and animal) and a single carbon atom, which is eventually involved in the writer's decision to end his book—the book that we are reading—in a certain way.

This embedding of the cosmic in the everyday is made possible by the strategic use of what I have called interconnectivity anchors. To reiterate, an interconnectivity anchor is a salient stylistic pattern or passage that calls attention to the relations among levels of reality, acting (at least potentially) as a magnet for readers' interpretation. We may compare interconnectivity anchors to T. S. Eliot's (1997) concept of "objective correlative," except that what is objectified is not a feeling but a sense of interconnection (which may, of course, take on affective qualities). Examples are image-schematic patterns in Joyce's "Ithaca," a diaper bin in Zoline's "Heat Death," and the writer's own brain and body in "Carbon." These situated conceptualizations of human-nonhuman interconnectivity will be more effective the more they can creatively reutilize bodily patterns—be they skeletal image schemata or more experientially rich somatic sensations. The narrative evocation of movement appears particularly conducive to interconnectivity, insofar as kinetic patterns straddle the divide between animate and inanimate entities: not only is exploratory movement constitutive of perception (from an enactivist perspective) and intrinsic to living beings, but the universe itself is in constant motion—at least until its hypothetical heat death. We can thus use our familiarity with animate movement in order to approximate the universe's own "round-dance of life and death." Narrative is ideally suited to capture this kinetic approximation, because of how it can incorporate movement into the affective contour of its progression—through the staccato rhythm of Joyce's questions and answers, Zoline's numbered descent into heat death, or the effortless flow of Levi's cosmic tale.

Notes

1 Contemporary fiction has deployed similar devices in engaging with the scale of the climate crisis. See Caracciolo (2020) on interconnectivity anchors in Don DeLillo's novel *Underworld* and Alexandro Gonzáles Iñárritu's film *Babel*.
2 Both schemata have been frequently reprinted. See, for instance, Joyce (2008, 735–39).
3 I discuss more at length this distinction between conscious and unconscious embodied involvement in the "Routes into Embodied Reading" section of the introduction. See also Caracciolo (2018).
4 As noted by Fritz Senn, "'Ithaca' takes up five-sixths of all occurrences of 'reduce[d]' in *Ulysses*" (1996, 54).
5 I would like to thank Anežka Kuzmičová for bringing this psychological phenomenon to my attention.
6 The "epact" is the number of days to be added to the solar calendar to determine its equivalent in the lunar calendar.
7 For more on the publication history of *New Worlds*, see Stableford et al. (2015).
8 For more on Zoline's oeuvre, see Clute (2014).
9 According to Fauconnier and Turner (2002), a "conceptual blend" is a mental construct resulting from the integration of two distinct semantic domains, in this case entropy as a physical measure of disorder and the more tangible disorder of objects in human-scale space.
10 See Evans and Green (2006, 187–89) for an in-depth discussion of force image schemata.
11 Here is how Charlotte Ross describes this tension in a recent monograph: Levi called

> for the two cultures of science and literature, to which he contributed, to be conceived as a continuum of interrelated intellectual and practical activity. Yet he also insisted that his scientific and literary selves were not only distinct, but fundamentally irreconcilable.
>
> (2011, 63)

12 "The dialectic of enlightenment is culminating objectively in madness," Horkheimer and Adorno (2002, 169) write.
13 For more on materialist or "physicalist" (as this position is also known) approaches to the mind-body problem, see Stoljar (2009).

3   Sex and the Cosmos

In an essay on the role of metaphorical language in the history of psychology, David Leary (1990) argues that, with the rise of modern science, mental phenomena have typically been understood via a comparison with physical objects interacting in space. The mechanical worldview of physics has been used to conceptualize the intangible realities of mental life and social interaction. There is an interesting exception to this tendency, however, and it is Newton's theory of universal gravitation: in some of Newton's early writings on the topic, the metaphors travel in the opposite direction, from the social domain to physics. As Leary argues, when

> Newton first pondered the fact that no detectable mechanical force accounted for the tendency of masses of matter to move toward one another, he conceptualized this mysterious movement as analogous to the "attraction" of human persons toward one another. In his early notebooks he even used the term "sociability" in addition to "attraction."
>
> (1990, 9–10)

Social interactions were thus being invoked to model *physical* interactions. Nowadays it would be unusual (though perhaps not altogether impossible) for a scientist to draw on social metaphors for physical phenomena in a scientific publication. Novelists are more at liberty to engage in comparisons of this kind: they can build on our experience of the intermediate world—including human intersubjectivity—to explore processes existing at other levels of reality. We've seen a few examples of this conceptual dynamic in the previous chapter; here we turn to three novels published in the 1980s and 1990s in which the distinctively embodied experience of sexuality and sexual desire is used to probe nonhuman realities ranging from quantum physics to the birth of the universe. The novels in question are John Updike's *Roger's Version* (1986), Jeanette Winterson's *Gut Symmetries* (1997), and Michel Houellebecq's *The Elementary Particles* (1998).

With these case studies I shift the focus from embodied cognition in reading to embodiment as it is thematized by literary texts and used as a resource for style and narrative form. As I indicated in the introduction, our bodies are multidimensional constructs, and it would be a mistake to segregate the biological and cognitive from the cultural dimension. Sexual attraction is not only located in the body—it gives rise to a wide array of bodily feelings—but it has another person's body as its object, and it is deeply influenced by socio-cultural factors. I will be adopting here Alan Goldman's broad definition of sexual desire as "desire for contact with another person's body and for the pleasure which such contact produces" (2002, 40). Surely, this desire is central to human-scale reality: as an intrinsically biocultural phenomenon, sex shapes our affective landscape and orients our lives. While grounded in our drive toward biological preservation, sexual desire is always already invested with diverse cultural meanings—which reflect our socio-cultural background as well as the practices in which we are participating. Sexuality can even take on spiritual significance, as in some strands of Christian mysticism or in the Tantric tradition in Buddhism.[1]

Sex challenges individuality at multiple levels: it confronts us with alterity in the form of another person's body; the intense feelings it elicits can take us beyond ourselves (or at least our usual selves). Sex also plays a pivotal role in natural selection and therefore the continuation of our species. Through this challenge to individual consciousness, sex puts pressure on the intermediate world: potentially, it decenters the self and encourages us to attend to a temporal scale far larger than our lifespan. This biocultural complexity explains, at least in part, why several cultural traditions have traced a link between sexuality and spirituality. My case studies in this chapter harness this link as they bring their characters' sexual experiences to bear on cosmic questions concerning the nature of physical reality. Scientific knowledge is blended with Christian theology in *Roger's Version*, alchemy and magic in *Gut Symmetries*, and a faith in "love" as a metaphysical principle in *The Elementary Particles*. The gap between sex as an embodied phenomenon and cosmic realities that are far removed from our bodies is thus addressed via a sophisticated syncretism of scientific and prescientific thinking—a conceptual operation that reveals the inherent limitations of scientific knowledge as we confront anxieties about the cosmos, our role in its history, and our future as a species. Put otherwise, narrative turns to spiritual notions as it seeks to fill in the many gaps in contemporary scientific views on the cosmos. In the process, the human body becomes strange and unfamiliar, the physical world is partly and uneasily re-enchanted. The defamiliarization plays out in ethical terms in the novels I examine in this chapter: one of Updike's characters views carnal sin as a cosmological bridge toward God, Winterson's narrative explores the violence of masculine domination, and Houellebecq's novel features a controversial posthuman narrator. Through these ethically charged scenarios, the three novels demonstrate that integrating scientific thinking into a satisfying narrative progression requires striking a balance between formal closure and the open-ended nature of the questions pursued by science.

Groping for God

In an article in *Religion and Literature,* Thomas Dicken summarizes the plot of *Roger's Version* (1986) as follows:

> Dale Kohler, a computer virtuoso,...claims that computers could now do the work of building a natural theology based on scientific evidence, citing the extreme improbability of a world like ours without an intelligent Creator. There are, of course, the assorted domestic tensions, the problems with women and children, which always fill out Updike's novels. But much of the narrative involves the Barthian God, known only through revelation, never through any human ladders reaching up to God, versus the possibility of human reason attempting to build an argument for God.
>
> (2004, 70)

By evoking Swiss theologian Karl Barth, Dicken hints at the epistemological tension that underlies Updike's novel—namely, the tension between God as an idea that can be demonstrated through empirical and scientific means (Dale's computer program) and God as a mystery knowable only through faith and revelation. But it is another aspect of the quotation that interests me here. It is the sentence about the "assorted domestic tensions"—which Dicken describes, dismissively, as a "filler" that distracts from the narrative's theological concerns. Yet the intriguing formal challenge tackled by Updike in *Roger's Version* has to do with the integration of wide-ranging questions about God and the cosmos into the "assorted domestic tensions" that—pace Dicken—take center stage in the plot.

In essence, the novel revolves around four characters: Roger, the narrator and a Divinity School professor of Barthian persuasion; Esther, Roger's wife; Dale, a researcher who wants to demonstrate God's existence via a computer model of the universe; and Verna, Roger's niece—a nineteen-year-old single mother with a history of drug abuse. With Updike's characteristic bent for geometrically arranged human relations, these four characters enter what can be described as a love rectangle: at the beginning of the novel, Dale contacts Roger to talk about his research, inquiring about the possibility of obtaining a grant from the Divinity School to complete his work. Over the course of that conversation Dale, who knows Verna, mentions her difficult circumstances. Roger then decides to seek her out to offer help, an opening that slowly builds up to an incestuous sexual liaison. At the same time, Esther begins a clandestine relationship with Dale in Roger's house—or so Roger imagines, in vivid and sometimes explicit sequences, but we never have any direct evidence for this affair (hence the title, *Roger's Version*).

Whether we see these social and sexual transactions as occupying the background (as Dicken implies) or the foreground of the novel, the question remains how exactly they are connected to the theological and cosmological questions considered by Dale and Roger. Put otherwise, how are levels of reality as different as those of cosmology and (extra)marital relationships brought together by Updike's plot? How are cosmological concerns embedded in the earthly world of these four characters? Of course, we cannot take for granted that they *are* successfully embedded. A lesser writer than Updike could use the cosmological theme to add some (possibly spurious) depth to a story of marital infidelity; or, on the contrary, the four characters' psychological and physical transactions could only serve as a narrative "hook" for the philosophical questioning. If Updike's novel avoids a neat split along these lines, it is to a large extent thanks to the author's use of metaphors and similes derived from the domain of bodily—and specifically sexual—experience. These stylistic devices carry out the work of what I called "interconnectivity" in the previous chapter: they reduce the gap between the four characters' vicissitudes and the very fundamental questions Dale is raising about the cosmic order.

This interconnectivity can already be seen at work in the initial exchange between Dale and Roger, in the latter's office. Dale begins by pointing out "three main problems with the Big Bang theory" (2006, 12). One of these problems is that the early universe expanded at a seemingly ideal rate, allowing for the formation of macroscopic objects such as stars and planets:

> A little, really little, bit less outward push, and the universe would have collapsed back onto itself in a couple million years—that's nothing, in cosmic terms. I mean, the human species has been around that long. A little bit more, and the stars and galaxies never could have formed; matter would be blowing away too fast, out the window, so to speak. The odds of its working out the way it did are just about as long as you taking some kind of a supergun and hitting an inch-high target on the other side of the universe, twenty billion light-years away.
>
> (2006, 12–13)

Note how this account is interwoven with dynamic metaphors that, ultimately, point to embodied image schemata: in metaphors such as the "outward push," the universe "collapsing back onto itself," matter "blowing away too fast," and in the final analogy of hitting a target from a cosmic distance, the universe is turned into a human-scale space that shrinks and expands in a reassuringly familiar way. The twist is that these images are evoked to stress the *unlikelihood* of things having happened in this way; this is a passage about the apparent "fine-tuning" of the universe, as cosmologists call it. Philosopher Richard Swinburne explains this idea as follows: "rather special laws and boundary conditions are required if the Universe is to be human-life-evolving" (2003, 106); since life as we know it could not have developed if physical constants had been even slightly different, the fact that those "boundary conditions" are met is highly improbable. This is the thrust of Dale's argument: the fine-tuning cannot be understood as mere coincidence but must be taken as proof for intelligent design. Embodied metaphors are employed to evoke the idea of a universe that is commensurable with human life, if not in temporal and spatial proportions, at least because of the recognizability of the divine impulse that created it: God made the universe so that it could support biological beings like us.

Roger resists this view, but in doing so he inadvertently puts forward another embodied analogy for God's creation:

> I do worry a bit about this concept of probability. In a sense, every set of circumstances is highly improbable. It is highly improbable, for instance, that a particular spermatozoon out of the millions my father ejaculated that particular day...would make its way to my mother's egg and achieve my particular combination of genes; but some such combination, given their youth, attitude toward birth control, et cetera, was likely, and mine as probable as any other. No?
> (2006, 15)

The biological mechanisms underlying sexual reproduction are thus used to critique Dale's notion of probability and, ultimately, challenge his explanation of the universe's fine-tuning. To this objection, Dale responds that "babies are born all the time, and there's only one universe, that we know of" (2006, 15). In Updike's novel, as in this exchange between the two characters, metaphors and motifs drawn from bodily experience work as a probe into cosmological questions, alternatively supporting and questioning religious belief—or particular versions thereof.

Indeed, as I said above, the novel contrasts two views of the divine: Roger's belief in a Barthian God that is fundamentally unknowable and does not sit well with the discoveries and methods of science; and Dale's faith in empirical knowledge and technology as means to prove God's existence. Interestingly, this divergence is far from being only conceptual, because it is mapped onto different ways of understanding—and "using"—the human body. Roger's comparison between theology and pornography in the following passage is quite telling:

> I have a secret shame: I always feel better—cleaner, revitalized— after reading theology, even poor theology, as it caresses and probes

every crevice of the unknowable. Lest you take me for a goody-goody, I find kindred comfort and inspiration in pornography, the much-deplored detailed depiction of impossibly long and deep, rigid and stretchable human parts interlocking, pumping, oozing.

(2006, 41)

This is a defamiliarizing portrayal of the human body, one in which anatomic differentiations are lost: in their quest for God, bodies have to grope their way around a space that resists the cognitive distance afforded by vision, oozing into one another—and almost fusing with the physical world of matter that mechanically "stretches," "interlocks," and "pumps." The physical and affective tangle of sex becomes an equivalent for the narrator's struggle with a God that remains concealed in "every crevice" of the universe, never revealing Himself in a recognizable form. We find a similar image before the first sexual encounter between Roger and Verna:

> The girl was studying. Her head, seen from above, was a depth of partly brown, partly blond curls, circle upon perfect circle like what cyclotrons reveal of matter's deep collisions. An aroma of shampoo arose from these deeps, and a faint tang more purely animal, the powdery warmth of her scalp.
>
> (2006, 138)

First it is the shape and physical weight of Verna's curly hair that attracts Roger's attention, as if those circles held a promise of embracing "raw" matter, not unlike a particle accelerator ("cyclotrons"); then this feeling is compounded by sensations that imply physical closeness (odor, in "tang," and touch, in "powdery warmth") and intensify the narrator's sexual desire. Physical—and, in this case, compromising—proximity is thus the embodied stance that signifies Roger's cognitive involvement with the mysteries of the universe: to attempt to know the cosmos is to struggle with it in a quasi-sexual embrace.

In his reading of *Roger's Version*, James Schiff (1992) argues that vision serves as a central metaphor in the novel, and that this is largely the result of intertextual dialogue with one of Updike's models—Nathaniel Hawthorne's classic adultery narrative, *The Scarlet Letter* (1850). I here shift the emphasis from vision to proximal sensory modalities such as touch and smell, at least as far as Roger's figure is concerned. It is true, as Schiff suggests, that Roger's fantasies have a visual component, but they employ vision as a bridge toward the haptic intimacy of sex. Contrast this with Dale's visual imagination of God as he works on his computer simulation of the universe. The premise of that modeling is that Dale can "simulate our actual world, not in its content so much as in its complexity, at a level that would yield graphical or algorithmic clues to an underlying design, assuming one exists" (2006, 216). The "underlying design" that Dale brings to light in the second half of the novel is different from what one might expect, however, since the computer simulation shows glimpses of a human—or at least anthropomorphic—body. At first it is a face:

> His fingers flicker with their rat-scrabble on the feather-light plastic keyboard, crashing together yet two more agglomerations of vertices and parametric cubic curves. Out of the instant ionic shuffle a face seems to stare, a mournful face. A ghost of a face, a matter of milliseconds.
>
> (2006, 244)

Struck by this fleeting vision, Dale starts looking for statistical patterns in the data and finds that "his statistical dusting of the biologically derived models had revealed, if not one of God's fingerprints, a whorl or two" (2006, 246). Now God is embodied not diegetically, as in the appearance of the mysterious face, but stylistically, through the metaphor of the "fingerprints," which are part of an embodied scenario that compares Dale's own investigative work to "dusting." The work continues, and as he enters commands on the machine Dale is again hoping to catch a glimpse of God's body:

> The new display resembles the one before, save that its patches are finer in scale and have been subjected to a torque that has generated whirlpools, concentric intensification of color layers that appear to tunnel downward like the fingers of a rubber glove.
>
> (2006, 248)

Note how the abstract shapes of the simulation materialize in the (embodied) simile of the "fingers of a rubber glove," which grounds our imagination of what's on the computer screen. At the same time, this simile paves the way for the subsequent appearance of a mysterious hand:

> The anomaly, in shades of green intermixed with orange, appears to be illegibly foreshortened; he maps its image on a plane tilted first 85° on a vertical axis, and then a more cautious 72°, and thus arrives at an image he can read. It is a hand. A hand, patched of colors as if dabbled with glowing camouflage paint but its form emergent, even to palm creases: a hand relaxed on its back and its fingers curled together and not strictly distinguishable, but the knobbed form of the opposed thumb unmistakable.
>
> (2006, 248–49)

Is this anthropomorphic hand really there, a symbol of God's presence and intervention, or is it just a figment of a credulous man's imagination? We will never know, of course. But the difference from Roger's vision of the body in the passages examined above is striking. While Roger looks for God in the messy proximity of sex, Dale chooses the mediation of abstract symbols and computer simulation. While Roger explores "crevices" where embodiment is reduced to fleshy but indistinct "human parts" and can be sensed only through touch and smell, Dale's research reveals clear-cut organs, such as faces and hands, available to visual perception. Despite these discrepancies, however, both Roger and Dale tend to "body forth" the cosmos as they grapple with the apparent fine-tuning of the universe where life, and the human species, developed. Our knowledge of God is understood in terms of embodied interactions with the world—whether these involve the intimacy of sex or the mediated (also in the technological sense) vision of distinctly human-like body parts.

Where does this conceptual mapping leave us with respect to the "love rectangle" that constitutes the plot of *Roger's Version*? How does Updike address the divide between the cosmological scale of the questions raised by Dale and Roger and their sexual encounters with (respectively) Esther and Verna? Updike pulls off this feat by implementing a double vision similar to the one we've seen at work in *The Shrinking Man* (in Chapter 1) but of a more conceptual nature: Dale's and Roger's embodied accounts of God are simultaneously embraced, albeit at different levels. We have to keep in mind that the novel is "Roger's version," meaning that it is not only relayed by Roger's voice but filtered through his imagination. This is particularly true for the passages narrating Dale's sexual affair with Esther, which took place in Roger's absence and yet is described in painstaking detail. There is something morbid about this husband's prying into his wife's infidelities, complete with obscene descriptions of Dale's penis and the many attentions Esther devotes to it (see, e.g., Updike 2006, 151–52). We may question the reliability of these sequences, and we may understandably wonder if these sexual encounters took place at all, but doing so would be missing the point of Roger's narrative: just as the parallel between theology and pornography was prefixed by the words "I have a secret shame," Roger is here indulging in a shameful use of his imagination where truth value is beside the question for the real purpose is *closing in on God through sin*. As Roger says of his own incestuous relationship with his niece, Verna,

> I was guilty of heresy, the heresy of which the Cathars and Fraticelli were long ago accused amid the thunders of anathema—that of committing deliberate abominations so as to widen and deepen the field in which God's forgiveness can magnificently play.
>
> (2006, 289)

Immersing oneself in sin thus becomes a way of celebrating the bound-lessness of God's love for His erring creatures.

This moral dynamic goes hand in hand with the *bodily* dynamic of using the imagination to step into one's wife's adulterous bed. Recall Roger's reference to "impossibly long and deep, rigid and stretchable human parts" in the passage about pornography. It is as if Roger turned his own imagination into an "impossibly long" probe with which to explore the possibility of Esther's marital infidelities—and simultaneously gain embodied insight into God's existence. Along the same lines, the narrator's "sensation of peace *post coitum*" (after sex with Verna) is seen as "sweet theistic certainty" and "living *proof*" (2006, 289, italics in the original). For Roger, embracing the abject messiness of reality offers a way to God, and in that sense the somatic transactions (in act and thought) that occupy the foreground of Updike's novel are not re-moved from cosmological questions: only through existential and ethi-cal "gropings" effected by way of deviant sexual encounters can we fully understand our position vis-à-vis cosmic realities.

Yet science is not completely unhelpful in this project of cosmic understanding—but it is science augmented by a keen awareness of our own status as embodied creatures. This is where Dale's computer-assisted investigations enter the picture. These investigations, as we've seen, were based on the recognition of visual and statistical patterns, and the geometric configuration of Updike's plot—the love rectangle—serves as a structural equivalent to these patterns.[2] At the end of the novel, a character named Kriegman, Roger's neighbor and a biologist, dismisses Dale's ideas about the logical necessity of divine intervention in the Big Bang. Armed with impassionate rhetoric and colorful meta-phors, Kriegman argues that the universe came into existence because the four dimensions of space-time, initially a mere potentiality, were bound to unravel and express themselves in actuality. In his words:

> A lesser number of spatial dimensions, it just so happens, couldn't provide enough juxtapositions to get molecules of any complexity, let alone, say, brain cells. More than four, which is what you have with space-time, the complexity increases but not significantly: four is plenty, sufficient. O.K.?
>
> (2006, 302–3)

Dale then draws the key conclusion (but, as always, it is possible that Roger is only projecting his own thought processes): "Dale nods, think-ing of Esther and myself, himself and Verna. Juxtapositions" (2006, 303). The configuration of sexual desire and social bonds that underlies the novel's plot is mapped onto the fundamental forces of nature, as if the variable geometry of human relations could help shed light on why there is something rather than nothing. Social "juxtapositions" are a matrix for plot through their high narrative potential: an unfaithful wife, an inexperienced lover, a jealous husband, and a young seductress are stock elements of narrative. Updike blends them with the four dimensions of space-time, thus tinging cosmic realities with a proto-narrative quality: just as these four characters "naturally" give rise to a plot, time and space are bound to give birth to a universe.

Ultimately, the origin of the cosmos is presented as the result of forces that are affective and performative—and therefore deeply embodied—rather than coldly scientific. We can read this idea into the theatrical clout of Kriegman's critique of Dale's theism: "Kriegman is shrinking, growing stooped; his chins are melting more solidly into his chest; he bobs like a man being given repeated blows on the back of his head" (2006, 303). If Dale feels defeated and humbled by Kriegman, it is not because the latter's explanation is particularly impressive from a technical or scientific viewpoint—after all, Kriegman, as Dale timidly points out and Kriegman himself concedes, has spoken in metaphors. But the rhetorical force of Kriegman's speech is such that Dale has the distinct "sensation of having been intellectually flattened" (2006, 307)—where another embodied metaphor ("flattened") reflects the inevitable centrality of the body in approaching, and debating, scientific questions.

All in all, embodiment operates at multiple levels in Updike's novel, showing—through the careful coordination of these levels—the close interrelation between our biological being and our attempts at penetrating the mysteries of the universe. Diegetically, the physical proximity of sex becomes a blueprint for cosmological knowledge as Roger insists that God can be found only by way of crude feelings and morally problematic gropings. At the level of plot, the "juxtapositions" between the novel's four protagonists generate narrative instabilities that are shown to be structurally analogous to the forces that tilted the universe itself into existence before the Big Bang—thus implying that narrativity and ontology are part and parcel of the same process of dynamic, and spontaneous, becoming.[3] While this conclusion appears to go against the grain of Dale's theistic understanding of the universe, it actually extends Dale's interest in formal patterns and therefore offers a more "distant" kind of knowledge than Roger's sex-inflected reflections. Yet even this relatively abstract analogy between social interaction and the physics of the Big Bang should not be divorced from the body, for it is steeped in embodied metaphors and histrionically performed by Kriegman in one of the novel's pivotal scenes. Thus, stylistically, metaphors derived from somatic experience resolve the tension between Roger's and Dale's conceptions of the cosmos (and our knowledge thereof). "This is all metaphor," Dale objects, and "What isn't?", Kriegman boldly responds (2006, 304), reasserting the epistemic and cognitive value of metaphor as an answer to the problem of interconnectivity. The body, with its openness to affect (including shame and sexual desire), can thus serve as a bridge between our intermediate world and the cosmos at large.

Thinking GUTs: From Alchemy to Quantum Physics

Intellectual history is full of surprises. Jungian psychology and quantum physics would seem to be worlds apart, and yet Jung had a decade-long correspondence with Nobel-prize winning physicist Wolfgang Pauli, one of the founding fathers of quantum physics (Jung and Pauli 2001). Suffering from intense psychological distress, Pauli wrote to Jung to seek advice in the 1930s. But the epistolary exchange soon strayed from Pauli's personal life, touching on central aspects of the work of both Pauli and Jung. And here, unexpectedly, one finds the scientist sympathetic to the premodern (and prescientific) discourses that inform Jung's psychology—particularly the language of alchemy. In the preface to the Jung-Pauli correspondence, Beverley Zabriskie writes:

> For Pauli, symmetry was the archetypal structure of matter. Just as the alchemists looked for the substratum of reality beneath matter, he came to the view that the elementary particles were not themselves the ultimate level of reality. As he became more familiar with alchemy as a psycho-physical unity, Pauli saw the same *lumen naturae*, the light of nature, or the "spirit in matter," glimpsed by Paracelsus and Jung.
>
> (2001, xxxvii)

The discourse of alchemy allows psychological phenomena to be reconciled with insights into the nature of reality at the subatomic level. Take Jung's key notion of "synchronicity," which denotes events that appear to be connected in semantic but not in causal terms. Coincidence is a good example of synchronicity: when I think of a friend that I haven't seen in a long time and shortly afterward I run into him or her, I know that my chance encounter hasn't been *caused* by my thinking but I am still likely to assign special significance to it. Along similar lines, the theory of so-called "quantum entanglement" posits interactions between particles in situations where—from the perspective of Newtonian mechanics—causality would seem impossible; Einstein famously called it "spooky action at a distance" (see Markoff 2015). This parallel between psychological synchronicity and quantum entanglement reflects the "psycho-physical unity" highlighted by alchemic thinking. It is on overlaps of this nature that Jung and Pauli focus in their interchanges. Of course, just because Pauli was an eminent scientist we don't have to take at face value everything he writes about the deep significance of quantum physics: at times his considerations come across as no less speculative and fanciful than Jung's.

The problem derives from the fact that quantum phenomena—including entanglement and that other controversial idea of quantum physics, indeterminacy—occur at a subatomic level of reality, without extending into the world of everyday experience, where physical reality seems to follow an entirely different, deterministic logic. To be sure, there have been serious attempts at "scaling up" quantum phenomena without losing scientific credibility—recently, by Karen Barad in *Meeting the Universe Halfway* (2007), which charts the ramifications of quantum physics (in Niels Bohr's version) for domains such as ethics and politics. But bridging the gap between these levels of reality remains a challenge, possibly as a result of the incompleteness of physics itself, which has yet to find a convincing way to integrate quantum phenomena with Einstein's general theory of relativity. In the words of mathematical physicist Roger Penrose,

> it turns out that the principles of gravitational physics are in fundamental conflict with those of quantum mechanics...As yet, no appropriate union between quantum mechanics and Newtonian gravity—which fully takes into account Einstein's Equivalence Principle...—has yet come to light.
>
> (1997, 92)

The "union" envisaged by Penrose would require what physicists refer to as a "theory of everything" (Deutsch 1997)—namely, a theory capable of resolving the conflict between the physics of subatomic phenomena (quantum physics) and the physics of larger spatial scales, including the human scale and the cosmos as a whole.

Jeanette Winterson's novel *Gut Symmetries* (1997) takes its cue from this theoretical divide; like Pauli in his correspondence with Jung, Winterson builds on the prescientific discourse of alchemy to integrate quantum physics and human-scale, intermediate reality. Two of the novel's protagonists are physicists who consider fundamental questions about the nature of reality and are engaged in a quest for a "grand unified theory" (abbreviated "GUT"). The title is thus a pun connecting physics with the human body, the cosmic scope of a grand unified theory with the affective, visceral mode of experience that we associate with the gut (hence "gut reactions," etc.). To fully understand the logic of this association we have to say more about the novel's plot, which—not unlike *Roger's Version*—revolves around an extramarital affair. But while in Updike the four protagonists enter a slightly unusual, rectangular configuration, here we are in more familiar territory, with a love triangle taking shape already in the novel's first chapter: Jove, a physicist based at the prestigious Institute for Advanced Study at Princeton, meets Alice, a younger British physicist, on a cruise. Jove is married, but this doesn't keep him from courting Alice and starting a sexual affair with her. The twist in this rather clichéd scenario is that Jove's wife—Stella—and Alice eventually fall in love, in a lesbian relationship that builds on some of the themes of Winterson's previous works (for instance, *Sexing the Cherry* and *Written on the Body*; see Farwell 1996, Chap. 6).

As Helena Grice and Tim Woods (1998) point out, like Winterson's previous novels, *Gut Symmetries* seeks to destabilize heteronormative conceptions of love, targeting in particular Jove's sexism. What distinguishes *Gut Symmetries* is that Winterson's feminist critique is conducted via an exploration of gender difference in scientific practices (a dimension investigated by McClellan 2004), practices that bring in a set of cosmological questions that are entirely new to Winterson's work. The novel comes to grips with these questions by intertwining three different discourses, with the middle one creating a tentative bridge between the other two: first, human subjectivity, and specifically the gendered experience of the novel's two female protagonists; second, the pre- and pseudoscientific theories of alchemy and tarots; and third, the discourse of quantum physics itself. Interestingly, these three domains fall into a pattern that is closely reminiscent of the triangular relationship between the protagonists; however, only Alice has access to all three forms of knowledge, thanks to her bisexual relationship with Jove and Stella. Structurally, then, Alice plays a mediatory role in the novel's narrative economy analogous to the function of alchemy on a more interpretive level. To see how this process unfolds, let us turn to the novel's prologue, which focuses on Paracelsus, a Renaissance thinker and astrologist whose works had enormous influence on Jung's psychology.

This prologue takes the form of a condensed, and poeticized, account of Paracelsus's life and philosophy. It begins with a date and place ("November 10 1493. Einsiedeln, Switzerland") and with the narrator zooming in on Paracelsus's whereabouts before his birth, in a Russian doll-like progression with a surprising reversal at the end: "First there is the forest and inside the forest the clearing and inside the clearing the cabin and inside the cabin the mother and inside the mother the child and inside the child the mountain" (1997, 3). This displaced "mountain" begins to challenge our sense of distinctions between inside and outside, large and small. The mother's womb, like the titular gut, can contain the extremely large, whose existence is not only spatial but psychological (we are told that Paracelsus was "driven by a mountain in his soul"). After a few paragraphs, the link between embodiment and cosmology is asserted even more explicitly:

> The mediaevals were entrail-minded and Paracelsus often delivered his lectures over a scalpelled corpse. This was not the nineteenth-century model of diagnosis by pathology. It was, if it was anything, diagnosis by cosmology. Paracelsus was a student of Correspondences: "As above, so below." The zodiac in the sky is imprinted in the body. "The galaxa goes through the belly."
>
> (1997, 4)

This points to a first, and still incipient, trade-off between the discourses of magic and twentieth-century science: the realization of the continuity between our embodied subjectivities and the material world suggests a sense of connectedness ("correspondences") that science is unable to interpret by itself; the language of alchemy and magic serves to address this epistemic gap and the cosmological anxieties that result from it.

The prologue thus sets the stage for the novel's plot, introducing its main elements while using Paracelsus's prescientific worldview as an interpretive key: "Here follows a story of time, universe, love affair and New York. The Ship of Fools, a Jew, a diamond, a dream. A working-class boy, a baby, a river, the sub-atomic joke of unstable matter" (1997, 7). Arguably, the literary and mythological allusions (here to the Ship of Fools, to canonical literary works such as *Moby Dick* and *The Tempest* elsewhere in the novel) have the function of "grounding" the protagonists' epistemological quest, helping them make sense of the strange revelations of quantum physics. This strangeness is at the heart of the first chapter, narrated by Alice and beginning with a "digression" on the history of cosmological thinking from the ancient Greeks to Einstein. This account is prefixed by Alice's feelings of existential unease, a device that blurs the boundary between the "external" history of the cosmos and her psychology:

> This has been my difficulty. The difficulty with my life. Those well-built trig points, those physical determinants of parents, background, school, family, birth, marriage, death, love, work, are themselves as much in motion as I am. What should be stable, shifts. What I am told is solid, slips. The sensible strong ordinary world of fixity is a folklore.
>
> (1997, 9)

This feeling of instability—the chapter is fittingly set on a boat—undermines the world of everyday experience, which is shown to be shallow and illusory, our bodies and brains making constant mistakes as they attempt to appraise reality:

> I know that the earth is not flat but my feet are. I know that space is curved but my brain has been cordoned by habit to grow in a straight line. What I call light is my own blend of darkness. What I call a view is my hand-painted trompe-l'oeil. I run after knowledge like a ferret down a ferret hole. My limitations, I call the boundaries of what can be known. I interpret the world by confusing other people's psychology with my own.
>
> (1997, 11–12)

These errors and confusions stand in an interesting contrast with Paracelsus's idea—articulated in the prologue—that "as above, so below," for Alice seems to be barred from insight into the fundamental symmetry of reality: there is a rift between the worldview of modern physics and the intermediate world that her "brain" is struggling to close; yet her efforts are unsuccessful, like a ferret running "down a ferret hole"—an instinctive behavior that doesn't push back the limits of what can be known, but only reconfirms them. Contrast the pointlessness of the running (which is underscored by the repetition of "ferret," as if this were a tautological activity) with Roger's parallel between theology and pornography in Updike's novel: while Roger's image hints at a substantive—if morally controversial—form of knowledge, Alice is stuck in a dead end that is at the same time personal, ethical, and epistemological.

What shakes Alice out of this existential impasse is her sexual relationship with Jove and Stella, which coincides with a shift from the "brain" of the above-quoted passage to the "the visceral place between mouth and bowel, the region of digestion and rumination" (1997, 12–13). Only in and through this "thinking gut" can Alice come to a reconciliation between the instability of quantum physics and her everyday reality, resolving the tension between her identity as a scientist who tries "to work towards certainties" and her personal life, which moves "away from them" (1997, 28). To reach this dialectical conclusion, Alice has to become gut-like, digesting and ruminating the subjectivity and life history of both husband and wife. This is what the novel as a whole attempts to accomplish, and if the three characters' voices all sound alike—as reviewers haven't failed to notice (see Makinen 2005, 141)—it is not a shortcoming but rather a stylistic equivalent of Alice's psychological work: the novel's uniformity in tone and register demonstrates how, through her relationship with Jove and Stella, Alice digests and absorbs their worldviews into her own sense of self, creating an impression of undifferentiated subjectivity. In turn, only this diffuse selfhood can close the divide between the subatomic world of quantum physics and the macroscopic world of human-scale objects and relations. Giving up the self as an autonomous, clear-cut entity allows Alice to both embrace the fundamental uncertainty of quantum physics and perceive the complexity of the intermediate world:

> our place in the universe and the place of the universe in us, is proving to be one of active relationship. This is more than a scientist's credo. The separateness of our lives is a sham. Physics, mathematics, music, painting, my politics, my love for you, my work, the star-dust of my body, the spirit that impels it, clocks diurnal, time perpetual, the roll, rough, tender, swamping, liberating, breathing, moving, thinking nature, human nature and the cosmos are patterned together.
>
> (1997, 99–100)

Yet this sense of the co-patterning of reality is never, in Winterson's novel, a purely abstract realization, because it draws inspiration from bodily experiences, including the experiences of intersubjective contact in sex. This point is neatly illustrated by the following passage:

> What did we hope for, heating and re-heating ourselves to absurd temperatures? As matter heats up it is subject to demonstrable change. Boiling in our vessel, our water molecules would begin to break down, stripping us back to elemental hydrogen and oxygen gases. Would this help us to see ourselves as we really are?
>
> Heated further, our atomic structure would be ripped apart. He and she as plasma again, the most common state of matter in the universe. Would this bring us closer together? At about a billion degrees K, give or take a furnace or two, he and she might begin to counterfeit the interior of a neutron star and could rapidly be heated further into sub-atomic particles. You be a quark and I'll be a lepton.
>
> If we had the courage to cook ourselves to a quadrillion degrees, the splitting, the dividing, the ripping, the hurting, will be over. At this temperature, the weak force and the electromagnetic force are united. A little hotter, and the electroweak and the strong force move together as GUT symmetries appear.
>
> And at last? When gravity and GUTs unite? Listen: one plays the lute and another the harp. The strings are vibrating and from the music of the spheres a perfect universe is formed. Lover and beloved pass into one another identified by sound.
>
> (1997, 102–3)

Here Paracelsus's idea of "correspondences" between celestial and human bodies is more than a conceptual premise, as in the novel's prologue, insofar as it is *performed* by the characters' sexual encounters. Temperature stands, metaphorically, for the intensity of the lovers' feelings, but it also points to the alchemical furnace and the particle accelerator, signaling the successful integration of the three discourses of love, alchemy, and modern physics. The references to the increasing heat give a dynamic, processual quality to the narrative: eventually, distinctions between the speaker, "he," and "she" are reduced—boiled down—to pure pattern, "the music of the spheres." To reach this climactic ending, the human body has to open up and lose its familiar shape, fusing not just with subatomic particles but with the fundamental forces of nature.

I mentioned Alaimo's (2010) concept of "transcorporeality" in the previous chapter; this idea can help us shed light on Winterson's approach to the body. To borrow from Harold Fromm's critique of the notion of "environment," transcorporeality stands for a particular kind of realization—namely, that the

> "environment"…runs right through us in endless waves, and if we were to watch ourselves via some ideal microscopic time-lapse video,

we would see water, air, food, microbes, toxins entering our bodies as we shed, excrete, and exhale our processed materials back out.

(2009, 95)

In Winterson's novel, this discovery is located within the "thinking gut," the organ in which the separation between inner and outer, self and otherness breaks down. Alice comes to realize that subjectivity should mimic the porousness of the gut, its being an interface between the macroscopic (food) and the microscopic (the biochemical transactions that sustain life).

This openness of the gut makes it inherently more compatible with the instability of quantum phenomena than the cerebral cognition that Alice appeared to favor at the beginning of the novel, before her encounter with Jove and Stella. As a mode of thinking, the gut can thus relieve the tension between human-scale reality and scientific knowledge, even though this revelation comes at a cost, since it does away with the self as a stable, autonomous entity: "'we' and the sum universe cannot be separated in the way of the old Cartesian dialectic of 'I' and 'World.' Observer and observed are part of the same process" (1997, 164–65).[4] This is a patterned process, one that traces a rhythm (visual and auditory) that Winterson's writing pursues through stylistic and thematic means. Ultimately, the abstraction of rhythm and pattern serves as a bridge between the cosmos ("the music of the spheres"), subatomic realities, where "our seeming-solid material world dissolves into wave-like patterns of probabilities" (1997, 163), and our own embodied subjectivity ("What physicists identify as our wave function may be what has traditionally been called the soul"; Winterson 1997, 164).

Of the three characters constituting the novel's love triangle, Jove, locked in his masculine, dualistic worldview, would seem cut off from this enactivist insight into the patterned coupling of mind and world. Yet in the novel's pivotal episode he discovers—traumatically—the significance of the gut's transcorporeality. On a yacht trip with Stella, they find themselves unable to steer the boat after a severe storm. They drift at sea for several days, until they run out of food and water. When Stella loses consciousness and appears to be near death, Jove resolves to eat her flesh in order to avoid the same fate. This horrific act has been read, in a feminist vein, as "a desperate attempt [on Jove's part] to reinstate the patriarchal possession of his wife" against her lesbian relationship with Alice (Makinen 2005, 149). Yet Jove's consumption of Stella is more complex than this interpretation suggests, for Jove is forced to ignore dualistic distinctions between his body and Stella's, human flesh and meat, in order to ensure his own survival. In this sense, Jove's desperate act contradicts his own (patronizing) critique of Stella's failure to distinguish "between inner and outer" (1997, 195). Jove thus enacts the transcorporeal logic of the gut, coming to understand the affective power of this mode of thinking, even though his realization is horrific and guilt-ridden instead of liberating (as it is for the female characters).

This acute distress is signaled by the verbatim repetition of the following lines, which appear five times in the chapter narrating Jove's cannibalism:

> I had to do it. She was dead. She was nearly dead or I would not have done it. If I had not done it she would have died anyway. I did it because I had to. What else could I have done?
>
> (1997, 195)

Through its alliterations (do/done/did/dead), the meandering syntax conveys a strong sense of rhythmicity, which signals that Jove may have intuited the wave-like nature of reality, and to some extent may join the female characters' fused subjectivities—even as the horrific nature of his act continues to set him apart.

The apparently disjointed and decentralized narrative of Winterson's novel operates through subtle stylistic patterns such as Jove's alliterative sentences. This strategy translates into formal terms the idea that underlies the novel—and Alice's psychological development: facing up to the interrelation between our bodies and cosmic realities (Paracelsus's "galaxa [going] through the belly") involves rethinking conventional notions of subjectivity. In *Gut Symmetries*, this is accomplished through a complex conceptual merger between the intersubjective reality of sex and the apparently incompatible discourses of quantum physics and alchemy. Love and sex, especially when they transgress heteronormativity (through homosexuality and queerness), decenter our sense of self and therefore pave the way for a fuller acceptance of our position vis-à-vis cosmic realities—and these realities' position *within* us. In that sense (and in that sense only), it doesn't really matter that quantum physics is a serious scientific endeavor, alchemy an outdated and groundless pseudoscience: both resonate with, and can reinforce, the destabilization brought about by confronting otherness in intimate contacts.

Sex, Consciousness, and Elementary Particles

While *Gut Symmetries* integrates sexuality with a scientific understanding of the cosmos, Michel Houellebecq's novel *The Elementary Particles* (1998) builds on the opposite impulse—that of segregating sex and science by aligning them with two different characters, the half-brothers Bruno and Michel. Bruno is a high-school literature teacher who—the narrator implies—has taken up writing poetry as a way to compensate for his inability to find a sexual partner. Indeed, sex is a constant source of anxiety and frustration for him. Michel, by distinct contrast, is an eminent biologist who for the most part of the novel intentionally avoids—out of shyness but also sheer lack of interest—any sexual contact. At the same time, Michel's research yields the startling insight that sexual reproduction is largely responsible for humanity's slow, and inefficient, evolution: for Michel, sexuality is "a useless, dangerous and regressive function" (2000, 220). In fact, the novel posits that Michel's pioneering work on the possibility of asexual reproduction allows humanity to evolve into a new species, freeing them from frustrations such as those experienced by Bruno: the narrator, we find out at the end of the novel, belongs to this posthuman species whose existence is made possible by Michel's discoveries.

We'll have to keep in mind that the narrator speaks from this posthuman vantage point, since his views on contemporary society are largely responsible for the controversies that the novel has sparked in France (see Abecassis 2000). Concretely, the posthuman setup translates into an unreliable narrative where Bruno's misfortunes are grotesquely—and sometimes cruelly—exaggerated, since he is taken as an expression of an outdated, sex-obsessed humankind, whereas Michel is celebrated as the harbinger of a new species, a brilliant scientist capable of "giving mankind the gift of physical immortality" (2000, 250). Yet if we read against the grain of this unreliable narrator's evaluations, a significantly different picture emerges. I will argue in this section that in order to appreciate the complexity of *The Elementary Particles* we have to mentally compensate for the one-sided narrative, learning to see the merits of Bruno's worldview as well as the risks entailed by Michel's philosophy.

In the biographical sketches of Bruno and Michel that form the first part of the novel, Michel comes across as a timid boy who seeks solace in the formalized language of mathematics: "Human reality, he was beginning to realize, was a series of disappointments, bitterness and pain. He found in mathematics a happiness both serene and intense" (2000, 56). As we read the narrator's account of Michel's life, we realize that his distrust in "human reality" derives from his lack of control over—and understanding of—other people's behavior. There is an element of unpredictability in human interaction that Michel tries to avoid by turning to mathematical models—hence, of course, Michel's deep interest in science as an alternative to the muddle of social interactions.

Interestingly, however, the novel underscores that even in science unpredictability and randomness cannot be completely eliminated. This is where quantum physics enters the picture: as in *Gut Symmetries* and in a number of other twentieth-century novels (see, e.g., Coale 2012), quantum phenomena offer a valuable resource (and set of metaphors) for fiction exploring how the invisible worlds of science shape life on a human scale. At one level, Houellebecq's novel develops an analogy between human behavior and subatomic phenomena, implicitly comparing the protagonists to two "elementary particles" acting in and on society in different—and often, as we'll see, opposed—ways. But quantum physics also figures thematically in *The Elementary Particles*. Just as science is for Michel a way of asserting control over the uncertainty of everyday experience, Michel's research focuses on how the uncertainty at the heart of science itself—quantum indeterminacy—can be modeled and used to explain key features of human biology and psychology. In the following passage, for example, quantum physics helps solve the longstanding problem of reconciling free will with the deterministic worldview of science:

> In principle, the transfer of electrons between neurons and synapses in the brain—as discrete atomic phenomena—is governed by quantum uncertainty. The sheer number of neurons, however, statistically cancels out elementary differences, ensuring that human behavior is as rigorously determined—in broad terms and in the smallest detail—as any other natural system. However, in rare cases...a different harmonic wave form causes changes in the brain which modify behavior, temporarily or permanently. It is this new harmonic resonance which gives rise to what is commonly called free will.
>
> (2000, 77)

Michel's groundbreaking contributions to biology also build on quantum physics. His point of departure is the observation that the

> existence of identical macromolecules and immutable cellular ultrastructures, which had remained consistent throughout evolutionary history, could not be explained by the laws of classical chemistry. In some way as yet impossible to determine, quantum theory must directly impact on biological events. This would create an entirely new field of research.
>
> (2000, 104)

The plot of *The Elementary Particles* traces the trajectory of this "new field of research," quantum biology, reconstructing its history and contribution to humanity's future. Yet, while Michel is widely credited for being the initiator of this field, the initial spark of intuition comes only when Michel overcomes his distrust in humankind and catches a glimpse of the sexual pleasures so stubbornly (and vainly) pursued by his halfbrother. This dynamic between the two characters and their respective ideologies drives the novel's plot. For most of the text, Michel and Bruno are "elementary particles" that follow parallel courses, converging rarely and only briefly. Even at the formal level, the narrative moves back and forth between the two protagonists, devoting a chapter to each, in alternating order. The logic of the narrative composition thus reflects the divergence in Bruno's and Michel's worldviews, which boils down to the characters' different attitudes toward their bodily experience.

Bruno's sexual drive goes hand in hand with a striving for the *intensification* of embodiment, which emerges repeatedly in the novel's style. Thus, when telling Bruno's life story, the narrator carefully teases out the phenomenological texture of the character's experiences, rendering them in strongly embodied terms. Consider, for instance, the following passage:

> It was about then that he began reading Kafka. The first time, he felt a cold shudder, a treacherous feeling, as though his body were turning to ice; some hours after reading *The Trial* he still felt numb and unsteady. He knew at once that this slow-motion world—riddled with shame, where people passed one another in an unearthly void in which no human contact seemed possible—precisely mirrored his mental world. The universe was cold and sluggish. There was, however, one source of warmth—between a woman's thighs; but there seemed no way for him to reach it.
>
> (2000, 52)

The experience of reading Kafka is rendered through a series of phenomenological similes ("as though his body were turning to ice") and metaphors ("this slow-motion world," "unearthly void") that are located in the protagonist's body, though they also tinge the "universe" around him—with the experience of Kafka becoming a stand-in, and a symbol, for an entire existential situation. Sex promises to turn this situation around, and while it remains physically inaccessible it never drops out of sight, orienting Bruno's experience through its "warmth." The character's worldview is thus marked by a stark, and vividly experienced, contrast between existential coldness and warmth.

Even later in the novel, when Bruno meets a woman named Christiane, the text continues to describe his bodily feelings with the same degree of almost lyrical intensity: during their first sexual encounter,

> Bruno pressed his body to [Christiane's], his face against her small, firm breasts...He could feel her drawing him toward the center of the pool, then slowly she began to turn. He felt the muscles in his neck give, his head suddenly heavy...He saw the stars as they wheeled slowly overhead.
>
> (2000, 115)

The phenomenology of sexual contact serves as a springboard toward cosmic realities (the stars overhead). Both this and the previous passage place value on embodiment, with sex (or the lack thereof) offering an opportunity to explore the "vitality affects" (Stern 2010) that make up Bruno's existential orientation toward the world.

Michel's resistance to social interaction is diametrically opposed to this exploration of Bruno's bodily experience, since it results in a sense of unbridgeable *distance* from the world—as if Michel's body was muted and, ultimately, made irrelevant. In a scene from the first part of the novel, the young Michel has just lost a chance to dance with the girl he loves, Annabelle; yet he seems utterly indifferent to what happens:

> He had a sudden premonition that all his life would be like this moment. Emotion would pass him by, sometimes very close. Others would experience happiness and despair, but such things would be unknown to him, they would not touch him...He felt separated from the world by a vacuum molded to his body like a shell, a protective armor.
>
> (2000, 72)

This "vacuum" that envelops Michel is similar to, and yet strikingly different from, the "void" experienced by Bruno. While the void has to be filled in through the intensification of experience (and notably through the warmth of sex), the vacuum creates a safe distance where bodily sensations are made numb, like raindrops deflected by a tent's waterproof canvas. Michel thus loses self-consciousness of his body, or the ability to attend to, and act on, his own experienced feelings.[5] This leads Bruno himself, in one of his rare encounters with his half-brother, to remark: "You're not human...I knew it from the start, from the way you behaved with Annabelle" (2000, 150). The dampening of embodiment coincides with a loss of humanity—an important point in light of the novel's ending, where Michel's denial of bodily consciousness becomes one of the distinguishing features of the posthuman species he creates.

For most of the novel, Michel and Bruno are thus separated by their attitudes toward somatic experience. The situation changes only when Michel reunites with Annabelle and begins a romantic relationship with her—a sui generis relationship, to be sure, but one that nevertheless confronts him with his own body. This passage describes Michel's intercourse with Annabelle, detailing the awakening of bodily experience in him:

> Annabelle helped him off with his clothes and masturbated him until he could penetrate her. He felt nothing except the softness and the warmth of her vagina. He quickly stopped moving, fascinated by the geometry of copulation, entranced by the suppleness and richness of her juices. Annabelle pressed her mouth to his and wrapped her arms around him. He closed his eyes and, feeling the presence of his penis more acutely, started to move inside her once again. Just before he ejaculated he had a vision—crystal clear—of fusing gametes, followed immediately by the first cell divisions. It felt like a headlong rush, a little suicide. A wave of sensation flowed back along his penis and his sperm pumped out of him; Annabelle felt it too, and exhaled slowly. They lay there, motionless.
>
> (2000, 226)

Initially, we're told that Michel "felt nothing"—in continuity with the indifference toward bodily sensations already registered by the novel. Yet the clause "except the softness and the warmth of her vagina" qualifies the previous statement: that "warmth" is, of course, what Michel's half-brother finds so attractive in sexual contacts, and it is significant that it should appear in this context. The text moves on to the "geometry of copulation," which points to Michel's preference for abstract, mathematical patterns similar to those we've seen foregrounded by *Roger's Version* and *Gut Symmetries*; yet Michel's geometric image is immediately offset by another reference to somatic experience (the "suppleness and richness of her juices"). These sentences are thus poised between Michel's usual denial of bodily experience and a budding awareness of his body. The balance shifts more decidedly in favor of embodiment when Annabelle's loving gestures cause Michel to feel "the presence of his penis more acutely" and, a moment later, a "wave of sensation"—a temporary, but remarkable, intensification of consciousness in a character who has so far sought distance from experience.

Michel's following vision of "fusing gametes" is crucial. On the one hand, it captures what is about to happen in Annabelle's body—the triggering of a basic mechanism of sexual reproduction, which results in her becoming pregnant. On the other hand, this realization anticipates Michel's major breakthrough: as we read in the novel's last chapter, Michel

> established, for the first time, on the basis of irrefutable thermodynamic arguments, that the chromosomal separation at the moment of meiosis which creates haploid gametes is in itself a source of structural instability. In other words, all species dependent on sexual reproduction are by definition mortal.
>
> (2000, 248)

This sense of mortality is made more poignant by the novel's plot: Annabelle dies from a devastating cancer diagnosed when she goes to the gynecologist to confirm her pregnancy (the result of the "fusion" of her gametes with Michel's). In this key episode, Michel takes on Bruno-like qualities for the first time, in that he is flooded with sensations—thus temporarily attenuating the polarization of embodiment and disembodiment that underlies the novel. Through Michel's feelings, embodiment is paradoxically asserted as a source of insight and discovery even as Michel paves the way for a species that has done away with the two defining traits of our bodies—their sexuality and their mortality.

It is only after having first-hand experience of such things—in the form of sex with Annabelle, and her death—that Michel is able to make the decisive step toward a sexless, immortal humanity. This breakthrough consists in a new cloning method whereby "any genetic code, however complex, could be noted in a standard, structurally stable form, isolated from disturbances or mutations" (2000, 254). Michel learns how to overcome the unpredictability and randomness that define human interactions (including sexuality) as well as quantum effects at the subatomic level: the analogy between human behavior and subatomic particles—which underlies the novel, right from the title—is thus definitively abandoned. This outcome, in turn, reflects Michel's preference for stable, mathematical structures over the messiness and open-endedness of embodied intersubjectivity. The way in which Michel reaches this conclusion is highly revealing. The last chapter of *The Elementary Particles* is devoted to Michel's work at a research facility in Ireland after Annabelle's death. Here the narrator suggests that Michel's careful observation of the Book of Kells—a medieval manuscript displayed at Trinity College in Dublin and well known for its elaborate illuminations—has had a key influence on his thinking, allowing him "to overcome the complexities of calculating energy stability in biological macromolecules" (2000, 250). This scientific discovery, made possible by a medieval Gospel book, highlights a notion that we've already encountered in my reading of Winterson's *Gut Symmetries*—namely, the notion that reality is patterned at a very fundamental level.

While in Ireland, Michel writes a book titled *Meditations on Interweaving*, where he argues that "Natural forms...are human forms. Triangles, interweavings, branchings, appear in our minds. We recognize them and admire them; we live among them. We grow among our creations—human creations, which we can communicate to men—and among them we die" (2000, 251). Yet these universal forms are not purely abstract, in the sense of being devoid of affective value: one of the most surprising aspects of Michel's philosophy as it is conveyed in this last chapter is that love—the love that Michel had known through his relationship with Annabelle—informs these geometrical patterns, endowing them with a conspicuous spiritual dimension (Buddhism is referenced twice in the novel's last chapter and in the epilogue). In another quotation from Michel's *Meditations*, we read that

> the lover hears his beloved's voice over mountains and oceans; over mountains and oceans a mother hears the cry of her child. Love binds, and it binds forever. Good binds, while evil unravels. Separation is another word for evil; it is also another word for deceit. All that exists is a magnificent interweaving, vast and reciprocal.
>
> (2000, 251)

Love is thus a unifying principle, and formal patterns—in nature, but also in human intersubjectivity—are a manifestation of this principle.

This universal love is different from sexual desire, whose greediness seems inextricably bound up with "separation" (i.e., individual, autonomous existence) and with the unpredictability of natural selection. And yet, the narrator himself stresses Annabelle's role in enabling Michel's intuition: "though [Michel] Djerzinski had not known love himself, through Annabelle he had succeeded in forming an image of it. He was capable of realizing that love, in some way, through some still unknown process, was possible" (2000, 251–52). In this sense, even Bruno's attraction to sexual "warmth" can be salvaged from the narrator's snide remarks, as an attempt—perhaps misguided and off-color—to move beyond the ruthless instrumentality of sex as a factor in natural selection. Sexual contacts contain a seed of the universal love that—when seen as a formal principle and elevated to an insight into the nature of reality—makes sexual reproduction itself superfluous. As in both *Roger's Version* and *Gut Symmetries*, sex becomes a means for grappling with questions about the nature of humanity and its stance in the larger cosmic theater. But while in those novels the epistemic value of sex is, ultimately, asserted, in *The Elementary Particles* it is both acknowledged and undercut as humanity prepares to outgrow its own reliance on sexual reproduction: as the narrator affirms in the epilogue, lifting the words of Michel's disciple and advocate Hubczejak, humanity should be honored as "'the first species in the universe to develop the conditions for its own replacement'" (2000, 263).

However, that replacement comes at a high ethical cost. The posthuman society based on Michel's philosophy and described by the narrator in the epilogue is clearly dystopian: if violence has become a thing of the past, so have individual differences—and the arts and humanities with them. "The rise to dominance of scientists in all fields of thought became inevitable" (2000, 262), the narrator declares. The benumbed distanciation from reality that accompanied Michel's life has now become a species-wide trait shared even by the last remaining humans: "It has been surprising to note the meekness, resignation, perhaps even secret relief with which humans have consented to their own passing" (2000, 263). Ultimately, what the narrator's posthuman species loses is precisely the embodied consciousness that Bruno aimed to intensify via his sexual pursuits. Through the lens of this ambiguous epilogue, the novel can thus be read as an exploration into the limits as well as the ineliminable richness of bodily experience. It is a "last tribute to humanity," as the narrator explicitly frames his account in the novel's last paragraph. It also serves as a powerful reminder of the ambivalence of our sexual, mortal bodies—which are both a source of insight (as Michel discovers in his intimacy with Annabelle) and a constraint (as Michel's scientific work shows) as we attempt to think beyond the confines of the human condition.

***

In his psychoanalytic account of plot, Peter Brooks writes that narratives

> both tell of desire—typically present some story of desire—and arouse and make use of desire as dynamic of signification. Desire is in this view like Freud's notion of Eros, a force including sexual desire but larger and more polymorphous.
>
> (1984, 37)

Desire as an engine of characters' actions thus works in tandem with readers' desire to know how the narrative ends, how it resolves the instabilities and problems that set the plot in motion. The novels I have analyzed in this chapter effectively exploit this duality of desire, its being both a thematic focus of storytelling and the force behind readers' engagement. The protagonists' social and sexual relations assume a geometric shape: a square in *Roger's Version*, which charts the parallel extramarital affairs of Roger and his wife; a triangle in *Gut Symmetries*, with Alice falling in love with both Jove and his wife; and a polar opposition between Bruno's sex obsession and Michel's sexless life in *The Elementary Particles*. These shapes are formal and thematic patterns that give the plot momentum and fuel readers' interest in its ending, as suggested by Brooks.

Yet, by incorporating scientific theories and discussions, these novels significantly complicate the "dynamic of signification" posited by Brooks. In fact, my case studies blend the protagonists' sexual experiences and romantic liaisons with fundamental questions about cosmic phenomena such as the Big Bang (*Roger's Version*), quantum physics (*Gut Symmetries*), and the evolution of life on Earth and its basis in particle physics (*The Elementary Particles*). These questions are in themselves involved in a dynamic of desire, since they capitalize on a deep-rooted need to understand the universe and our position in it. However, unlike its sexual and narrative equivalent, this *epistemic* desire cannot be easily fulfilled in the context of a novel. The integration of scientific knowledge in these texts leads to long argumentative or expository passages that resist the forward-looking logic of narrative, its investment in the ending as a privileged site for evaluation and interpretation.

Part of the problem is that scientific knowledge can be articulated only tentatively and imperfectly through the verbal, narrative means of the novel. Perhaps more importantly, however, the reader's epistemic desire is frustrated by the fact that scientific knowledge is in itself tentative and incomplete: Updike, Winterson, and Houellebecq confront us—more or less explicitly—with the shortcomings of current scientific answers to cosmological questions. *Roger's Version* asks whether the universe shows traces of divine intervention, and whether this God would be empirically knowable—and thus reconcilable with the revelations of science. *Gut Symmetries* focuses on the deeply counterintuitive worldview painted by quantum physics, attempting to connect it to—and investigate it through—sexual experiences unfolding in the intermediate world. *The Elementary Particles* inspects, through the ambivalent lens of narrative irony and unreliability, a posthuman future where the uncertainties of both quantum physics and natural selection have been eliminated—and the individuality of human consciousness with them. In the hands of these authors, literary narrative becomes a device for "problem-posing" rather than problem-solving: it demonstrates the personal and ethical relevance of scientific questions, but it also draws attention to how attempts to know everything—via the "grand unified theories" envisaged by Winterson—are bound to fail, at least for the time being.

The unsatisfactory answers offered by the novels' science are what justifies the inclusion of alternative models and frameworks, such as Roger's Barthian theology, alchemy in *Gut Symmetries*, and Michel's philosophy of love in *The Elementary Particles*. Despite their seeming incompatibility with the scientific method, these references serve the crucial function of mediating between sexual desire, which has to reach a conclusion (or at least a successful reconfiguration) by the end of the narrative, and epistemic desire, which is bound to remain unfulfilled. By triangulating between these distinct discourses, my case studies seek a balance between formal closure and openness of ethical questioning, with characters engaging in morally problematic or intersubjectively tangled sexual experiences, or even (in Houellebecq's novel) paving the way for a posthuman, postsexual dystopia. This balance between narrative form and ethics lies behind the "polymorphous" (to quote again Brooks) narrative interest they generate. The body—here seen as the locus of sexual feelings—stages this complex dialogue between science, culture, and the characters' intermediate-level reality. Embodiment provides these novels with a metaphorical repertoire—Updike's "human parts interlocking, pumping, oozing," Winterson's "thinking gut," Houellebecq's "fusing gametes"—whereby they can weave together various levels of reality into a plot: through the imaginative associations they create, these embodied metaphors can alleviate the epistemological tensions and ethical ruptures between scientific models, prescientific beliefs, and everyday experience.

Notes

1 Robert Fuller explores the connection between sexuality and religious feelings in Chapter 5 of Fuller (2008).
2 Updike builds on this geometric view of human relationships throughout his oeuvre. The short story "Problems" (in Updike 1979) develops the geometric analogy even further, since the plot is presented as a series of mathematical problems.

3 For an account of narrativity that is broadly consistent with this view emerging from Updike's novel, see Askin (2015).
4 Without referring to Winterson's novel, Elizabeth Wilson (2015) outlines a strikingly similar account of how "gut thinking" blurs dualistic distinctions.
5 Cf. my reading of Vladimir Nabokov's *The Defense* in Caracciolo (2014d, Chap. 8), where I argue that Nabokov's protagonist is affected by a similar lack of bodily self-consciousness.

4 Posthuman Time Faces the Hard Problem

While Chapter 1, and to some extent all previous chapters, dealt with differences in spatial scale, this chapter shifts the focus to temporality, investigating how fictional narrative can integrate *temporal* scales incommensurable with the intermediate world. A good point of departure for this discussion is a diagram included by British physicist Roger Penrose in *The Large, the Small and the Human Mind* (1997; see Figure 4.1). This diagram compares different temporal and spatial scales in physical reality and shows how they relate to humans' average lifespan and body size. The two logarithmic scales are aligned so that an object traveling at the speed of light would cover in a given amount of time (left-hand scale) the spatial distance shown on the right-hand scale.

Penrose notes a striking difference in humans' position vis-à-vis time and space:

> [The] number of human lifetimes which make up the age of the Universe is very, very much less than the number of Planck times, or even lifetimes of the shortest lived particles, which make up a human lifetime. Thus, we are really very stable structures in the Universe. As far as spatial sizes are concerned, we are very much in the middle—we directly experience neither the physics of the very large nor the very small.
>
> (1997, 6–7)

Penrose's observation about the midway position of the human body in spatial terms resonates with the notion of intermediate world I have used throughout this book. But the fact that the human lifespan falls so close to the top of the temporal scale raises some intriguing questions. Might it be that our experience of temporality puts us in a better position to understand phenomena that occur over extremely long time periods than extremely short-lived ones? Surely, while the literary imagination has equally probed very small and very large spatial scales, it has shown a marked preference for largeness in the temporal domain. The three narratives I will examine in this chapter follow this trend: they are J. G. Ballard's short story "The Terminal Beach" (1964),

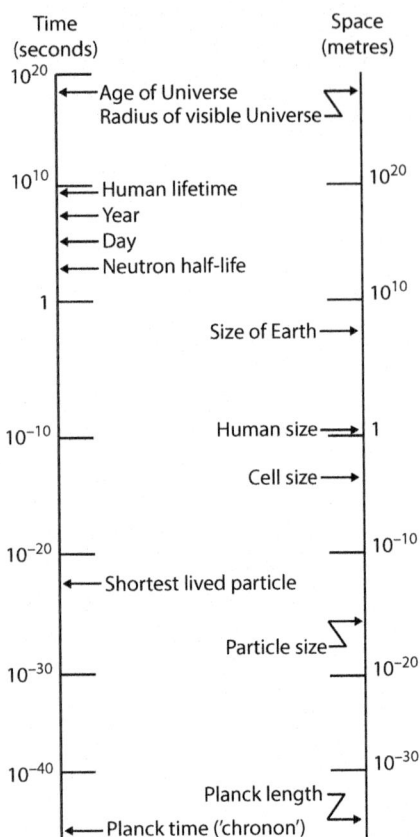

Figure 4.1 Temporal and spatial scales in comparison, from Penrose (1997, 5). Cambridge University Press © 1997. Reprinted with permission.

Kurt Vonnegut's *Galápagos* (1985), and Jorge Luis Borges's "The Immortal" (1947). I have chosen to tackle these texts in this order because it reflects the increasing temporal scales they involve: a postapocalyptic (but relatively near) future for Ballard, the remote futurity of human evolution for Vonnegut, and infinite time for Borges's immortal protagonist. These narratives bring into play posthuman temporality insofar as they are premised on a radical break in human life as we know it— whether this break entails extinction (Ballard), evolution into a different species (Vonnegut), or immortality (Borges).

Building on this posthuman perspective, these narratives defamiliarize human subjectivity and embodiment by probing the divide between psychological phenomena and physical, material processes; they ask how subjectivity may emerge from raw matter, grappling with the so-called "mind-body problem" (see, e.g., Maxwell 2000) or "hard problem of consciousness" (Chalmers 1995). In short, the problem has to do with the fact that we tend to experience a fundamental difference between entities that are inert and inanimate (for instance, a rock or a plastic cup) and entities that behave in ways that evince subjectivity (for instance, a human being or a dog). This intuition would seem to go in the direction of so-called Cartesian dualism—the idea that mind and matter are irreducibly distinct substances. However, as Thomas Nagel puts it in a recent contribution to the philosophical debate, the scientific consensus nowadays is that dualistic accounts of the mind are on the wrong track: "Among the scientists and philosophers who do express views about the natural order as a whole, reductive materialism is widely assumed to be the only serious possibility" (2012, 4). "Reductive materialism," in this context, means that—at a certain level of description—subjectivity can be reduced to objective, physical processes without any explanatory residue: consciousness is just matter arranged in particularly complex ways. The difficulty is that, even if we assume (as most scientists do) that materialism is indeed "the only serious possibility," we are still far from having a complete understanding of how matter can lead to consciousness and the subjective texture of our psychological life.

Even if we place faith in materialism as a philosophical and scientific outlook, experientially we will still perceive a difference between entities that we construe as subjects and entities that we construe as "mere" objects. Edward Slingerland argues along these lines: "The dualism advocated by Plato and Descartes was not a historical or philosophical accident, but rather a development of an intuition that comes naturally to us, as bearers of theory of mind: agents are different from things" (2008b, 394). Hence, there is a tension between the dualism of our day-to-day experience and the materialism that underlies scientific efforts at understanding the mind. This tension runs through, and periodically surfaces in, this chapter's case studies, bringing in its wake fundamental questions about the embodiment of mind. Crucially, these questions are bound up with the adoption of a posthuman timeframe: as we think beyond human existence, we are bound to ask if and how consciousness may be realized in different ways from the biological bodies we (and other animals) inhabit. The cosmic perspective of posthuman time is thus deeply interconnected with the problem of how consciousness emerges from our material bodies. This is, after all, the core message of Nagel's above-mentioned book: "the mind-body problem is not just a local problem, having to do with the relation between mind, brain, and behavior in living animal organisms, but...it invades our understanding of the entire cosmos and its history" (2012, 3). Fiction can serve as a privileged site for envisioning the cosmic ramifications of the hard problem—as my guiding texts do by taking on the stylistic and narratological challenge of representing large-scale temporalities.

In fact, engaging with posthuman temporalities raises a significant challenge for narrative. The problem is not just with the sheer *amount* of time to be put in narrative form, but with the distortions that the act of narrativization tends to create. Narrative is, in Herman's (2003) phrase, a "tool for thinking": we use it to compress temporal experience into acts of meaningful communication, by singling out the facts or events that appear relevant in a given context. But recall the discussion of narrative's built-in anthropomorphic bias in the introduction: the criteria for narrative relevance tend to be *human* criteria. Past a certain point, when the events to be related exceed the scope of human existence and history, it becomes difficult for narrative to avoid introducing a sense of anthropomorphic intentionality and teleology where there are only biophysical processes. A good example is the temporality of evolution by natural selection: as Porter Abbott has argued in a seminal essay, "there is no unencumbered way of packaging [evolutionary processes] in narrative form without serious distortion" (2003, 144). This is because evolution doesn't have a teleological endpoint and doesn't have the particularized agents that we associate with narrative: not only are individual animals unable to intentionally shape evolutionary processes, but even treating species as the "protagonists" of evolution would be a misrepresentation of Darwin's account, as Abbott shows.

In my case studies in this chapter, authors have to overcome or at least sidestep narrative's built-in bias for teleology and agency. If fiction is to confront readers with the large-scale, cosmic time posited by scientific theories of evolution or the history of the universe, it must find ways to resist readers' tendency to look for familiar human meanings. As I will show, vast temporalities can be imagined in narrative form only by putting pressure on the human, by distorting it through bodily defamiliarization and by questioning the divide between mere physicality and mental life.[1]

Sense of Place and the Place of Mind

Like Pamela Zoline, whose short story "The Heat Death of the Universe" I have discussed in Chapter 2, J. G. Ballard is one of the exponents of an experimental "new wave" in science fiction writing of the 1960s, which marked a sharp departure from previous models. And like "The Heat Death," my guiding text in this section appeared in the British magazine *New Worlds* (in 1964, three years before Zoline's short story). "The Terminal Beach" tells the story of Traven, a military pilot stranded on Eniwetok atoll in the Pacific Ocean. Eniwetok was the site of a series of US nuclear tests in the 1950s, and the narrative is haunted by the specter of nuclear disaster. The narrative charts Traven's rapid mental deterioration as he is exposed to the atoll's desolate landscape: for example, he catches glimpses of his dead wife and son or hallucinates speaking with the corpse of a Japanese doctor. When a rescue party arrives on the atoll, Traven decides to hide from his rescuers and remain behind. The story concludes as it begins, with Traven listening to "the waves breaking along the shore" while his mind brims with "images of burning bombers falling through the air" (2009, 589; cf. 604).

Yet more than Traven's delirium is at stake here. The protagonist's mental and physical decline fuses with the destiny of the human species, until it becomes impossible to distinguish between Traven's "terminal" condition and the impending extinction of humankind. Thus, in his hallucinations Traven envisions his life as the watershed between two species of human beings. The first is embodied by Claude Eatherly, a US military pilot who flew over Hiroshima in a weather reconnaissance mission before the fateful dropping of the atomic bomb: "Often, however, he thought of Eatherly: the prototypal Pre-Third Man—dating the Pre-Third from August 6, 1945—carrying a full load of cosmic guilt" (2009, 599). The "cosmic guilt" is an allusion to the posttraumatic stress disorder that Eatherly allegedly experienced after his involvement in the bombing of Hiroshima—a story that gained wide publicity in the late 1950s, with Eatherly becoming "a symbol of American guilt" over the bomb's victims (S. K. Johnson 1988, 51).

In Ballard's short story, Eatherly's guilt is elevated to a cosmic feeling that transcends national borders and historical responsibilities, indicating humanity's deep unease at the atomic forces unleashed by the bomb. As the manifestation of events unfolding well below the intermediate world (in the case of the Hiroshima bombing, nuclear fission), nuclear power stirs anxieties related to humanity's uncertain and fragile position vis-à-vis the laws governing the cosmos as a whole. The antithesis to these anxieties is what the short story calls "*Homo hydrogenensis*" or "Eniwetok Man" (2009, 599; emphasis in the original). While Eatherly is the timid and tormented precursor of the bomb, the Eniwetok Man is its offshoot: he has learned to live with the consequences of nuclear catastrophe and has adjusted to its wasteland not just psychologically but (Ballard's narrative suggests) biologically. Traven dreams up this posthuman creature and at times appears to edge close to it—but, ultimately, he is unable to let go of his human feelings.

For instance, in a surreal theatrical dialogue between Traven and the dead Japanese doctor at the end of the novel, the latter declares: "Each of us is little more than the meagre residue of the infinite unrealized possibilities of our lives. But your son, and my nephew, are fixed in our minds forever, their identities as certain as the stars" (2009, 603). This equation between personal identity and the stars contradicts the "cosmic guilt" experienced by Eatherly (and, indirectly, by Traven): it stands for a posthuman embrace between subjectivity ("our minds," "their identities") and the far-off materiality of the cosmos. Yet Traven is, as indicated by the italicized stage direction that follows, "*not entirely convinced*" (2009, 603).

He cannot reconcile himself to his son's absence, and therefore he stops short of becoming the *Homo hydrogenensis* whose posthuman viewpoint the Japanese doctor articulates in this scene. Suspended between the Cold War and a posthuman future, the protagonist is psychologically and physically trapped on the atoll. In fact, he adds that the doctor's cosmic view of human identity "leads to a dangerous conclusion in the case of this island" (2009, 603).

A full understanding of the nature of this conclusion requires confronting the spatiality of this atoll and how Ballard conveys it to his readers. Eniwetok presents a bare, desolate landscape reminiscent of a warzone. At the beginning of the story we are told that Traven sleeps "on the floor of the ruined bunker" and that decommissioned warplanes loom by the emergency airstrip (2009, 589). The sea can be heard from Traven's standpoint, but it cannot be seen due to the sand dunes that separate the bunker from the beach. We later discover that a vast swathe of the atoll is dominated by concrete blocks, geometrically arranged and rigorously identical to one another. These "blockhouses" were probably built as nuclear shelters, though the narrative says little about their original function: they emanate a mystery that goes far beyond their practical use, and in fact the text compares them to "a continuous concrete cap upon the island, a functional, megalithic architecture as grey and minatory (and apparently as ancient, in its projection into, and from, time future) as any of Assyria and Babylon" (2009, 591). Like ancient ruins, these blocks bring to the narrative a "deep," remote temporality—except that here the arrow of time is reversed: the island's landscape points not to the past but to a "time future," and thus to the posthuman creature imagined by Traven.[2] This semantic association is made even more explicit in the following passage: "Typically the island inverted the geologist's maxim, 'The key to the past lies in the present.' Here, the key to the present lay in the future. This island was a fossil of time future" (2009, 591). This final oxymoron ("a fossil of time future") neatly summarizes the nature of Ballard's island, where space and time merge in an inseparable whole, an excellent illustration of Mikhail Bakhtin's (1981) notion of "chronotope."

The bleakness and repetitiveness of this landscape make it particularly vivid and memorable for the reader. Space is broken down into very simple, quasi-geometrical elements, which the text describes as "quantal" (i.e., discrete and discontinuous, though of course a reference to quantum physics can't be ruled out). The narrator returns to these building blocks with regularity, as if to drill them into readers' mind and thus facilitate their imagination of the atoll: "Elements in a quantal world: The terminal beach. The terminal bunker. The blocks" (2009, 596). Not only is this world pared down to easily imaginable shapes, but its uniformity of color—everything is covered in concrete, even the beach—may tinge our mental imagery and give it a black-and-white quality. In an analysis of online commentaries on Cormac McCarthy's *The Road*—a novel characterized by similarly bleak and monochrome spatial descriptions—I found that several readers reported imagining McCarthy's landscape in black and white (see Caracciolo 2013c, 431). As in *The Road*, the chromatic uniformity of the atoll in "The Terminal Beach" helps make this space more distinctive—and therefore easy to visualize. Finally, our imagination is aided by Ballard's style, which underlies the affective significance of this place through associations with death and mourning, as in the following passage: "a sepulchral light lay over the concrete bunkers and causeways, and the basins seemed like ornamental lakes in a city of deserted mausoleums, abandoned even by the dead" (2009, 593–94). Because emotions increase the memorability and psychological significance of places, the affective cues deployed by Ballard's language have the effect of heightening the vividness of readers' imagination.

These strategies result in a concrete "sense of place," to borrow a concept from the field of human geography (see Tuan 1977; Foote and Azaryahu 2009). Sense of place is what defines a place and sets it apart from other locations; it encapsulates a place's distinctive (and often ineffable) qualities, which Ballard's narrative excels at conveying. Through this emerging sense of place, readers are given the chance to experience the full emotional and sensory impact of the atoll, almost as if they were there in person, alongside Traven.

This illusion may, in turn, be complicated and compounded by empathetic perspective-taking for the character—a phenomenon already examined in Chapter 1 in relation to Matheson's shrinking man. Consider, for instance, the following description:

> Half a mile further along the atoll [Traven] found a group of four submarine pens, built over an inlet, now drained, which wound through the dunes from the sea. The pens still contained several feet of water, filled with strange luminescent fish and plants. The warning light winked at intervals from the apex of a metal scaffold. The remains of a substantial camp, only recently vacated, stood on the pier outside.
>
> (2009, 596)

The first sentence of this passage adopts a spatial framework centered on Traven's body—a "body tour," as psychologists call it (see, e.g., Levinson 2003, 26). This strategy is announced by the opening words, "Half a mile further along the atoll," which suggest what we may think of—in cinematic terms—as a tracking shot: readers are asked to follow the character's linear movement as he walks half a mile further. Implicitly, this character-centered frame of reference continues into the following sentences, which—we infer—focus on Traven's visual perception.

In sum: not only is our imaginative reconstruction of this place particularly vivid and tangible, but it is likely to coincide—at least in part—with the character's own perceptual point of view. When this happens, we develop not only a sense of place but a sense of *presence* in the story-world (see Kuzmičová 2012), an embodied feeling of being there known as "immersion."

The striking aspect of Ballard's narrative, however, is that at the same time as it makes the island so visually and somatically concrete, other strategies work toward *dematerializing* this space. Many passages imply that the island is to be read psychologically, as either a projection or an extension of Traven's psyche: "This island is a state of mind," declares one of the scientists working on Eniwetok. And the narrator adds, approvingly, in a parenthetical comment:

> if primitive man felt the need to assimilate events in the external world to his own psyche, 20th century man had reversed this process; by this Cartesian yardstick, the island at least existed, in a sense true of few other places.

> (2009, 590)

What does it mean to "reverse this process"? It means that psychological states are assimilated to—in the sense of being both compared and integrated with—physical features of the island. In this way, Eniwetok becomes a spatial extension of Traven's existential feelings: by exploring the topography of the island we draw closer to the protagonist's sense of alienation and troubled personality, shaped by the possibility of a nuclear catastrophe and by the attendant "cosmic guilt." A few lines later, an italicized quotation from *War, Sadism and Pacifism* (1947) by psychoanalyst Edward Glover strengthens this psychological reading of the landscape: "The actual and potential destructiveness of the atomic bomb plays straight into the hands of the Unconscious" (2009, 590). If Eniwetok is a "state of mind," it is because—for Ballard—this nuclear wasteland taps directly into Traven's unconscious, to the extent that any clear-cut differentiation between mental states and physical features of the landscape is lost.

These ideas point in two radically different directions, however, and Ballard amplifies the effect of his short story by leaving this tension unresolved. If the island holds a mirror up to the protagonist's psychology, then we may well be within a Cartesian, dualistic view of the mind—where the mirroring and the blurring of boundaries work precisely because the existence of these boundaries is assumed: the mind and physical processes are fundamentally distinct, and the connections between them can only be metaphorical (note the allusion to the "Cartesian yardstick" in the passage quoted above). This reading would emphasize the symbolism of the island as it reveals certain features of the human psyche, and particularly our deep-seated interest in envisioning a posthuman future—the future foreshadowed by the atomic bomb. The text hints repeatedly at this symbolic dimension of Eniwetok: "Above him, along the crests of the dunes, the tall palms leaned into the dim air like the symbols of a cryptic alphabet. The landscape of the island was covered by strange ciphers" (2009, 589); "The landscape is coded. Entry points into the future = Levels in a spinal landscape = zones of significant time" (2009, 597). These symbols, ciphers, and codes dissolve the physicality of the landscape into abstract associations that function in a dualistic way; psychological significance is superimposed on the island as if it belonged to a different sphere of existence. Through this symbolic strategy, the narrative evokes mind-matter dualism, and with it our tendency to distinguish between the character's psychology (and human psychology more generally) and the island's physical landscape.

The story can be approached from an alternative angle, which avoids this difficulty by embracing the idea that our mental processes are deeply, and constitutively, material. From this perspective, the island is not an allegorical reflection of Traven's state of mind; it actively *shapes* or (alternatively) *extends* his mind in fully material terms. For instance, the narrative explores the effects of the concrete blocks, with their regular layout, on Traven's psychology:

> As he entered the first of the long aisles, Traven felt the sense of fatigue that had dogged him for so many months begin to lift. With their geometric regularity and finish, the blocks seemed to occupy more than their own volumes of space, imposing on him a mood of absolute calm and order.
>
> (2009, 595)

The key phrase here is "seemed to occupy more than their own volumes of space": the blocks influence Traven's mood by invading his body (and mind) with their "absolute calm and order." In the mind-world continuum, the mind has no priority: the world determines what Traven feels. A few paragraphs later this impact is couched in even more explicitly neurophysiological language:

> Since the discovery of the blocks he had become a creature of reflexes, kindled from levels above those of his existing nervous system (if the autonomic system was dominated by the past, Traven sensed, the cerebro-spinal reached towards the future).
>
> (2009, 596)

The physical landscape latches onto the character's "cerebro-spinal" system, which is future-oriented like the island itself, "a fossil of time future." This and similar statements emphasize the continuity between the geography of the island and the nature of Traven's mind, for both are—without any need for metaphors or symbols—material through and through.

In other instances the short story comes close to Clark and Chalmers's (2010) influential "extended mind hypothesis," which is another materialist way of looking at the mind, falling within the broader framework of embodied cognitive science.[3] The idea behind this hypothesis is that the mind doesn't stop at the physical boundaries of our body, but extends into the world through artifacts that play a substantive role in cognition. Writing instruments are a prime example: think of how writing (or otherwise recording information externally) greatly expands our ability to remember things. Clark sees this process as one of "continuous reciprocal causation" based on "continuous, mutually modulatory influences linking brain, body, and world" (A. Clark 1997, 163). To the extent that the world is causally involved in our mental processes, it *is* part of our mental processes. In Ballard's story, the blocks make up for Traven's psychological shortcomings, taking on work that his mind cannot handle:

> The system of megaliths now provided a complete substitute for those functions of his mind which gave to it its sense of the sustained rational order of time and space. Without them, his awareness of reality shrank to little more than the few square inches of sand beneath his feet.
>
> (2009, 597)

This is an overblown version of the extended mind hypothesis: just as we use clocks or measuring instruments to complement and objectify our experience of time and space, the blocks completely take over functions normally carried out by Traven's mind; he needs their monolithic materiality to give spatio-temporal order to his existence.

This order is, as we have seen, "quantal" insofar as it is based on discrete units—the blocks themselves. This idea is further developed in an important episode from the second part of the short story, when Traven finds himself "unable to leave the blocks" (2009, 600):

> *"Goodbye, Eniwetok,"* [Traven] murmured.
>
> Somewhere there was a flicker of light, as if one of the blocks, like a counter on an abacus, had been plucked away.
>
> *Goodbye, Los Alamos.* Again, a block seemed to vanish. The corridors around him remained intact, but somewhere in his mind had appeared a small interval of neutral space.
>
> *Goodbye, Hiroshima.*
>
> *Goodbye, Alamagordo* [sic]. *"Goodbye, Moscow, London, Paris, New York…"*

Shuttles flickered, a ripple of lost integers. He stopped, realizing the futility of this megathlon farewell. Such a leave-taking required him to fix his signature upon every one of the particles in the universe.

(2009, 601)

As Traven, in his delirium, takes leave of cities variously connected with the atomic bomb (as real or potential sites of atomic blasts), the blocks seem to vanish one by one—and at the same time a blank appears in Traven's "inner," mental space. The blocks are part of Traven's mind and even stand for spaces beyond the atoll, but in a very different sense from the "codes" and "ciphers" we have seen above: here the mental is not externally superimposed on the physical; on the contrary, the physical enters the mental and actively participates in Traven's train of thought. Eventually, however, Traven decides to abandon his "megathlon farewell," because he realizes that the interconnectedness between the physical world and his psychology is constitutive: his mind is bound up with "every one of the particles in the universe." This scene suggests something akin to Nagel's idea that "the mind-body problem...invades our understanding of the entire cosmos." In his attempt to rid himself of the blocks, Traven discovers that the material world is always already part of our minds, just as our minds are always already part of the cosmos: no liberation is possible, but only the acceptance of the continuous reciprocal causation between our physical bodies and the material world.

Yet Traven doesn't seem to accept this realization completely. This is what emerges in his final dialogue with the Japanese doctor. The two characters are talking about a fly that is buzzing around the doctor's corpse. The doctor warns Traven:

You can't accept the plurality of the universe—ask yourself why, Traven. Why should this obsess you? It seems to me that you are hunting for the white leviathan, zero...Have a proper humility, pursue a philosophy of acceptance. TRAVEN: Then may I ask why you came here, Doctor? YASUDA [the doctor]: To feed this fly. "What greater love—?"

(2009, 603–4)

The doctor's last comment is a reminder of the materiality of our bodies, whose ultimate goal ("why you came here") is that of sustaining an ecological cycle. This insight contradicts Traven's quest for a "white leviathan, zero," which is perhaps an allusion to consciousness as an immaterial, illusory substance. For the Japanese doctor, there can be no "greater love" than accepting that there is no fundamental difference between our minds, our bodies, and the material world—they are all part of a physical continuum, not unlike the humble fly.

During the time spent among the mysterious blocks, which enter Traven's mind and even replace some of his cognitive functions, the character comes close to this realization, but eventually he cannot fully face up to it. He does manage to escape from the blocks, however, and returns to the beach—and to the same situation he was in at the beginning of the narrative:

> Patiently Traven waited for [his wife and son] to speak to him, thinking of the great blocks whose entrance was guarded by the seated figure of the dead archangel [the Japanese doctor], as the waves broke on the distant shore and the burning bombers fell through his dreams.
>
> (2009, 604)

The blocks are now only a thought, kept at a safe distance by the Japanese doctor's corpse, and Traven is free to indulge in memories of his family and in traumatic war images (the burning bombers). We can thus map dualism and materialism onto the two human species discussed above, Eatherly and the Eniwetok Man. Traven has a fleeting glimpse of the Eniwetok Man's posthuman materialism: he toys with the cosmic perspective, which involves accepting the physical nature of mind. Yet the character is unable to detach himself from Eatherly's cosmic guilt and cannot dispel the illusion of a separation between the world of physical things and the world of mental (and specifically human) happenings. Suspended between the human and the posthuman, Traven cannot leave the limbo of the terminal beach, remaining locked in a dualistic understanding of reality.

The protagonist is not alone on this terminal beach, however. The sense of place created by Ballard's spatial descriptions transports readers to the world of Eniwetok and invites them to share in the protagonist's epistemological drama. This is, on my reading, the tension probed by Ballard's narrative, and we experience it through a process of bodily defamiliarization: the postapocalyptic landscape of the island is so vividly described that we can develop an illusion of being there, in a fully embodied way. Yet it is also a highly symbolic landscape: it stages abstract ideas such as dualism and materialism and it takes on quasi-universal resonance by leveraging unconscious psychological predispositions—in particular, a fascination with the extinction of our own species. Like Traven himself, Eniwetok is caught between two states, physical existence and symbolism, and this interpretive dilemma plays out in bodily terms—through Traven's starved body, the Japanese doctor's corpse, and readers' own body to the extent that they come to inhabit the island during their engagement with the narrative. We feel the island's materiality, but we also grasp its symbolic significance, and we remain suspended between these interpretations even as we realize—as Traven begins to do—that there should be no difference between mental symbols and physical realities. Put otherwise: the reading experience enacts the very split that the character, and the narrative as a whole, are struggling with. The defamiliarization lies in this textual mechanism, which confronts us with the surprising continuity between the body, the world, and our allegedly autonomous mental life. In this way, Ballard's short story joins a number of literary texts that, in the twentieth century, have attempted what Russell Samolsky (2011, 5) conceptualizes as the "incorporation of apocalypse": they associate catastrophic scenarios with marked, distorted, or otherwise problematized forms of embodiment.

Why We Don't Need Big Brains

Taking issue with the unimaginativeness of much science fiction at the beginning of the 1960s, Ballard argued in an essay-manifesto for the "new wave" that the genre should "turn its back on space, on interstellar travel, extraterrestrial life forms, galactic wars and the overlap of these ideas" (1996, 197). Instead, he made two suggestions: first, science fiction authors should begin exploring the "inner space" of characters' psychology (hence the title of the essay, "Which Way to Inner Space?"); second, biology should take a central role in this exploration. "The Terminal Beach" neatly exemplifies the first claim, since as we have seen the narrative blurs the boundary between the physical features of the setting and the character's mental states. The turn to biology is less explicit in the short story, but it arguably underpins the narrator's references to Traven's "cerebro-spinal" system or the evolutionary promise of a *Homo hydrogenensis*. A writer who, two decades later, would respond to Ballard's call for a more prominent role of biology in science fiction is Kurt Vonnegut, whose novel *Galápagos* uses evolution by means of natural selection as its main plot device. The literary mode favored by Vonnegut is satire: by adopting the large-scale temporality of evolution, *Galápagos* pokes fun at humanity and reveals its parochial, faulty, and ultimately expendable nature. In doing so, Vonnegut's novel presents a striking image of how the human mind evolved, investigating how it is deeply connected to a body of a certain size and structure.

Vonnegut achieves a remarkable integration of narrative and thematic dynamics by anchoring these questions about the evolution of mind to the novel's narrative progression. The plot is set off by a combination of disasters: a global financial crisis wreaks havoc on the economies of South America (including Ecuador, where part of the novel is set); meanwhile, a virus spreads through the planet and makes all women sterile, seemingly condemning humanity to an early, abrupt extinction. Humanity starts disappearing off the face of the Earth, with only one exception: a handful of people who, in an attempt to escape from Ecuador's social and economic turmoil, sail off the Ecuadorian port of Guayaquil and are eventually shipwrecked on Santa Rosalia, an island in the Galápagos archipelago. Being cut off from the rest of humankind, these survivors do not contract the virus and therefore ensure the continuation of the human species.

The plot brims with ironic references to Darwin's theory of evolution, but also to the Biblical narrative.[4] Darwin famously visited the Galápagos islands and made there a series of key observations that laid the groundwork for his account of natural evolution. The ship on which the survivors escape is called the "Bahía de Darwin" and is repeatedly compared to Noah's ark. The ship's captain, the only man on Santa Rosalia and therefore the father of all future human beings, is dubbed by the narrator a "latter-day Adam" (2011, 51). The narrative is retrospective, with the narrator (named Leon Trout) looking back on the events that made the survival of humankind possible. More precisely, the narration takes place "a million years" in the future, as the novel's first sentence indicates: "The thing was: One million years ago, back in 1986 A.D., Guayaquil was the chief seaport of the little South American democracy of Ecuador, whose capital was Quito, high in the Andes Mountains" (2011, 3). If the narrator has witnessed events unfolding on such a vast timescale, his identity poses something of a problem. In fact, this is one of the novel's central puzzles: as we read, it becomes gradually clear that the narrator is a disembodied entity, the ghost of a man who died on the Bahía de Darwin while it was still in the shipyard. Curious to know the fate of these last humans and see what will become of humanity, the narrator passes up an opportunity to leave the Earth and decides to haunt the ship for a million years. The picture he paints is startling: from the cosmic viewpoint of a million years into the future, humanity has "survived," but only by turning into a species of seal-like creatures incapable of speech or tool use.

This outcome, which the narrator announces relatively early on in the novel, undercuts any form of human exceptionalism and speaks to recent debates about the Anthropocene, an era defined by the impact of human activities on the planet's ecosystems (see Introduction). For Vonnegut's posthuman narrator ("posthuman" both because of his disembodiment and because he narrates after the end of humanity as we know it), even the Anthropocene is likely to seem a short-lived reality: we are an animal species subject to evolutionary pressures like any other species; language and technology, long thought to be human prerogatives, are the result of a particular evolutionary history and may be abandoned as evolutionary pressures change with the environment. The narrator explains that, having to survive in a place where food only comes from the sea, human hands

> have become flippers...Those parts of people's brain which used to control their hands, moreover, simply don't exist anymore, and

human skulls are now much more streamlined on that account. The more streamlined the skull, the more successful the fisher person.

(2011, 202)

This point resonates with one of the narrator's pet theories, which he develops throughout the novel: namely, that our "big brains" are anything but an asset to our evolutionary success; they are at the root of humanity's calamities and constitute "nearly fatal defects in the evolution of the human race" (2011, 9).

A series of parallels with nonhuman animals support the narrator's pessimistic view of human brains. For instance, we learn that one of the characters stranded on Santa Rosalia, the biology teacher Mary Hepburn, used to tell her students about Irish elk, which "survived for two and a half million years, in spite of the fact that their antlers were too unwieldy for fighting or self-defense" (2011, 26). For Mary Hepburn, Irish elk are an example of "how tolerant nature could be of clearly ridiculous mistakes in evolution" (2011, 26). A similar use is made of one of the Galápagos islands' distinctive bird species, the blue-footed boobies. In another of Mary Hepburn's classes, the students watch a documentary showing these birds' elaborate courtship ritual, which the narrator describes in detail:

> Already breast to breast and toe to toe, they made their sinuous necks as erect as flagpoles. They tilted their heads back as far as they would go. They pressed their long throats and the undersides of their jaws together. They formed a tower, the two of them—a single structure, pointed on top and resting on four blue feet. Thus was a marriage solemnized.
>
> (2011, 112)

For Mary, this striking behavior, which has no survival value, is closely reminiscent of human art or even religion (2011, 115). But the narrator puts a different spin on this analogy between the birds' behavior and human culture: from his posthuman perspective, art and religion are as gratuitous and extravagant as the birds' garish blue feet and elaborate courtship dance; they are costly evolutionary add-ons that humanity had to shed as soon as the material conditions changed.

So much for the narrator's evolutionary account of our "big brains." Of course, this account should not be taken literally, for it is highly likely that our social intelligence did play a role in the evolutionary success of humankind. But there is an aspect of evolutionary science that Vonnegut does get right, and that aspect is precisely what keeps the novel's plot moving: namely, the idea that natural evolution is a fundamentally chance-driven process. As Andrea Bixler explains in an article about how science fiction can be used to teach evolution, Vonnegut's novel "incorporates genetic drift as well as natural selection: Future human evolution is modified not only through adaptation to a new environment, but also by random changes in a small gene pool" (2007, 339). It is the combination of environmental pressures (the animals that possess survival-enhancing traits are more likely to reproduce) and random genetic mutations that drives natural evolution. In Richard Dawkins's words, evolution "occurs because, in successive generations, there are slight differences in embryonic development. These differences come about because of changes (mutations—this is the small random element in the process that I spoke of) in the genes controlling development" (1996, 73). This "small random element" goes hand in hand with the fact that evolution doesn't have a teleological endpoint: it doesn't "lead" anywhere—not even to human big brains—but is rather an ongoing, open-ended process. As Porter Abbott argues in the article discussed in the introduction to this chapter, this lack of agency and teleology, compounded by the large scale of evolutionary processes, makes natural selection particularly difficult to pin down in narrative form.

Vonnegut's answer to this challenge is twofold and involves the strategies that I will call "mindless progression" and "nonlinear temporality." Through these literary devices, Vonnegut is able to offer a radically materialist solution to the hard problem of how complex minds came into being (and can disappear without a trace). Mindless progression refers to the way in which the plot mirrors the randomness and haphazardness of natural evolution. If humanity does not become extinct, the narrator reminds us, it is only thanks to a long series of coincidences. Take, for example, the shipwreck on Santa Rosalia: this will turn out to be a lucky circumstance, because the island's remoteness protects the survivors from the virus outbreak that is taking place on the mainland. But the narrator makes clear that this shipwreck was caused by the captain's sheer incompetence at maneuvering the ship. This, in turn, happened because the first mate, who had the skills to actually steer the ship, decided to disappear before the situation in Guayaquil took a sharp downward turn. Hence the narrator's comment:

> The combination of the Captain's incompetence and the decision of Hernando Cruz to go to the aid of his own flesh and blood, although the stuff of low comedy at the time, has turned out to be of incalculable value to present-day humankind.
>
> (2011, 149)

If things go in a certain way, and humanity survives, it is not thanks to the survivors' actions but *despite* them—that is, because of the unintended consequences of those actions.

To signal the precarious and serendipitous nature of the narrative progression, the narrator makes frequent use of counterfactuals, through what Gerald Prince has called the "disnarrated": "events that *do not* happen but, nonetheless, are referred to (in a negative or hypothetical mode) by the narrative text" (1988, 2; emphasis in the original).[5] A particularly spectacular example of this strategy can be found halfway through the novel, when a mentally disturbed soldier breaks into a souvenir shop and kills two major characters. The narrator adds that "the soldier who shot them is another person who should be credited with having done a little something whose effects are still visible after a million years" (2011, 159). Ironically, this has nothing to do with the cold-blooded killing of the two characters. Rather, the soldier's action that makes a difference (again, unwittingly) is his breaking open the shop's backdoor—which allows six young girls belonging to an indigenous people of the Ecuadorian rain forest to join the other survivors via the shop. These girls, the narrator points out, "would grow to womanhood on Santa Rosalia, where…they would become the mothers of all modern humankind" (2011, 164). This result explains the narrator's previous counterfactual comment that, if the soldier "had not burglarized that shop, there would almost certainly be no human beings on the face of the earth today. I mean it. Everybody alive today should thank God that this soldier was insane" (2011, 160). Two things are worth noting here: first, the disnarrated serves to emphasize how humanity's survival was an unpredictable outcome hanging on a series of fortuitous circumstances—an idea that injects into the novel's plot the chance-driven logic of natural evolution; second, just as the captain lacks the ability to steer his ship, the soldier who unintentionally "saves" humankind is mentally deranged. This coincidence further separates the progression of the narrative from any sense of goal-oriented intentionality (which, of course, reflects the lack of intentionality in evolution itself).

This is a radical plotting strategy in that it does away with the link between plot and characters' mental states. One of the clearest formulations of this link in narratology can be found in Marie-Laure Ryan's *Possible Worlds, Artificial Intelligence, and Narrative Theory* (1991): for Ryan, plot is produced by the interaction between the storyworld and characters' "private worlds"—that is, the worlds reflecting their beliefs and desires. But in *Galápagos* the narrative advances *despite* the characters' mental states, through unintended consequences and coincidences. The novel's "mindless plotting" is uncoupled from the characters' mentalistic agency and intentionality. What the narrator says of the Bahía de Darwin thus turns out to be true of the narrative as a whole, at least as far as the characters are concerned: "there had been absolutely nobody at the top who had understood how things really worked, what it was all about, what was really going on" (2011, 150).

In another sense, however, the narrator (and behind him the author) *are* in charge. How the narrator handles the novel's temporality makes this abundantly clear. Commenting on this aspect of the novel, Jerome

Klinkowitz argues: "By a combination of specific focusing and virtually infinite extrapolation, Vonnegut is able to put much more into a novel than would normally fit...In doing so, he speaks cosmically, using the voice of a million-year-old ghost" (2004, 132). From his cosmic viewpoint, this ghostly narrator has complete control over the novel's timespan; he conveys it to the reader by relating in detail the events that led to the shipwreck off Santa Rosalia (Klinkowitz's "specific focusing") and by condensing the slow evolutionary processes that resulted in humanity becoming a seal-like species ("infinite extrapolation"). The formal device that enables the narrator to embrace this large-scale temporality is the constant use of prolepses or flash-forwards. The narrative keeps moving back and forth between three distinct temporal planes: the events that unfold in Ecuador and later on the ship, what happens to the survivors once they get to Santa Rosalia, and what becomes of humanity one million years into the future, long after the survivors' death. This nonlinear temporality makes for a particularly fragmented narrative experience, in which readers' interest in the survivors' fate is continuously displaced by references to future events. For instance, in introducing a young girl named Selena, the narrator remarks in passing: "Little did young Selena know in Guayaquil, as she listened to her sociopathic father wheel and deal on the telephone, that her destiny was to pair off with Hisako Hiroguchi, two rooms away, and to raise a furry baby" (2011, 74–75). In many other cases the narrator drops casual references to how human bodies changed over the course of a million years, explaining that humans would no longer be able to perform actions that were routine for the characters onboard the Bahía de Darwin: "No person living today has hands clever enough or a brain big enough to operate a [computer]. Nobody can thread a needle, either—or play the piano, or pick his or her nose, as the case may be" (2011, 61).

The wide temporal scale of evolution is thus captured by destabilizing the linearity of the narrative through the strategic anticipation of future outcomes. The effect of these temporal shifts is ironic, in the sense that they undermine any suspense the reader may experience. Further, the shifts reinforce the impression that the plot proceeds—like natural evolution—in a haphazard fashion, directed as it is by the whims of an unpredictable narrator: in his reading of the novel, Peter Freese argues that the novel's decentralized narrative method traces "a cosmic round dance" (2009, 601). The nonlinearity is a discourse-level equivalent to the apparent randomness and mindlessness that govern the progression of the story.

What picture of the human mind does the narrative paint through these sophisticated strategies? For the narrator, our rich mental life is only a prank of evolution, the result of oversize brains capable only of bombarding us with worthless ideas in a state of constant flux:

> the Galápagos Islands could be hell in one moment and heaven in the next, and Julius Caesar could be a statesman in one moment and

a butcher in the next, and Ecuadorian paper money could be traded for food, shelter, and clothing in one moment and line the bottom of a birdcage in the next, and the universe could be created by God Almighty in one moment and by a big explosion in the next—and on and on.

(2011, 16–17)

In another important passage, the ship's captain is seen looking at the stars and contemplating the insignificance of his planet and species vis-à-vis cosmic realities, but these sublime feelings are also put down to big brains with "excess capacity." The narrator wryly adds: "You won't catch anybody thinking thoughts like that today" (2011, 216). Everything in human mentality—politics, material culture, cosmological hypotheses—is dismissively reduced to a hyperactive brain being "diverted from the main business of life" (2011, 17): namely, the evolutionary business of finding food, shelter, and sexual partners. No wonder, then, that in Vonnegut's novel humanity avoids extinction only thanks to a series of unintentional mistakes made by the brain—with the implication being that if the characters had consciously *wanted* to save our species, they would have failed miserably. (A grim lesson to be taken into account as the specter of an ecological disaster looms larger and larger.)

Nowhere in the novel is this point demonstrated more clearly than in the description of the body of our evolutionary descendants. The narrator repeatedly draws our attention to the fact that the seal-like humans are unable to form words, use tools, or mentally handle complex scientific theories. Natural selection has even solved our notorious tooth problems, though it's been a "draconian" solution, as the narrator admits: "It hasn't made teeth more durable. It has simply cut the average human life span down to about thirty years" (2011, 85). In this and many other descriptions throughout the novel, irony is accompanied by bodily defamiliarization, insofar as the shape and structure of human bodies have changed so dramatically in a million years that it would be hard to see these creatures as "human," were it not for our trust in the narrator's evolutionary account. Further, the "streamlining" (2011, 201) of our descendants' bodies and brains has led to a "streamlining" of their mentality, a correlation that implies an embodied view of psychological processes: the richness of human thinking can be mapped onto physical properties of our bodies, which are in turn the result of a particular evolutionary history. Vonnegut thus embraces reductive materialism as a solution to the mind-body problem. Crucially, this position is not so much spelled out as implicated in the plot through its close mirroring of the logic of natural selection—a mirroring made possible by the narrator's cosmic viewpoint, mindless progression, and nonlinear temporality.

Yet Vonnegut's engagement with the mind-body problem is more complex than this materialist reading of the novel suggests. Through its ironic narrative, the novel comes close to the tension between dualism and materialism we have seen at work in Ballard's "The Terminal Beach." The ambivalence, in *Galápagos*, begins with a character's remark about a "soul" supposedly independent from the brain:

> "I'll tell you what the human soul is, Mary," [Roy Hepburn] whispered, his eyes closed. "Animals don't have one. It's the part of you that knows when your brain isn't working right. I always knew, Mary. There wasn't anything I could do about it, but I always knew."
>
> (2011, 45)

Of course, it would seem easy to dismiss this character's words as naïve: the novel's Darwinian narrative outlines a much more plausible, empirically grounded view of mental processes. It doesn't help that, in one of Vonnegut's many sarcastic twists, Roy Hepburn will soon die of brain cancer. But references to a mysterious "soul" can be found throughout the novel, as noted by Freese:

> This chain of references to a brain-soul dichotomy is another example of Vonnegut's quite unabashed technique of eating his cake and having it, too. By adopting Roy Hepburn's childishly simple distinction that humans have a "soul" and animals do not, Trout [the narrator] can solve his evaluative problems by charging everything he rejects in human beings to their faulty brains and by granting everything he likes to the praiseworthy souls.
>
> (2009, 596)

What is even more important, Roy's dualistic account of mental processes finds implicit support and narrative legitimization in the narrator's figure—for what is this ghostly narrator but a disembodied mind? The narrator keeps talking about an afterlife and a "blue tunnel" that would lead to it: a religious, dualistic conception of consciousness that flatly contradicts the narrative's apparent Darwinian materialism.

Surely, these images of the afterlife are ironic, but everything in the novel is, including the idea of a posthuman species endowed with fur and flippers. This tension between reductive materialism and metaphysical dualism cannot be easily resolved. Vonnegut is confronting readers with the schism between science and the residual dualism of our psychological makeup. This implicit dualism depends on cultural and linguistic biases; even more fundamentally, it reflects how cognition is skewed toward a worldview in which subjects are inherently and irreducibly distinct from "mere" objects. This goes hand in hand with Slingerland's intuition, discussed in the introduction to this chapter, that the "dualism advocated by Plato and Descartes was not a historical or philosophical accident, but rather a development of an intuition that comes naturally to us, as bearers of theory of mind: agents are different from things" (2008b, 394). This intuition lies at the root of religious worldviews based on the possibility of consciousness after biological death, for this position assumes that what makes us agents (our minds) can survive our thing-like bodies. The novel thus exploits the tension between religious narratives (the afterlife, the references to Noah's ark and Adam, etc.) and the scientific framework of Darwinism to point up the ambivalence of our conception of mind. This ironic move leaves readers in an epistemological no man's land: the hard problem is brought up but ultimately goes unanswered; in the process, readers are reminded of the limitations and inadequacy of their "big brains," which are prone to experience a categorical distinction between mind and body where there should be none. One thing is certain: for Vonnegut, if we did not have brains of this size, we could not afford the luxury of pondering the mysteries of the universe—or of our own minds. Two narrative strategies work jointly toward revealing this cognitive impasse: the cosmic timescale introduced by the narrator and the defamiliarizing perspective he offers on the future evolution of human bodies.

Infinite Loops of Selfhood

If Vonnegut engages closely with the science of evolution, the main inspiration for Jorge Luis Borges's short story "The Immortal" is philosophical. The short story is part of Borges's lifelong interest in the philosophy of temporality.[6] Just one year before the publication of "The Immortal" in 1947, Borges had published an essay entitled "A New Refutation of Time," where he offered a metaphysical *scherzo* in the tradition of Bishop Berkeley's idealism. Claiming to take the philosophies of Berkeley and Hume to their logical (if radical) conclusion, Borges argues that time is, like everything else in the universe, the product of a universal mind uncoupled from subjectivity; to this God-like mind, everything—including the temporal expanse of the universe—is available at once:

> I deny, with the arguments of idealism, the vast temporal series which idealism admits. Hume denied the existence of an absolute space, in which all things have their place; I deny the existence of one single time, in which all things are linked as in a chain.
>
> (2007, 222)

If there is no temporal succession, then our experience of temporality is an illusion; narrative, as an attempt at capturing time through a sequence of signs, must be equally misguided. And yet, at the end of the essay, this metaphysical edifice falls apart, with the author conceding that his insight into the nature of time is deeply counterintuitive. The apparent philosophical detachment of Borges the essayist gives way, and the author starts sounding much like one of the troubled characters we are familiar with through Borges's fiction:

> *And yet, and yet...*Denying temporal succession, denying the self, denying the astronomical universe, are apparent desperations and secret consolations. Our destiny (as contrasted with the hell of Swedenborg and the hell of Tibetan mythology) is not frightful by being unreal; it is frightful because it is irreversible and ironclad. Time is the substance I am made of. Time is a river which sweeps me along, but I am the river; it is a tiger which destroys me, but I am the tiger; it is a fire which consumes me, but I am the fire. The world, unfortunately, is real; I, unfortunately, am Borges.
>
> (2007, 233–34; italics in the original)

Remarkably, this paragraph—which closes the essay—weaves together the destiny of the self and the destiny of the universe at large. The puzzle of time as an intrinsic dimension of our subjectivity cannot be uncoupled from time as a feature of the physical universe. If we deny the sequentiality of time, then the existence of both the self and the "astronomical universe" is put into jeopardy. This connection between selfhood and the universe emerges in the paradoxical images at the end of the quotation: if time is a river—an analogy that goes back to Heraclitus—how can one be the river, too? To phrase the question otherwise, how can the self be both contained by and equal to the universe? And how can time be both the self and that which destroys the self (a tiger, the fire)? The analogies through which Borges expresses these ideas take a peculiar spatial form; they trace what Douglas Hofstadter would call a "strange loop"—that is, "a paradoxical level-crossing feedback loop" (2007, 102). They resemble, for instance, M. C. Escher's famous image of two hands drawing each other, which Hofstadter takes as an example of a strange loop in his influential *Gödel, Escher, Bach* (1999). In Borges's paragraph, however, the level crossing doesn't involve the distinction between creator and creation but ideas of containment (being *in* the river of time and being the river) and destruction (being what destroys and what is destroyed). These blurred distinctions give rise to what Hofstadter calls a "sense of topological wrongness" (1999, 686), which is evoked by many of Borges's stories. This wrongness depends on the fact that strange loops contradict image schemata (in this case, CONTAINMENT and CYCLE) derived from embodied interactions with the world.

Originally published in 1979, Hofstadter's *Gödel, Escher, Bach* has earned widespread critical acclaim. Yet, as Hofstadter himself laments in the preface to *I Am a Strange Loop* (2007), the intrinsic appeal of the idea of "strange loops," and their ubiquity in human cultures, have upstaged the central message of his earlier book. That message was concerned with the hard problem of consciousness: how can "things" as immaterial as consciousness and selfhood arise from physical processes in our brains and bodies? For Hofstadter, the conscious self is an emergent phenomenon that cannot be pinned down in any brain area or individual neural process but depends on complex patterns of activity. In this respect, Hofstadter's argument is aligned with the account of the self that Daniel Dennett has offered in *Consciousness Explained* (1991). The self is not something that exists in any physical sense: it is a subjective illusion produced by brains wired up in certain ways. Hofstadter suggests that the abstract pattern of selfhood is fundamentally similar to a strange loop in its organization: "Our 'I''s are self-reinforcing illusions that are an inevitable by-product of strange loops, which are themselves an inevitable by-product of symbol-possessing brains that guide bodies through the dangerous straits and treacherous waters of life" (2007, 292). How does this strange loop work? In our psychological development we are exposed to "an extensive web of linguistic and cultural conventions that collectively and subliminally insist that we each are exactly one person" (2007, 308). Symbolic animals that we are, we interiorize these conventions to the extent that we reinterpret our disparate experiences by assuming that a self was "there" in the first place. The self thus seems to underlie our life experiences, while it was in fact *created* by them. This is precisely the level-crossing, counterintuitive logic that we find in Borges's paradoxes about temporality.

My case study in this section—the short story "The Immortal"— combines Borges's interest in temporality with an exploration into selfhood as a fundamentally "loopy" phenomenon. In this text Borges engages with the paradoxes of the self by doing away with temporal succession. The narrative thus functions—as many of Borges's short stories—as a thought experiment on the nature of self and its relationship with the temporal scale of human experience. What happens, the story asks, when a character does not just *imagine* the posthuman futurity of Ballard and Vonnegut, but can actually experience it because he has become immortal? This is the premise of Borges's short story, and its implementation in narrative form employs, as we'll see, a number of embodied cues and strategies. In this way, the text hints at the deep-seated connection between human subjectivity, embodiment, and temporalities beyond the human.

"The Immortal," first published in 1947 and later included in the collection *The Aleph*, is one of Borges's best-known short stories.[7] It starts with a familiar trope: in 1929, the princess de Lucinge acquires the original edition of Pope's translation of the *Iliad* from the rare book dealer Joseph Cartaphilus; when the princess opens the sixth volume, she discovers a handwritten document by Marcus Flaminius Rufus, a military tribune in one of Rome's legions at the time of the emperor Diocletian.

The bulk of Borges's story is presented as a verbatim transcript of Rufus's account. Dissatisfied with life in the army, Rufus embarks on a quest for a legendary City of the Immortals he has heard about from a dying soldier. This city lies next to a river whose waters are thought to give the gift of immortality. Rufus travels eastward, into "barbaric lands...where the Earth is the mother of monsters" (Borges 2000, 5). After several harrowing days in the desert, abandoned by his companions and about to die from thirst, Rufus falls unconscious. When he comes to, he discovers that he has been taken captive by a tribe of Troglodytes whose existence (material *and* mental) is so rudimentary that they live in caves and cannot communicate verbally. Rufus repeatedly compares them to animals, insisting on their abject, repulsive nature. Surprisingly, however, "the patent City of the Immortals" (2000, 6) is now clearly visible on the horizon, perched on a stone plateau. Taking advantage of the Troglodytes' indifference to his fate, Rufus escapes and quenches his thirst in a "noiseless, impure stream" that runs at the foot of the city (2000, 6). Only later does the character realize that this stream is the fabled river of immortality.

Rufus decides to venture into the City of the Immortals; to do so, he has to make his way through a subterranean labyrinth. Here he experiences the first distortion in his time consciousness:

> I know not how long I wandered under the earth; I do know that from time to time, in a confused dream of home, I conflated the horrendous village of the barbarians and the city of my birth, among the clusters of grapes.
>
> (2000, 8)

Unbeknownst to Rufus, this conflation is the first sign of how the character's immortality distorts his self-consciousness and undermines his identity: the present merges with the past. Rufus comes to grips with the devastating effects of immortality in a series of stages. The Troglodytes play an important role in this realization: after visiting the city, Rufus discovers that one of the Troglodytes has followed him. Rufus calls him Argos because it reminds him of "the moribund old dog of the *Odyssey*" (2000, 11), and imagines him to be locked in a mental world where "there were no objects, but rather a constant, dizzying play of swift impressions" (2000, 12). And yet, after days of silence, Argos suddenly starts speaking—and he even seems to recognize the name of Ulysses's dog. Not only that: Argos, it turns out, is Homer himself. Asked how much of the *Odyssey* he knows, Argos replies: "*Very little...Less than the meagerest rhapsode. It has been eleven hundred years since last I wrote it*" (2000, 12; italics in the original).

Rufus now understands that the Troglodytes are the Immortals, and that their apathetic, mindless life is the result of their losing the temporal horizon of mortality: "In their self-absorption, they scarcely perceived the physical world" (2000, 13). Rufus goes on to explain that, *sub specie aeternitatis*, it becomes impossible to judge the merits of human action: "Much as the way in games of chance, heads and tails tend to even out, so cleverness and dullness cancel and correct each other" (2000, 14). Even something as remarkable as writing the *Odyssey* loses any significance, because "given infinite time, with infinite circumstances and changes, it is impossible that the *Odyssey* should *not* be composed at least once" (2000, 14; italics in the original). This explains the Troglodytes' lack of interest in external reality—so that the story as a whole has been read as a critique of the notion of immortality in Christian theology (see Stewart 1993).

But it is more than that. The narrative demonstrates how the experience of selfhood breaks down as soon as we leave behind the orientation toward death of human life—what Martin Heidegger (1996) called Dasein's "being-toward-death"—and embrace the timescale of infinity. As Rufus puts it, having fully realized the consequences of his own immortality: "a single immortal man is all men. Like Cornelius Agrippa, I am god, hero, philosopher, demon, and world—which is a long-winded way of saying that *I am not*" (2000, 14; italics in the original). In the language of Borges's "A New Refutation of Time," immortality denies temporal succession, or at least meaningful temporal succession, and this in turn—as a domino effect—denies selfhood. My interest here lies in how Borges's narrative succeeds in translating this insight into a particular kind of experience that we go through as we read the story. I will focus on two strategies, one of which is spatial (and therefore reminiscent of the sense of place evoked by Ballard's "The Terminal Beach") while the other has to do with metalepsis qua the blurring or destabilization of narrative levels (and therefore points to the "loopiness" of the self as discussed by Hofstadter).[8]

Rufus, as I said above, visits the City of the Immortals. But the city's architecture is nothing like what he had expected. Far from being the eternal dwelling place of god-like creatures, the city defies all purpose or meaning, and only inspires sensations of "oppressiveness," "horror," and "complex irrationality" in the visitor (2000, 9). Rufus's description is worth quoting in full:

There were corridors that led nowhere, unreachably high windows, grandly dramatic doors that opened onto monklike cells or empty shafts, incredible upside-down staircases with upside-down treads and balustrades. Other staircases, clinging airily to the side of a monumental wall, petered out after two or three landings, in the high gloom of the cupolas, arriving nowhere...*This City, I thought, is so horrific that its mere existence, the mere fact of its having endured—even in the middle of a secret desert—pollutes the past and the future and somehow compromises the stars. So long as this City endures, no one in the world can ever be happy or courageous.* I do not want to describe it; a chaos of heterogeneous words, the body of a tiger or a bull pullulating with teeth, organs, and heads monstrously yoked together yet hating each other—those might, perhaps, be approximate images.

(2000, 9–10; italics in the original)

Before examining this description more closely, we should keep in mind that our conceptualization of time is intimately connected to spatial patterns. Not only do we keep track of time through motion in space (for instance, the sun's apparent movement, or the mechanical motion of a clock's hands), but we think and talk about time through spatial metaphors (see Evans and Green 2006, 75–87). In the dead of winter, for instance, we can say that the summer seems impossibly *far*. We are thus associating a temporal relation (between two times of the year) with a spatial one (the distance between two points). This association has become so conventional in language that it is likely to strike most speakers as completely nonmetaphorical. Yet cognitive linguists and psychologists working in the wake of Lakoff and Johnson (1980) remind us that the conceptual metaphor "time is space" has profound consequences for our experience of time: "those aspects of time that are specified through spatial metaphors will be shaped by the metaphors used…The spatial schemas invoked by these metaphors will provide the relational information needed to organize events in time" (Boroditsky 2000, 4).[9]

Borges's description of the City of the Immortals builds on this cognitive link between time and the experience of space. The visual incongruity of this space aligns itself closely with the impossible spaces depicted by Giovanni Battista Piranesi or M. C. Escher (see Lapidot 1991). But given the story's focus on temporality, one may suspect that this space stands for something beyond itself—namely, the eternity that the narrator, having just drunk from the river of immortality, is beginning to experience. The city's architecture thus becomes an allegory drawing on, and dramatizing, the spatial metaphors we typically use to conceptualize time. Through the spatial language of the city, with its lack of linearity and purposefulness, Borges conveys the horror and disorientation of losing the bearings of human mortality. This idea comes to the foreground in the italicized portion of the quotation. Here Rufus brings into focus the source of the horror: it is the fact that the city has endured in time, and that it "pollutes the past and the future." Its unsettling architecture drains human emotions (here represented by happiness and courage) of their significance, which is precisely what Rufus says of immortality. In this way, the city leaves its mark on the whole universe, it "somehow compromises the stars."

Insofar as our experience of space is always based on the body, Borges's characterization of the City of the Immortals does not only employ space to make the horror of immortality more concrete, but it also appeals to readers' bodies in the process. The sense of place evoked by the description plays into this embodied involvement, much like what we have seen for Ballard's atoll. Note also that the last sentence of the quotation uses grotesque, monstrous bodies to convey what it is like to experience this place, thus tying low-level responses to distorted embodiment—fear and disgust—to our imagination of the city.[10] In reflecting on Rufus's words on immortality, readers may then connect them with their embodied apprehension of the space of the city. An abstract insight into the undesirable consequences of immortality is rendered as a spatial experience that reflects embodied modes of engagement with the world—particularly perception and basic emotions. Just like Ballard's Eniwetok, Borges's City of the Immortals is a powerful chronotope insofar as it demonstrates "the inseparability of space and time," to quote Bakhtin (1981, 84). Crucially, however, the temporality involved here is the infinite time of immortality.

The second device through which Borges's narrative probes a more-than-human timescale has direct implications for the question of the self. Having realized that immortality is a curse rather than a blessing, Rufus starts looking for a river whose waters can make him mortal again. After finding it and drinking from it, he is overjoyed that he can again experience the bodily sensations that immortality had blunted:

> As I scaled the steep bank beside [the river], a thorny tree scratched the back of my hand. The unaccustomed pain seemed exceedingly sharp. Incredulous, speechless, and in joy, I contemplated the precious formation of a slow drop of blood.
>
> (2000, 16)

Immortality produces bodily defamiliarization, since it questions the familiar association between injury and pain. The new timescale of eternity had thus altered the character's consciousness to the extent that he had lost full awareness of his body. This awareness is crucial to the constitution of a minimal or, to use Antonio Damasio's (2000) term, "core" self: developmentally, it is because we recognize the body as ours through sensations of comfort or discomfort that we develop an inchoate sense of who we are. There is broad consensus for this in various areas of the mind sciences: to quote George Butterworth, who writes in the tradition of Gibson's ecological psychology, "there is tactile, auditory, and kinesthetic identity of the bodily self early in life" (1995, 93). While significant, the alteration produced in Rufus's bodily self by immortality is only a first symptom of the revelation that will follow soon, and that concerns Damasio's "autobiographical self"—the self as a coherent construct based on concepts and narratives about oneself.

On rereading his account one year after regaining mortality, Rufus notes that "in the first chapters, and even in certain paragraphs of others, I believe I detect a certain falseness" (2000, 17). These deviations from the truth could be seen as the result of poetic license or literary embellishment, but—the narrator points out—there is "a more private and inward reason" for them: "I will reveal it; it does not matter that I may be judged a fantast. *The story I have told seems unreal because the experiences of two different men are intermingled in it*" (2000, 17; italics in the original). In fact, the narrator proceeds to unravel the complex intertextual web of Rufus's narrative, finding a wealth of Homeric phrases and quotations: Rufus's voice thus seems to merge with the voice of his companion, Argos, who turns out to be Homer himself. From the viewpoint of immortality, individual identity loses any meaning, and selves expand beyond themselves, absorbing others' experiences and language without any concern for factual truth.

Starting with Ronald Christ (1969), critics have seen this intertextual appropriation as integral part of Borges's artistic method. In "The Immortal," this strategy coincides with a disruption in narrative form, which in turn has important ramifications for Borges's engagement with the notion of self. In Rex Butler's words, "Borges suggests this confusion of personalities *formally*, with a subtle and at first reading almost indiscernible shift between first- and third-person forms that takes place throughout the narrative" (2012, 184–85; emphasis in the original). In discussing the Homeric turns of phrase in Rufus's account, for instance, the narrator twice refers to Rufus in the third person, as "Flaminius Rufus"—which is a puzzling move, since readers have been assuming that the narrator *is* Rufus all along. The narrator's identity thus remains suspended: he is Rufus, and yet at the same time he adopts an external viewpoint. This is a first intimation of how the logic of strange loops informs Borges's narrative. A short postscript appended to the text by an anonymous editor raises the ante even further, suggesting that Rufus is none other than Joseph Cartaphilus, the rare book dealer who had sold the volume of Pope's *Iliad* containing Rufus's manuscript. This revelation is an example of "ontological metalepsis" (Pier 2010): a disruption of narrative boundaries, in this case between the frame narrative and Rufus's embedded account, which conflates characters (the rare book dealer and Rufus himself) previously presented as ontologically distinct. As a rhetorical and narrative strategy, metalepsis has already been linked to Hofstadter's "strange loops" by Brian McHale (1987, 119–21): according to McHale, there is a structural analogy between the level-crossing logic of strange loops and the workings of metalepsis in postmodernist narratives. Further, Debra Malina's *Breaking the Frame* explores the connection between metalepsis and selfhood in a number of twentieth-century literary narratives: "because [metalepsis] disrupts narrative hierarchy in order either to reinforce or to undermine the ontological status of fictional subjects or selves, it provides a model of the dynamics of the essential self" (2002, 2).

What is missing in narratological discussions of metalepsis, and what Borges's short story allows us to perceive, is how the strange loop is more than a figure for the metaleptic constitution of the self: it is its underlying principle. Indeed, as argued by Hofstadter, the self always emerges from a boundary-crossing gesture whereby socio-culturally circulating models of selfhood are internalized into a relatively stable (illusion of) self. In turn, because of the influence of these models, the self is thought of as existing prior to the socio-cultural interactions that, as a matter of fact, have played an active role in shaping it. This is the dynamics that I take Borges's short story to be staging through its embedded narrative, and by opening up Rufus's identity to apparently "extraneous" voices (Homer, the rare book dealer). Rufus writes that as "the end approaches, there are no longer any images from memory—there are only words" (2000, 18). These "words" here stand for literary models, such as those that can be found in Homer's works, and more generally for the socio-cultural templates from which the very idea of an autobiographical self is born. But this autobiographical self is entangled with the embodied sense of self that we develop from proprioception and perception: a breakdown of the latter (signaled by Rufus's bodily defamiliarization) necessarily leads to an implosion of the autobiographical narrative through which we weave the illusion of a stable identity. Rufus thus dissolves into the identity and experiences of neighboring characters: "I have been Homer; soon, like Ulysses, I shall be Nobody; soon, I shall be all men—I shall be dead" (2000, 18).

Borges's narrative works by radicalizing the looping logic of the self to the point that the absence of any underlying "self-substance" comes to light: the self *is* the strange loop, though its strangeness is much less apparent in everyday contexts than it is here. Via Rufus's immortality, the timescale of infinity allows the narrative to expose this process of self-constitution. The adoption of a cosmic temporality—here in the broadest possible sense of the word "cosmic," the time that encompasses everything—creates the conditions for investigating the puzzles of selfhood. This brings us back to the quotation from Nagel's *Mind and Cosmos* discussed at the beginning of this chapter: questions about the nature of mind and its relation to the physical world cannot be uncoupled from questions about the nature of reality and particularly, in this short story, the elusive phenomenon that we call "time." While this connection between mind and cosmos takes on full significance *sub specie aeternitatis*, Borges's narrative succeeds in staging it within the limited medium of human experience, through Rufus's physical and emotional distress as he explores the impossible spatiality of the City of the Immortals and becomes intimate with an immortal body. The defamiliarization inherent in Rufus's experiences—and the conception of selfhood that it exposes—are communicated to readers as they engage with these narrative offerings in bodily and affective terms.

***

Focusing on one novel and two short stories published between 1947 and 1985, this chapter sought to trace the complex interactions between cosmic temporality (i.e., a timeframe beyond the human scale) and a set of philosophical questions about the nature of mind. On the reading I have offered here, Ballard's "The Terminal Beach" charts the boundaries of mind, collapsing the Cartesian distinction between an "inner space" and material realities and anticipating contemporary theories that posit the embedding and extension of mental processes. Vonnegut's *Galápagos* takes an evolutionary perspective, suggesting—through the lens of satire—that our big brains, the locus of consciousness and cultural experience, are faulty machines that will be "streamlined" in future iterations of humanity. Finally, Borges sets up a thought experiment on what it would be like to lose the "being-toward-death" of living creatures: he shows how immortality would wreak havoc on what we call a "self" and reveals how the self is an illusion created over the course of our exposure to socio-cultural practices, in a looping, metaleptic process. In all these texts, cosmic temporality—and the posthuman perspective that comes with it—are evoked to offer a defamiliarizing view of mental processes and their material, bodily basis.

Bodily defamiliarization thus works in these case studies by connecting embodied responses to fiction (such as sense of place and empathy for characters) with the mind-body problem: forms of bodily involvement are used to question readers' conceptual understanding of the relation between physical bodies and seemingly intangible mental experiences. Large-scale temporality is crucial to this effect because it forces us to reframe humanity in light of the evolutionary events that preceded and will follow it. When dealing with such temporalities, I have argued, narrative has to develop innovative solutions to overcome its own anthropocentric bias: Ballard's characterization of Traven's psychology, Vonnegut's mindless plotting, and Borges's metaleptic narrative are among these solutions. Further, *space* plays a central role in all these narratives dealing with large-scale time. Think of Ballard's atoll, Vonnegut's Santa Rosalia, and Borges's City of the Immortals: these locations serve as spatial allegories for cosmic time, enabling fiction to encapsulate the defamiliarizing effects of phenomena that unfold over a timescale too large for readers to experience directly. In short, spatiality as well as temporality play into this cosmic framework and allow mind and consciousness to be recast in material terms.

Of course, this defamiliarizing operation cannot by itself *solve* the mind-body problem. But that would be asking too much of fiction.

Literary narrative, I suggested in the last chapter, is better suited for problem-posing than for problem-solving: by embedding philosophical questions in concrete contexts of human action and interaction, it can demonstrate their relevance and significance in experiential, affective terms. Put otherwise, fiction can effectively explore the ramifications of the hard problem and show how it brings in its wake a number of ethical and epistemological issues—first and foremost, those concerning our attitude toward the nonhuman world that we tend to dualistically oppose to human existence, but that is just as material as our mental states (at least if we accept insights into the embodiment of cognition).

Perhaps more clearly than Borges, Ballard and Vonnegut envision the extinction of the human species as a result of a complex interplay between environmental and human factors (nuclear power, a virus outbreak, etc.). Ecocriticism has carefully explored this interplay in relation to a wide gamut of literary texts dealing with catastrophe and disaster (see, e.g., Rigby 2013). My focus on embodied cognition allows us to see how deeply interrelated these concerns are with questions regarding the materiality of human minds. Philosophical approaches that go under the heading of "New Materialism" (Dolphijn and van der Tuin 2012) or "nonhuman turn" (Grusin 2015b), as discussed in the introduction, have so far tended to leave the question of subjectivity on the sidelines. Jane Bennett's move in the preface to her seminal *Vibrant Matter* is representative of how questions about mind have been dismissed in this area of research:

> In what follows the otherwise important topic of subjectivity...gets short shrift so that I may focus on the task of developing a vocabulary and syntax for, and thus a better discernment of, the active powers issuing from nonhuman subjects. I want to highlight what is typically cast in the shadow: the material agency or effectivity of nonhuman or not-quite-human things.
>
> (2010, ix)

I believe this shortshrifting is highly problematic: rethinking our attitude toward environmental realities necessarily involves rethinking the ways in which we conceptualize our own mental processes, and literature—through its problem-posing power—can greatly contribute to this reconceptualization.

Notes

1 Science fiction has often explored this connection between time and the posthuman, as a recent wave of scholarship has highlighted: science fiction, Ralph Pordzik writes, "seems particularly suited to come to terms with the difficult issues raised by posthuman theorists" (2012, 157). See also Gomel (2010) for a wide-ranging discussion of temporality in postmodern science

fiction. Many of Gomel's readings resonate with a posthumanist perspective. Even closer to my focus in this chapter, Benjamin Kohlmann (2014) looks at how the concern with posthuman futurity was accompanied, in science fiction from the 1960s and 1970s, by forms of literary engagement with animal experience. In these texts, the "world without humans" that must follow a nuclear catastrophe was probed by way of animal subjects, such as rats, that are able to survive the radiation. From a Heideggerian perspective, Kohlmann notes that these animals serve "as intermediaries between the realm of human life and the sphere of inanimate matter" (2014, 660), and can therefore help readers imagine the end of human subjectivity caused by species-wide extinction. The narratives I will analyze in this chapter follow in this tradition of literary inquiry.

2 See Gould (1987) for an authoritative discussion of the time's arrow metaphor and the "discovery" of deep time by geologists such as James Hutton and Charles Lyell in the eighteenth and nineteenth centuries.

3 However, not all the assumptions made by researchers working on the extended mind are consistent with the enactivist approach I outlined in the introduction. For discussion, see Menary (2010).

4 Several Vonnegut critics have focused on this juxtaposition of mythology and evolutionary science; see Mustazza (1991) and McInnis (2005).

5 Hilary Dannenberg (2008) has explored the role of counterfactuals in various kinds of plots, arguing that this device is far more pervasive than narrative theorists have tended to think. See also Laura Karttunen's (2008) reappraisal of the disnarrated.

6 For more on Borges's engagement with philosophical themes, see at least Bossart (2003) and Griffin (2013).

7 Butler (2012, 182–86) offers a useful survey of critical work on Borges's short story.

8 Along with John Pier's (2010) entry in the *Living Handbook of Narratology*, recent narratological treatments of metalepsis can be found in Fludernik (2003) and Kukkonen and Klimek (2011).

9 In the article from which these words are lifted, Boroditsky offers suggestive empirical evidence for this idea.

10 I expand on this embodied account of the grotesque in Caracciolo (2014a).

5 Bodies from Outer Space

So far in this book we have examined fictions that stage an encounter between human embodiment and cosmic spatio-temporal scales. Sometimes the embodiment I investigated was that of readers, through embodied simulations and narrative's affectivity; in other cases, I focused on characters' bodies and how they serve as a bridge toward the nonhuman at the diegetic (or thematic) level. But throughout my discussion of bodily defamiliarization, the body was always the familiar element brought into tension with unfamiliar and deeply unsettling cosmic realities. Put otherwise, in the narratives I have analyzed the defamiliarization builds on knowledge that is to a large extent *external* to the human body, such as Calvino's Big Bang, Zoline's entropy, or Vonnegut's natural evolution. Only at a later stage are these conceptual frameworks injected into the body itself, which becomes a medium for imagining and experiencing cosmic realities. This dynamic is at the heart of the defamiliarizing effect of these narratives.

This chapter changes tack and looks at three novels where the body is presented as—or is discovered to be—constitutively alien and unfamiliar, without any need for the incorporation of "foreign," scientific knowledge into human (or human-like) experience. The cosmos is not *brought to bear on* the body but rather shown to be already bound up with it, as part of the basic postulates of a fictional world: these are all novels that represent and explore—at the level of plot and theme—bodies from outer space. The texts I will examine are H. P. Lovecraft's novella *The Shadow Out of Time* (2004), first published in 1936, Stanisław Lem's novel *Solaris* (2011), originally published in Polish in 1961, and Michel Faber's *Under the Skin* (2000)—the latter being the most recent of this book's case studies. While radically different in tone and inspiration, these novels have one thing in common: they confront readers with alien bodies that depart from human modes and structures of embodiment. This defamiliarizing departure comes in varying degrees: it is subtle but deeply significant in *Under the Skin*, in which the protagonist is an alien whose body has been surgically modified to look like a human being's; it is more marked in *The Shadow Out of Time*, where a human narrator comes into contact with—and, as the narrative progresses, takes on—the horrifying body of an extraterrestrial species; finally, the departure from human embodiment is greatest in *Solaris*, in which the body and mind of a cosmic creature are so radically alien that all attempts at understanding them through human cognitive schemata are bound to fail. This is the order in which I will tackle my case studies over the following pages. To anticipate my argument, these figurations of nonhuman bodies converge on a vision of the material patterns that straddle the divide between subjectivity and physical realities. Patterns are, as we've seen multiple times in this book, central to the enactivist account of mind-world interactions. My case studies project such mind-like patterns beyond the domain of entities that we would normally recognize as living or animate—a process that puts pressure on everyday notions of embodiment and elicits distinctive forms of affect: consolation in Faber's novel, horror at the loss of human phenomenology in Lovecraft, and a disconcerting sense of intimacy with a sentient ocean in Lem's *Solaris*. In this way, these works challenge the connection between organismic life and mind that has always been at the root of the enactivist project since Varela, Thompson, and Rosch's *The Embodied Mind*.[1] The resulting defamiliarization of the body resonates with arguments advanced by nonhuman-oriented theorists such as Steven Shaviro and Graham Harman. But narrative, unlike philosophical reasoning, has to work hard to move from everyday notions of (human) embodiment to a metaphysical conception of mind and body as grounded in nonhuman materiality.[2]

Dissolving into the Inanimate

"Isserley always drove straight past a hitch-hiker when she first saw him, to give herself time to size him up. She was looking for big muscles: a hunk on legs. Puny, scrawny specimens were no use to her" (2000, 1). These are the first lines of Michel Faber's debut novel, *Under the Skin*. As we read further, we realize that the protagonist, Isserley, is cruising along the A9, a major road in Scotland's Highlands. She spots a hitch-hiker, drives past him a number of times to assess his body; then she decides to offer him a ride and start a casual—but probing—conversation, inquiring in particular about whether he "had a wife or a girlfriend waiting" (2000, 10). Because the car's heating is strategically on full blast, the hitchhiker is forced to take off his jacket while Isserley continues appraising his body. Isserley herself is wearing a skimpy top, her breasts on display (and readily noticed by the hitchhiker). We experience all this through the filter of internal focalization: we are privy to Isserley's thoughts even though we don't know what she is up to exactly. But as we read these pages for the first time it is hard not to interpret these interactions as some kind of complex (and, probably, pathological) mating ritual: Isserley could be anything between a nymphomaniac and a sex-obsessed serial killer. Little do we suspect that Isserley has no sexual interest whatsoever in these men. Gradually, the picture clears up: Isserley is an alien who has been surgically modified to look like a human being; her job is to kidnap muscular men so that they may be fattened, slaughtered, and eventually turned into specialty food to be shipped to Isserley's distant homeland. As commentators haven't failed to notice (see, e.g., Gymnich and Segao Costa 2006, 85), the novel draws an implicit parallel between how aliens inflict pain on human beings and how nonhuman animals are treated in the meat industry.

Linguistically, this parallel is underscored by the fact that Isserley refers to her own conspecifics as "humans," whereas she calls human beings "vodsels," making clear that they are inferior creatures with limited consciousness and cognitive skills.[3] As Sarah Dillon (2011, 142) points out in a thoughtful reading of the novel, the vodsels are consistently animalized by the narrator's figurative language, which reflects Isserley's own evaluation of her victims—and, more generally, the general perception of the vodsels among Isserley's conspecifics.[4] In hindsight, we can read in this light the "hunk on legs" and "puny, scrawny specimens" of the novel's beginning: this is not a sex addict's objectifying gaze, but the language of someone who sees human beings as little more than animals to be harvested.

Because of all this, Isserley is hardly a likeable character, and relating to her will initially prove difficult for many, perhaps most readers. And yet our relationship to Isserley develops as we are exposed to the character's profound sense of unease at being cut off not only from her home planet but also from her species: due to her human-like body, she is seen as an outcast by the aliens who work on the farm. Further, we find out that after the surgical operation her body has become a source of excruciating pain. These aspects of the character's psychology may reduce the distance between Isserley and the audience *despite* her apparent, and shocking, indifference toward the vodsels' (that is, human beings') suffering. The rapprochement between Isserley and readers is facilitated by Isserley's psychological development as she begins to realize—partially and reluctantly—that the vodsels may be more than "vegetables on legs" (Faber 2000, 171), as Isserley's boss describes them. A turning point in Isserley's transformation is a botched sexual assault, during which Isserley is held at knifepoint and almost raped by one of her hitchhikers. ("Almost" because, as the would-be rapist realizes to his dismay, Isserley's anatomy does not allow for intercourse.) After this episode, in Dillon's (2011, 146) words, the "division between herself [Isserley] and the vodsels breaks down. As a result, so too does her ability to distance herself ethically from them."

This realization puts Isserley in an ethical no man's land: it confronts her with the impossibility of bridging the gap between herself and other species—and perhaps more generally herself and other subjects.[5]

Locked in her personal trauma and sense of defeat, Isserley decides to commit suicide by setting off her car's self-destruct mechanism. This leads to the novel's last scene:

> The aviir [an explosive, in the aliens' language] would blow her car, herself, and a generous scoop of earth into the smallest conceivable particles. The explosion would leave a crater in the ground as big and deep as if a meteorite had fallen there.
>
> And she? Where would she go?
>
> The atoms that had been herself would mingle with the oxygen and nitrogen in the air. Instead of ending up buried in the ground, she would become part of the sky: that was the way to look at it. Her invisible remains would combine, over time, with all the wonders under the sun. When it snowed, she would be part of it, falling softly to earth, rising up again with the snow's evaporation. When it rained, she would be there in the spectral arch that spanned from firth to ground. She would help to wreathe the fields in mists, and yet would always be transparent to the stars. She would live forever. All it took was the courage to press one button, and the faith that the connection had not been broken.
>
> She reached forward a trembling hand.
>
> "Here I come," she said.
>
> (Faber 2000, 295–96)

This final scene reads as an irruption—sudden and dramatic but not, as we'll see, unprepared—of the cosmic into Isserley's experience. The cosmic dimension is evoked first by the meteorite simile, which points to the astronomical space beyond Earth, and then—with a shift to the microcosm—by the mention of the atoms and chemical elements ("oxygen and nitrogen") with which Isserley would intermingle. Her body dissolves into the inanimate particles that form the basis of meteorological phenomena such as snow, rain, or the mist: in this sense, she continues to exist—"she would live forever"—but at the cost of relinquishing her subjectivity. There is fear but also consolation in this gesture, which promises a radical transcendence of Isserley's subjective, embodied experience. This radical transcorporeality—to use again Alaimo's (2010) term—is what the cosmic perspective brings to the novel, allowing Isserley to evade the intractable ethical questions that her experiences with the vodsels had disclosed.

The novel's staging of embodiment is crucial to grasping the significance of this final scene: as I will argue below, the cosmic perspective resolves the tension between readers' affective responses to the vodsels' disfigured bodies and their somatic empathy for Isserley's sore and dysfunctional body. The novel starts with an implicit comparison between "big muscles" and a "hunk on legs"—where the word "hunk" suggests an object that is grotesquely attached to the body. This grotesque tone pervades Faber's approach to the human body in *Under the Skin*. As Mikhail Bakhtin notes in *Rabelais and His World*, the grotesque is defined by two features: the exaggeration of the body image "to disproportionate dimensions" (Bakhtin 1984, 312) and the weakening of the "limits between the body and the world" (1984, 313). Both features can be found, incipiently, in Faber's image of the "hunk," but later chapters of the novel scale up this grotesque element significantly. Consider, for example, this description of a man's disfigured body after a month of captivity in the aliens' farm:

> [The vodsel] had the typical look of a monthling, its shaved nub of a head nestled like a bud atop the disproportionately massive body. Its empty scrotal sac dangled like a pale oak leaf under its dark acorn of a penis. A thin stream of blueish-black diarrhoea clattered onto the ground between its legs. Its fists swept the air jerkily. Its mouth opened wide to show its cored molars and the docked stub of its tongue.
>
> (Faber 2000, 100)

Not only has the man's body become "disproportionately massive," but the physical boundaries of the body are made uncertain by the dangling scrotum (the vodsels are castrated to accelerate weight gain) and streaming diarrhea. The metaphorical language also works to a similar effect, associating body parts with vegetable life ("pale oak leaf," "dark acorn," "cored" like a fruit) in a way that opens up the human body to the natural environment. In terms of the Medieval hierarchy of the cosmos—the traditional doctrine of the "scala naturae" or "great chain of being" mentioned in the introduction, via Lovejoy (2001)—humans are thus demoted two ranks: they are not only animalized (as Dillon suggests) but reduced to living matter, like plants.

In a later passage, it is the boundary between one body and another that is called into question. This striking description culminates in another natural comparison, this time evoking the image of a sea anemone—an invertebrate, and visually plant-like, animal:

> The few remaining monthlings were huddled together in a mound of fast-panting flesh, the divisions between one muscle-bound body and the next difficult to distinguish, the limbs confused. Hands and feet spasmed at random, as if a co-ordinated response was struggling vainly to emerge from a befuddled collective organism. Their fat little heads were identical, swaying in a cluster like polyps of an anemone.
>
> (2000, 169)

The lack of differentiation between bodies points to an even more unsettling disruption of individual consciousness and identity: this is the human body reduced to an amorphous mass (or perhaps "hunk") of flesh that lives on without the centralized control of a self.

How are readers likely to respond to these grotesque representations? At one level, of course, there will be indignation over the aliens' treatment of these humans. This moral disgust will be compounded by physical disgust directed at these bodies—an emotion that is frequently associated with the grotesque (see Czachesz 2009).[6] However, because of the confusion of bodies and apparent lack of full-fledged subjectivity, it will be quite difficult to feel a more individualized kind of empathy or even sympathy for these characters. Through plot and metaphor, their bodies are grotesquely dissolved into the natural world so as to shift the reader's attention away from the pain that they must be experiencing. The external nature of these grotesque representations depends on the novel's adoption of Isserley's point of view: recall that, for Isserley's conspecifics, humans are fundamentally "vegetables on legs" (Faber 2000, 171), a view that explains the many debasing plant metaphors for human bodies and body parts. Part of the challenge of reading the novel consists in accepting this estranging viewpoint on our own species. The vehicle of that viewpoint is the vodsels' disgusting—and hence deeply unsettling—embodiment.

The human form is implicitly contrasted with the sleek and nimble body of the aliens, which is first described when Amlis Vess, the son of the farm's powerful owner, comes to visit the facility (2000, 109): the aliens, we learn, are four-footed creatures with a thick fur and a tail. Not unlike the humans' distorted bodies, however, the aliens' bodies are only depicted externally, from an observer's position. Our only reference point for the phenomenology of the body is Isserley, and her embodiment is fundamentally *hybrid* because of the surgical operation she underwent in order to look like a human being. Isserley herself acknowledges this problematic hybridity in an episode in which she hesitates about her bodily shape:

> She didn't know why she should need to see her limbs in order to exercise them, but she did. It was as if, in too profound a darkness, she could not be sure what sort of creature she was. She needed to verify what remained of her body.
>
> (2000, 144)

This situation of vague embodiment is reminiscent of a strategy adopted by Lovecraft in "The Shadow Out of Time," as we'll see in the next section.

Unlike Lovecraft, however, Faber captures Isserley's bodily sensations in great detail: most of the time, they are painful sensations.

For instance, we read that Isserley's "contorted back muscles [kept] her hostage in her bed with the threat of needle-sharp pains" (2000, 49), and that her "spine was jolted repeatedly, as if furious assailants were kicking her through the seat" (2000, 96); later on in the novel, pain is said to "[shoot] down her spine, like a skewer piercing her from ribcage to rectum" (2000, 232). These descriptions are particularly rich in metaphors and similes; yet this figurative language is radically different from the language Faber employs to characterize the vodsels' embodiment. Here Isserley's inner experience of pain is conveyed through metaphorical references to external activities that would *cause* a similar pain, such as the assailants' kicking or the skewer's (or needle's) piercing.[7] Note also that these scenarios imply a human or human-like subjectivity: they are intentional actions performed on Isserley's body. This figurative strategy affords readers an internal perspective on Isserley's consciousness— precisely the perspective that we were denied by the language associating the vodsels' bodies with plant-like things. Isserley's sore embodiment thus becomes a focus of our engagement with her: it is through descriptions like these, and through the sympathetic emotions that they are likely to elicit, that we establish an empathetic bond with the character despite our ethical resistance to her treatment of the vodsels.

But the exploration of Isserley's embodied phenomenology doesn't end here. The novel offers rich descriptions of the character's embodied encounters with the natural environment—and these encounters, unlike her inner sensations, are mostly positively connoted. Some of these outward sensations are visual: "One by one, feathery snowflakes started spiralling down from the sky" (2000, 69); "The endless night sky was all above her, glittering with a million distant stars" (2000, 222). Mostly, however, the environment is experienced through auditory, haptic, or even gustatory sensations that bring out its distinctive *texture*:

> The sensation of fresh snow crunching underfoot was deeply satisfying to Isserley. Just the idea of all that water vapour solidifying by the cloudful and fluttering to earth was miraculous. She couldn't quite believe it, even after all these years. It was a phenomenon of stupendous and unjustifiably useless extravagance. Yet here it lay, soft and powdery, edibly pure. Isserley scooped a handful off the ground and ate some. It was delicious.
>
> (2000, 56)

At one level, the focus on the Highlands' lavish natural beauty serves as a foil to Isserley's native planet, a place where even water and oxygen have to be artificially produced. Clearly, such passages have environmentalist overtones, implying that our planet looks increasingly like the dystopia of Isserley's homeland and that even Scotland's pristine nature is under threat.[8] This environmentalist message is bound up with—and, largely, pursued through—the phenomenology of Isserley's interactions with the natural world. This is a phenomenology of material pattern and texture, devoting meticulous attention to things such as the crunching sound of footsteps on fresh snow or the snow's powdery consistency. At times, these natural patterns infiltrate Isserley's inner experience— for example, in this passage: "Hours eroded by. Isserley's eyes swelled and itched with the imaginary grit of sleeplessness" (2000, 94). Metaphors such as "eroded" or "grit" are different from both the plant-like descriptions of the vodsels (which are external and reifying) and from the figurative scenarios that convey Isserley's pain (which build on intentional, anthropomorphic actions). These natural metaphors place the character's embodiment in a cosmic context, revealing the imbrication of her first-person experience with geological forces shaping Scotland's natural landscape.

The full significance of this metaphorical association comes to the fore in an important passage, in which we see Isserley walking on a desolate beach:

> The variety of shapes, colours and textures under her feet was, she believed, literally infinite. It must be. Each shell, each pebble, each stone had been made what it was by aeons of submarine or subglacial massage. The indiscriminate, eternal devotion of nature to its numberless particles had an emotional importance for Isserley; it put the unfairness of human life into perspective. Cast ashore, perhaps only briefly before being fetched back for another million years of polishing and re-shaping, the stones lay so serene beneath her naked feet.
>
> (2000, 61–62)

Again we find here an emphasis on the patterned complexity of natural landscapes, which consist in "numberless particles"—an idea that emerges for the first time in this passage, but was largely implicit in all previous contacts between Isserley and the nonhuman world: the stars, the snow or snowflakes, the grit itself are equally granular.

Three aspects of this beach episode are worth highlighting. First, this passage evokes a geological timescale that goes beyond the lifespan of any living creature, whether "human" (by which Isserley refers to her own alien species) or terrestrial. Second, nature is shot through with emotional values: because of its inherent "devotion," nature subjects things to a comforting "massage," making them "serene." Third, these emotional qualities can be directly experienced, as part of the phenomenological texture of the natural world: as the narrator points out a few lines after the end of this quotation, the "relief [Isserley] felt in allowing her long toes to splay over the rocky shore, curling round the stones, was inexpressible" (2000, 62). The passage runs together Isserley's embodied experience and the meanings associated with nature's nonhuman "devotion," leading to a comforting sense that the landscape puts "the unfairness of human life into perspective." This network of associations is summarized by the phrase "aeons of submarine or subglacial massage" since the word "massage" works at two levels: metaphorically, it stands for a nonhuman process of physical transformation, but it also hints at the literal action of the pebbles on Isserley's feet.

I suggest reading in this light the novel's finale: by turning her own body into particle-like "atoms," Isserley embraces the texture and patterns of the natural world, dissolving into the inanimate elements whose consoling power she had sensed through the phenomenology of the body. Ironically, however, this gesture entails giving up the bodily consciousness that had put her in touch with the nonhuman landscape in the first place. This irony makes the novel's engagement with environmental themes particularly poignant, in that it exposes the ambivalence of consciousness, which is both what enables us to appreciate the sublimity of the natural world (and potentially defend it against mindless exploitation) and what keeps us from attaining nature's deep-seated "serenity." This is another manifestation of the hard problem of consciousness discussed in the previous chapter—namely, the radical and seemingly fundamental difference between conscious subjects and inanimate things: this gap accounts for the emotional clout of Isserley's becoming "part of the sky" in the final scene. As readers overcome their initial resistance for Isserley and come to empathize with her, their engagement with the character's hybrid embodiment—along with her physical and emotional traumas—allows them to see how Isserley's individual destiny is woven into the fabric of the cosmos.

It is crucial to understand how this insight is made possible not only by the generic "alienness" of Isserley's embodied experience but by how it sits halfway between two other modes of embodiment depicted by the novel, the (to Isserley) familiar alien body and the grotesque vodsels. It is because Isserley's ordinary embodiment is disrupted—and therefore defamiliarized—that she develops a sensitivity for natural textures, which are uniquely able to counterbalance the excruciating pain she experiences throughout the novel. At the same time, the smoothness and cleanness of the natural landscape stand in stark contrast to the vodsels' bodies—bloated figures that ooze organic matter into the surrounding environment.[9] Each of these modes of embodiment has its own metaphorical regime, as we've seen: metaphors implying human-like intentionality for Isserley's pain and comparisons with plants (or animals and other foodstuff) for the vodsels' bodies. The tension between these metaphorical domains is overcome through the novel's appeal to a *third* domain, the textural patterning of the physical world. Faber's *Under the Skin* thus completes its downward movement along the great chain of being, from the human (in both the ordinary and Isserley's sense) to animals, plants, and finally the insensate world of "mere" physical matter—a process that results in the character's final dissolution into the inanimate. Even as it consistently explores Isserley's embodied experience of natural landscapes, the novel unravels the feeling body into its nonhuman building blocks and thus affords a defamiliarizing perspective on our own planet.

Object-Like Awkwardness

"The Shadow Out of Time," one of Lovecraft's best-known tales, starts with a situation that will be familiar to all readers of horror fiction: the narrator alludes to an unspeakable experience that might (or might not) have been a figment of his imagination. This trope takes a more intriguing, and quintessentially Lovecraftian, twist when the narrator notes that the implications of this alleged event are cosmic in scope: "If the thing did happen, then man must be prepared to accept notions of the cosmos, and of his own place in the seething vortex of time, whose merest mention is paralysing" (2004, 335). This statement takes us to the heart of Lovecraft's worldview, exposing what S. T. Joshi (1990, 186–90) has called Lovecraft's "cosmicism"—namely, his fascination for entities that transcend the human in both temporal and spatial terms. As Joshi explains, Lovecraft's thought is defined by "an unswervingly 'cosmic' point of view whereby all human actions are judged on the scale of both temporal and spatial infinity of an unknown and aimless cosmos" (1990, 171).

To understand how the tension between human bodies and cosmic realities plays out in Lovecraft's work—and in "The Shadow Out of Time" in particular—we need to factor in another feature of his worldview, also remarked upon by Joshi (among many other commentators): Lovecraft's cosmicism goes hand in hand with materialism. The horror, in his stories, is never a supernatural phenomenon, because it is produced by material entities that intervene in human history in entirely physical ways—even though our cognitive limitations have so far kept us from fully grasping these physical processes and the laws underlying them. In an influential essay on Lovecraft, Michel Houellebecq—the author of *The Elementary Particles*—puts this point as follows:

> What is Great Cthulhu? An arrangement of electrons, like us. Lovecraft's terror is rigorously material. But, it is quite possible, given the free interplay of cosmic forces, that Great Cthulhu possesses abilities and powers to act that far exceed ours.
>
> (2006, 32)

For Lovecraft, these alien species have been present—albeit mostly undetected—throughout human history; in fact, they have *shaped* our history from the very beginning: the evolution of our species can be properly understood only against this cosmic background. The inter-mingling of historical facts and fantastic (but material) cosmic entities constitutes the fundamental "weirdness" of Lovecraft's fiction.[10]

In recent years, Lovecraft's "non-supernatural cosmic art," as Mark McGurl (2012, 546) defines it, has turned him into a champion of object-oriented ontology and speculative realism—two of the approaches that participate in the "nonhuman turn" discussed in the introduction. In a special issue of the journal *Collapse* devoted to Lovecraft, Graham Harman—one of the key figures in object-oriented ontology—writes that Lovecraft's stories "revive a metaphysical speculation that embraces the permanent strangeness of objects" (2008, 6). In "The Shadow Out of Time," this "permanent strangeness" crucially involves the narrator's body as a result of his exposure to a radically alien life form. If, for Love-craft, the world is material through and through, then our body is no exception. But the body, we should not forget, is also the locus of hu-man subjectivity. A basic distinction in Merleau-Ponty's phenomenology is that between the body as "one object among all others" (2002, 49) and the body as subjectively perceived—the body as "the ground" for our consciousness, which makes possible "the relative permanence of disap-pearing objects, real objects" (2002, 80). Lovecraft's short story amplifies the former, objective aspect of the body as part of a broader strategy to decenter human subjectivity and reveal the parochialism of embodied ex-perience. I will claim that the confrontation with the *alien* body discloses the strange objectness (and perhaps abjectness) of our own, human body.

In "The Shadow Out of Time" an alien species, the Great Race, trav-els through time by taking over the bodies of other creatures and dis-placing their minds. The narrator is one of the victims. A "mind swap" along these lines does not sit well with a materialist view of mental pro-cesses, because it implies that mind can be dualistically detached from its physical basis. Lovecraft's answer to the hard problem of conscious-ness discussed in the previous chapter is, therefore, quite muddy: we find dualism where we would expect a radical materialism. But perhaps this dualistic mind swap serves as a mere narrative device; or perhaps its ap-parent dualism points to the limitations of current scientific knowledge and understanding. More than the device itself, it is the way in which the mind swap is conveyed to the reader that deserves attention; and this way, I will show, does tie in with materialism by building on the charac-ter's (and potentially the reader's) embodied experience.

Like many of Lovecraft's protagonists, the narrator of "The Shadow Out of Time," Nathaniel Wingate Peaslee, is an economics professor in New England. Peaslee's first brush with a cosmic force comes during one of his classes:

My head was aching, and I had a singular feeling—altogether new to me—that someone else was trying to get possession of my thoughts...I began to see strange shapes before my eyes, and to feel that I was in a grotesque room other than the classroom...Then I slumped down unconscious in my chair, in a stupor from which no one could arouse me.

(2004, 337)

This, we will learn in a moment, is a first sign of the alien entering Peaslee's body and supplanting his mind. Note how the mind swap is accompanied by a "singular feeling"—an unfamiliar phenomenology that paves the way for the protagonist's losing consciousness. When the narrator wakes up the next day, he is no longer himself—in fact, he will regain control of his body only after five years, and he will learn from others what happened during that time. At this stage, however, the narrator's account remains quite vague: he implies without stating that his body had been taken over by an alien mind.

The alienness manifests itself in directly embodied terms: the narrator's "eyes gazed strangely at the persons around [him], and the flexions of [his] facial muscles were altogether unfamiliar" (2004, 337). Peaslee's voice is equally affected: "I used my vocal organs clumsily and gropingly, and my diction had a curiously stilted quality, as if I had laboriously learned the English language from books" (2004, 337). Finally, as if to recapitulate how the mind swap involves bodily changes, the narrator adds: "I required an odd amount of re-education in the use of my hands, legs, and bodily apparatus in general" (2004, 338). There is something deeply disconcerting about these first-person references to changes that, despite the grammatical form, occurred outside of the narrator's awareness, and were only relayed to him at a later stage. The body is made strange through a double process of internalization: an external, cosmic force displaces the narrator's mental faculties; and the external viewpoint of those who observed the narrator after his sudden transformation is spliced into his retrospective account of those events. The narrator's body thus becomes contested territory, caught in a crossfire of perspectives that challenge the reassuring equation between embodiment and subjective experience. The awkward facial expressions and the stilted quality of the voice are the behavioral signs of this alien embodiment, which will become much more prominent as the novella progresses.

For now, we are told that the narrator's strange behavior is interpreted as a personality disorder and that he only comes back to himself after five years. But he never recovers fully. He is haunted by "vague dreams and queer ideas" (2004, 342), particularly ideas about time and how it may be possible to live "in one age and [cast] one's mind all over eternity for knowledge of past and future ages" (2004, 342). When he starts researching reports of sudden and protracted loss of consciousness, he finds a handful of cases strikingly similar to his own: people "seized with a strange secondary life and leading for a greater or lesser period an utterly alien existence typified at first by vocal and bodily awkwardness" (2004, 343). Even more worryingly, the "bodily awkwardness" continues even after the narrator has regained possession of his body:

> There was…a feeling of profound and inexplicable horror concerning myself. I developed a queer fear of seeing my own form, as if my eyes would find it something utterly alien and inconceivably abhorrent. When I did glance down and behold the familiar human shape in quiet grey or blue clothing I always felt a curious relief, though in order to gain this relief I had to conquer an infinite dread.
>
> (2004, 345)

Note how the feeling of awkwardness is here reversed vis-à-vis the previous part of the novella: it is not an alien mind that takes over the narrator's familiar human body but rather the body itself that morphs into an "utterly alien" form. Affect ("an infinite dread") is the vehicle of this realization, and its trigger is a subtle discrepancy between proprioception—the narrator's awareness of his own body—and actual perception (what the narrator sees when he glances down).

Soon even his perception will be affected by this alien embodiment. Initially, it is just *imaginary* perception, in the form of "fleeting visual impressions" that transport the narrator to a mysterious space. The first of these spatial descriptions is worth quoting in full, because of how it plays with the reader's own imagination of this environment:

> I would seem to be in an enormous vaulted chamber whose lofty stone groinings were well-nigh lost in the shadows overhead…There were colossal round windows and high arched doors, and pedestals or tables each as tall as the height of an ordinary room. Vast shelves of dark wood lined the walls, holding what seemed to be volumes of immense size with strange hieroglyphs on their backs…The dark granite masonry was of a monstrous megalithic type, with lines of convex-topped blocks fitting the concave-bottomed courses which rested upon them. There were no chairs, but the tops of the vast pedestals were littered with books, papers, and what seemed to be writing materials—oddly figured jars of a purplish metal, and rods with stained tips. Tall as the pedestals were, I seemed at times able to view them from above.
>
> (2004, 345–46)

Recall how, in Chapter 1, I argued that the reader is always asked to imagine narrative space from a particular viewpoint, which is occupied by what I refer to as the reader's "virtual body." However, this viewpoint may be more or less definite and more or less stable throughout a description.[11] I suggested that some of the descriptions in Ray Cummings's *The Girl in the Golden Atom* caused abrupt shifts in the scale of readers' mental imagery, problematizing their positioning with respect to the atomic reality of the golden atom. Lovecraft's passage operates in a partly similar way, but its effect is much subtler: the indeterminacy of readers' mental imagery is compounded by the indeterminacy of the narrator's own perceptual awareness of his body. The first two quoted sentences invite us to imagine a space of grandiose proportions. We take for granted that the narrator is a human being of average height, reading the detail of the "groinings" almost "lost in the shadows overhead" as confirmation of their size relative to the narrator's: the indistinctness of the ceiling suggests perceptual *distance*. Even the "pedestals or tables each as tall as the height of an ordinary room" or the "volumes of immense size" pose no particular difficulty: we just take these ordinary objects and scale them up, assuming that the narrator's perception of these objects reflects his diminutive size. Things begin to change with the sentence about the "dark granite masonry": the indication of the blocks' size is relatively unproblematic, but the detail of the description implies that the narrator is observing them from up close. Even more disconcertingly, how could a human-sized narrator see the "tops of the vast pedestals"? This incongruity might pass unnoticed if the narrator didn't make it explicit with the last sentence.

This final remark reveals how readers' imagination has been led down a garden path: they have been tricked into attributing to the narrator a normal human body, while in fact some elements of the description suggest otherwise—namely, that the reader has been adopting an alien body all along.[12] This blank at the heart of the description (what does the narrator's body look like?) resonates with his previous comment about the "infinite dread" that he experiences whenever he looks at his own body: suddenly, we realize that this apparently unemotional description may imply the same kind of fear, and that the vagueness of the narrator's position may in fact be an attempt at *denying* his nonhuman embodiment. Crucially, readers have been unwittingly drawn into this body (and, potentially, into the affect that goes with it) as they tried to form a spatially coherent mental image of this environment.

The same spatial vagueness surrounds the narrator's dreams. We read that these were "dreams of strange floatings over the city and through the regions around it" (2004, 348). This verb, "float," is repeated three times in the narrator's account, always in an effort to qualify his perception of his own motion. Note that while the narrator seems to observe things from a certain height, "floating" does not have the specificity of "flying": it does not imply or suggest a body of a certain kind. Thus, the word choice reflects the narrator's seemingly desperate denial of the obvious: "For a while my chief concern during dreams was to avoid looking down at myself, and I recall how grateful I was for the total absence of large mirrors in the strange rooms" (2004, 358). After a while, however, Peaslee cannot resist the temptation to look at his own body:

> At first my downward glance revealed nothing whatever. A moment later I perceived that this was because my head lay at the end of a flexible neck of enormous length. Retracting this neck and gazing down very sharply, I saw the scaly, rugose, iridescent bulk of a vast cone ten feet tall and ten feet wide at the base.
>
> (2004, 358)

By the time readers experience this revelation, the narrator has already provided them with an external description of the body of this alien species, known as the Great Race:

> They seemed to be enormous iridescent cones, about ten feet high and ten feet wide at the base, and made up of some ridgy, scaly, semi-elastic matter. From their apexes projected four flexible, cylindrical members, each a foot thick, and of a ridgy substance like that of the cones themselves.
>
> (2004, 356–57)

Two things are remarkable about the narrator's discovery that he is inhabiting an alien body. First, the mention of the flexible and extensible neck retrospectively accounts for the vagueness of the chamber's description (and of the "floating"): this bodily makeup affords a degree of perceptual freedom unparalleled in the human body. Second, the narrator's discovery had not just been foreshadowed in the passage about the chamber, but readers had been asked to *enact* his discovery in a first-person way through their embodied imagination of this space. The external description of the aliens' nonhuman (and nonanthropomorphic) body complements this experience, putting readers in a position to fully understand the narrator's horror when his true body shape is finally made explicit.

As the narrator makes these discoveries, the nature of the alien race he comes into contact with becomes clearer: the Great Race is a species of time-traveling creatures that swap their minds with those of other, lesser animals so as to avoid extinction. While the narrator's body was controlled by one of these aliens (that is, during the five years of his apparent "amnesia"), his mind was exiled in the alien's body. He was then free to consult "the Great Race's central archives"—which contain a vast amount of knowledge about distant times and places in the universe— and he even took on the task of writing a "history of [his] own age" (2004, 360) as a contribution to these archives. In an arresting demonstration of Lovecraft's cosmicism, the narrator adds: "My own history was assigned a specific place in the vaults of the lowest or vertebrate level—the section devoted to the culture of mankind and of the furry and reptilian races immediately preceding it in terrestrial dominance" (2004, 361). The human body—evoked by the mention of the "vertebrate level"—is treated here as little more than a curio, comparable to "furry and reptilian races." This is the last step in the bodily defamiliarization that started with the narrator's awkwardness. A turning point in that process was Peaslee's (and, potentially, the reader's) coming to occupy an alien body of the Great Race, with its markedly nonhuman features. This is quite different from—and indeed opposite in direction to—Faber's staging of the hybrid body in *Under the Skin*, in which human-like embodiment was painfully and violently imposed on Isserley. More significantly still, in Faber's novel the contact between the human and the nonhuman world was established through the phenomenology of the body, as we've seen. Lovecraft's "The Shadow Out of Time" works against the grain of phenomenology: it objectifies the human body by opening a rift between the narrator's physical body and his subjective experience. The alien body serves precisely to create and maintain this rift, which is implicit—but subtly active—in the vagueness of the description of the chamber or of the verb "float." The vagueness introduces a distance that is, first and foremost, experiential: the body becomes an inert object; even when it is observed, it is observed from a paradoxical position that is spatially internal but phenomenologically external.

Harman is right, then, to argue that Lovecraft's "horror comes...from the declared insufficiency of the description...The description is horrific only insofar as it undermines any distinct image" (2008, 27). My reading of Lovecraft's narrative brings to light how, if this effect is so powerful, it is largely because the vagueness enfolds not just the narrator's body, but the reader's own body as he or she empathizes with Peaslee and imagines his experiences. This point explains the power of the novella's conclusion. Peaslee discovers, in a remote desert in Western Australia, the entrance to a mysterious citadel that looks exactly like the place he visited in his dreams. For all the eerie familiarity of this place, one

> thing only was unfamiliar, and that was my own size in relation to the monstrous masonry. I felt oppressed by a sense of unwonted smallness, as if the sight of these towering walls from a mere human body was something wholly new and abnormal. Again and again I looked nervously down at myself, vaguely disturbed by the human form I possessed.
>
> (2004, 382)

At first glance, this experience suggests that the narrator has become habituated to the alien species' body (and body size) to the extent that his *human* body now appears strange to him in relation to these colossal structures. But there is much more than that at stake. Peaslee does not appear to be in full control of his body after he enters the citadel: there is still a trace of the alien in him, which explains his uneasiness with his human form. In fact, the narrator notes that his

> right hand, even as it shook with fright, still twitched rhythmically in its eagerness to turn a lock it hoped to find. My mind was asking itself questions whose origin and relevancy I was only beginning to guess. Would the shelf be reachable by a human body? Could my human hand master all the aeon-remembered motions of the lock?
>
> (2004, 387)

The "muscle memory" of the twitching hand is a further symptom of the objectification of the narrator's body, which responds to a logic of its own, beyond his conscious control or experience. This logic is object-directed: the body longs for a particular shelf, it is eager to turn a lock to have access to a certain object. Not only does Lovecraft's prose trace in vivid detail the contours of this architecture, but even the language through which he describes the protagonist's psychology draws on architectural (and therefore thing-like) elements: "Something was fumbling and rattling at the latch of my recollection, while another unknown force sought to keep the portal barred" (2004, 376). The protagonist's inner world mirrors the environment: there are no feelings but only things ominously interacting with one another. It is no wonder that the protagonist's fate hinges on the object that he retrieves from one of the library's shelves: a book, the only proof that he has visited this place in actuality and not just in his imagination. As the novel's last paragraph reveals, this book contained "the words of the English language in [the narrator's] own handwriting" (2004, 397): we realize that this is a dictionary that the narrator himself had compiled during his captivity in the alien body. This object mysteriously disappears during the narrator's frantic escape from the citadel, and with it the possibility of demonstrating the authenticity of his account.

More than this final hesitation between reality and hallucination—fairly conventional in a horror story—Lovecraft's account of the narrator's loss of consciousness is significant:

> I was in my conical, non-human body again, and mingled with crowds of the Great Race and the captive minds who carried books up and down the lofty corridors and vast inclines. Then, superimposed upon these pictures, were frightful momentary flashes of a non-visual consciousness involving desperate struggles, a writhing free from clutching tentacles of whistling wind, an insane, bat-like flight through half-solid air, a feverish burrowing through the cyclone-whipped dark, and a wild stumbling and scrambling over fallen masonry.
>
> (2004, 397)

As the narrator imagines returning to his former, alien body, he experiences a flurry of "non-visual" sensations that echo and expand the vagueness at the heart of his previous "floating." The struggling, writhing, burrowing, stumbling, and scraping are patterns of motion detached from any physical basis—even the flight is "bat-like," but not exactly a bat's flight. This is, in essence, bodily movement uncoupled from phenomenology and subjectivity, and it is the last step in the objectification of the body brought about by the narrator's exposure to the nonhuman: the body becomes an indistinct thing capable only of random, inchoate, insensate movement.

Human subjectivity is thus radically challenged from the viewpoint of a species much better adjusted to the cosmos than we are: a species of creatures that live "four or five thousand years" (2004, 363) and have mastered the art of time travel through mind swaps. Lovecraft's descriptive and stylistic prowess molds these ideas into a concrete experience readers can go through. In this way, Lovecraft appeals to a cosmic perspective to crack open human subjectivity *from the inside*, revealing the weird objectness not just of the world (as highlighted by Harman and others) but of our own body, and at the same time exposing the limitations of our embodied cognition: any confrontation with intelligent beings whose bodies are fundamentally different from our own is likely to elicit distrust and horror. In *Solaris*, Lem pursues some of the same concerns in relation to an even more spectacularly alien mode of embodiment, as we'll see in the next section.

Mimoid Minds

The alien life form that Lem stages in *Solaris* doesn't possess anything resembling a body in the everyday sense of the word. In fact, the Polish writer elevates the metaphor—already encountered in Chapter 2—of the "celestial body" to a literal (if fictional) reality: the narrative centers on a planet known as Solaris, and more specifically on the fluid mass that extends over the surface of this planet. This is no ordinary ocean: it is, biologists discover, "a highly organized structure, perhaps exceeding terrestrial organisms in its complexity, since it was capable of actively influencing the orbit of its planet—for no other cause had been discovered that might explain Solaris's [unstable orbit]" (2011, 296–98).[13] In this sense, *Solaris* can be productively read alongside recent discussions on the Anthropocene: just as the planetary impact of human activities exposes the interaction between different time scales—human, evolutionary, and geological (see, e.g., Chakrabarty 2014)—Lem's ocean has shaped its host planet to the point of altering its astronomical characteristics. Yet these effects on the planet, as the novel points out, are not a historical contingency (as in humanity's becoming a quasi-geological agent) but intrinsically bound up with the ocean's existence: "unlike terrestrial organisms it did not adapt to its surroundings over the course of hundreds of millions of years, so as only then to produce a rational species, but it had gained control over its environment from the start" (2011, 312–14).

The seemingly intentional deviation in the planet's orbit points to the conclusion that the ocean is a creature capable of purposeful and intelligent behavior. Despite this intimation of mind, however, the novel dramatizes the impossibility of establishing communication with the ocean or knowing its motives: the ocean appears to fall outside of humankind's "window of contact," as Lem would put it in a later novel, *Fiasco* (Weissert 1992, 161).[14] Because humanity and this alien life form are at different stages of cognitive evolution, the gap between them becomes virtually unbridgeable in the conceptual terms of science. This is what we learn in a number of passages where the first-person narrator, the psychologist Doctor Kelvin, summarizes the many hypotheses and theories that have marked the history of the academic field devoted to Solaris, known as "solaristics." These sections of the novel read like an "allegory of the scientific process," in Fredric Jameson's (2005, 112) words: ultimately, scientific research on Solaris contributes only to a narcissistic project of human self-affirmation, mirroring anthropocentric biases and presuppositions without producing any substantive knowledge about the ocean itself. As one of the novel's scientists puts it in a passage discussed by many commentators,

> We see ourselves as Knights of the Holy Contact. That's another falsity. We're not searching for anything except people. We don't need other worlds. We need mirrors. We don't know what to do with other worlds. One world is enough, even there we feel stifled.
>
> (2011, 1295–97)

This "world" that we inhabit—the anthropocentric world of human-scale experience—keeps us from genuine contact with Solaris. Even if we somehow managed to overcome this narcissistic concern with our own species, it is doubtful whether we would ever be able to *know* the ocean in any meaningful way, due to its irreducible alterity. Lem conveys this point by describing in minute detail the structures that the ocean spontaneously generates, labeled by scientists "mimoids" and "symmetriads." These impressive structures can be compared to meteorological phenomena on Earth, but they are clearly purposive. Mimoids imitate the shape of whatever object happens to be available, whether natural (a cloud) or human-made (a reconnaissance aircraft). Yet the exact purpose of this imitation remains mysterious. As for symmetriads, they are storm-like events of astounding mathematical complexity, pointing to a mind that is by several orders of magnitude more advanced than our own:

> This configuration constitutes, as a whole, a three-dimensional solution to a higher-order equation...Occupying an area of several cubic

miles, it constitutes the solution to an entire mathematical system; this solution, furthermore, is four-dimensional, since certain essential coefficients in the equation are also expressed in time, that is to say, in the changes brought about by its passing.

(2011, 2150–56)

Described in pages of rarefied prose, mimoids and symmetriads demonstrate the ocean's power to give material expression to mathematical relations that human beings would never be able to perceive directly, as part of the intermediate world. Thus these spatio-temporal structures serve as a visual equivalent of the ocean's radical otherness: "A symmetriad is millions [of simultaneous processes], no, billions, to the nth power; it is unimaginability itself" (2011, 2176). Against this background, we may wonder whether it makes sense to see the ocean as possessing some kind of body at all. After all, the idea of "body" is closely bound up with how life on Earth evolved and how intelligent behavior (and therefore mind) developed over the course of that evolutionary history. Perhaps Lem's representation of a mathematically minded ocean wants to challenge precisely that conception of embodiment whereby we think of mind and physical organisms as integrally related. In that sense, the anthropocentric (or at least Earth-centric) presuppositions that surround our notions of embodiment may be one of the factors that bar us from insight into the ocean's real nature. This point is made by Grattenstrom, a scientist whose work is discussed in one of Lem's scholarly digressions:

> Grattenstrom examined the formulas of relativity theory and of the theorem of force fields; he looked at parastatics and the hypotheses of a unified cosmic field, in search of traces of the human body—all that comes from and is a consequence of the existence of our senses, the structure of our organism, and the limitations and weaknesses of humankind's animal physiology. He reached the conclusion that there cannot now, nor in the future could there ever be, talk of "contact" between human beings and any non-humanoid civilization.
>
> (2011, 3154–59)

Even our best and most abstract scientific theories can't be uncoupled from the human body, whose presence subtly ("traces") but radically undermines our ability to make contact with a disembodied mind like the ocean's.

Yet, if it is clear that the ocean doesn't have a body in the usual sense of the term, the novel does not close the door on embodiment as a possible way of *knowing* the ocean. Perhaps the problem with scientific theories is that they imply the human body without openly acknowledging its significance—and its power. Indeed, the ending of *Solaris* suggests that an alternative mode of understanding—a fully embodied one—may be more successful in opening a dialogue with the ocean than the conceptual templates of science. This final scene injects new meaning into the metaphor of the "contact" with an alien mind, for it is *through* the body and physical contact with the ocean that some kind of communication, however tentative, is established. The narrator, Kelvin, is exploring a mimoid shaped like "an ancient city half in ruin,...an exotic Moroccan settlement" (2011, 3727–28). Here, he attempts to touch one of the ocean's waves and describes how the water-like substance

> hesitated, withdrew, then flowed over my hand yet without touching it, in such a way that a narrow layer of air remained between the surface of my gauntlet and the inside of the covering, which instantly changed consistency, turning from liquid to almost fleshy.
> (2011, 3745–47)

Commenting on this scene, Melody Jue argues that "the narrative ends with the possibility of a new practice of gathering knowledge that shifts from an aerial/visual sense to a liquid/tactile one" (2014, 232). Kelvin's close encounter with the ocean does mark a radical departure from all previous descriptions, which were dominated by vision and by the abstract nomenclature of science (including such neologisms as "mimoids" and "symmetriads").

Kelvin's haptic perception of the ocean signals a shift from a conceptual to an embodied mode of apprehension of the ocean's otherness. Nor is this merely a unilateral change in Kelvin's stance, because the water itself responds to the character's gesture by taking on an "almost fleshy" texture that it didn't have before—where "fleshy" is, of course, a metaphor evoking the domain of embodied experience. This "somatization" of the ocean—as we may call it—continues into the next sentence: "I then raised my arm; the wave, or rather its narrow tongue, followed it upwards, continuing to encase my hand in an ever more transparent dirty green encystment" (2011, 3747–48). The wave is described as tongue-like, its wrapping around Kelvin's hand is likened to an "encystment"—two more embodied cues. These are all variations on the embodied metaphor of the "contact" with an alien species, and yet they are variations that force us to take the metaphor seriously, as if the body served as a bridge between human beings and the ocean, whereas all scientific attempts failed. Some metaphorical distance is still involved, of course, corresponding perhaps to the ineliminable "narrow layer of air" that prevents *actual* contact with the ocean. But this metaphorical filter is nothing compared to the mystifications of science, which only held a mirror up to human cognition. The protagonist's encounter thus suggests an alternative reading of the novel, one focusing on the "traces" of embodiment that prepare this ending and at the same time help us disclose its significance.

The plot of Lem's novel begins with Kelvin arriving on a research station that was built on Solaris to study the ocean. Here he learns that one of the station's scientists, Gibarian, committed suicide shortly before his arrival. Something is clearly amiss on the station, but it takes Kelvin some time to find out exactly what is going on: all the station's members have been having "guests," as they euphemistically put it. A guest is an apparent replica of a person they have met in the past, and to whom they've had a particularly strong attachment, usually in difficult or painful circumstances. Kelvin's guest is his late wife, Harey, who killed herself after Kelvin threatened to leave her—a decision over which he feels intense guilt. At first Kelvin takes Harey for a dream or a hallucination, but to his dismay he discovers that she has a flesh-and-blood body. In the words of Sartorius, another of the station's scientists, these guests "are not persons, nor are they copies of specific individuals, but rather materialized projections of what our brain contains regarding a particular person" (2011, 1860–61). The only possible explanation is that the ocean has somehow read the characters' memories and created these doppelgängers, who put an enormous amount of psychological strain on the station's crew members. The purpose of these projections remains unclear, but Harey and the other guests can be seen as a literal embodiment of the ocean—an attempt at making contact with the scientists in a recognizably human (if unsettling) form. Through this strategy the novel begins to reduce the gap between the ocean and the human body.

Harey's physical body plays a major role in Kelvin's relationship with her, which goes from disbelief (when she appears for the first time) to hatred (when he realizes that she is a "copy") to uneasy, guilt-ridden affection. For instance, Kelvin caresses Harey's foot and realizes that it is "soft as the skin of a new-born baby" (2011, 994); this is taken as evidence for her being a mere copy or simulacrum. Later on, Kelvin takes a sample of Harey's blood and examines it under the lens of a powerful microscope, in a scene reminiscent of the Chemist's voyage in *The Girl in the Golden Atom* (discussed in Chapter 1). Here is what Kelvin observes: "I saw from above, sharply foreshortened, a vast wilderness flooded by a silvery glow. On it, in a hazy mist there lay flat round rocks that looked shattered and weather-beaten. These were the red corpuscles" (2011, 1780–82). As Jue notes, Harey thus "becomes, for [Kelvin], a landscape" (2014, 229). Jue goes on to discuss this scene in terms of the male character's objectifying gaze, which "forcefully [penetrates] into the secrets of a feminized 'nature'" (2014, 229). But the scene involves much more than that gendered contrast: by revealing a landscape in Harey's body, the microscope undermines the distinction between a living creature and inanimate "things" such as the apparent "wilderness," the "rocks," or—later in the passage—the "rocky crater" perceived by Kelvin. The body is thus shown to be made from inanimate "stuff," not unlike the ocean itself. Yet when Kelvin sets the microscope to maximum zoom only a silver field comes into view: "This body, seemingly so slender and frail—in fact indestructible—at its deepest level had turned out to be made of nothingness?" (2011, 1796–97). This "nothingness," the scientists hypothesize, proves that the ocean has created Harey out of building blocks—possibly neutrinos—too small to be seen through this microscope, or any other human-made apparatus. The opaqueness of the ocean's mind leaves its mark on its creation, Harey, whose bodily structure destabilizes an intuitive ontological distinction between animate and inanimate entities.[15] Through Harey and the other guests, the ocean opens a first channel of bodily communication with the humans on the station, even as this contact proves traumatic for Kelvin because of the affective baggage that comes with seeing a look-alike of his wife. Diegetically, the guests thus function as embodied, anthropomorphic stand-ins for the ocean's alienness.

Lem's novel brings together the ocean and embodiment through stylistic means, too. This is the effect of repeated metaphorical associations between the ocean and parts of the human body. Consider, for instance, this description from the novel's first chapter: "Stretches of slimy foam the color of bone were gathering in the troughs between the waves. For a split second I felt a twinge of nausea in the pit of my stomach" (2011, 150–51). Not only does the ocean elicit an embodied response from the narrator (disgust), but this response is linked to the bone-like (and therefore bodily) color of the foam itself. Therefore, a direct connection is established between the ocean's metaphorical body and Kelvin's physical one. Similar emotional connotations emerge in a later description of the mimoids, in which the ocean's waves are compared to "shrinking mouths, like living, muscled, closing craters" (2011, 2049). These mouths and muscles detached from an identifiable organism evoke an unstable and disconcerting form of embodiment. One of the many theories surrounding the ocean holds that it is "a neoplasmic glioma which, having come into existence within the bodies of former inhabitants of the planet, had consumed them all and swallowed them up, fusing the remains together in the form of an everlasting, self-rejuvenating, supracellular element" (2011, 409–11). The ocean is thus presented as a metastasis, a deviant form of embodiment that has spread itself out on a planetary scale. This theory, if accurate, would place the association between the ocean and embodiment beyond the realm of mere metaphor.

Whether the somatization of the ocean is metaphorical or not, its affective connotations of horror and repulsiveness are stable throughout the novel. This is, no doubt, a result of the disturbing alienness of the ocean's mind: the ocean and its embodiments (the "guests") challenge basic ontological distinctions between living beings and material things. The situation begins to change only toward the end of the novel, when Kelvin's dreams defamiliarize *his own* embodiment: "I [was] shrunken or imprisoned in a substance that was alien to me, as if my whole body had become part of some half-dead, unmoving, shapeless lump" (2011, 3289–90). In a later passage, Kelvin has a puzzling experience of being created by a mysterious "hand" whose touch pervades his body and that of another being present on the scene, possibly "a woman":

> Our bodies, naked and white, started to flow, blackening into streams of writhing vermin that emerged out of us like air, and I was—we were—I was a glistening, febrile mass of wormlike motion, tangling and untangling, but never-ending, infinite.
>
> (2011, 3308–10)

In a striking experience of transcorporeality, Kelvin's dreams turn his body into a shapeless mass that erases all boundaries and dissolves itself into pure pattern ("streams," "wormlike motion"). A hint of that shapelessness was present in Lovecraft's depiction of the Great Race. Yet in Lovecraft the link between body, living organism, and mind is to some extent preserved: it is the impossibility of distinctly *experiencing* the alien body that creates the horror. In Lem, the body of the alien, the ocean, becomes in itself indistinct and amorphous: as massive as a geological formation, as unpredictable as a meteorological phenomenon. Thus, the narrator counters all attempts at anthropomorphizing the ocean directly by suggesting that its "protuberances," the mimoids, "are no more its limbs than an earthquake is gymnastic exercise for the earth's crust" (2011, 2105–6). Kelvin's dreams put him in touch with this alien regime of embodiment, bringing him closer in his imagination to the ocean's paradoxically inanimate mind.

Ultimately, this experience severs the connection between mind and common-sense notions of what a biological organism is. We find here another unambiguous formulation of the hard problem of subjectivity. What gives rise to mind, the novel suggests, is a certain kind of patterning of matter; in this patterning, the human body and the ocean's alien mind converge.[16] This, we learn, is Kelvin's key contribution to solaristics:

> taking as my starting point the innovative research of Bergmann and Reynolds, who from the mosaic of cortical processes had succeeded in identifying and "filtering out" the components accompanying the most powerful emotions—despair, pain, joy—I went on to juxtapose those recordings with discharges emitted by currents in the ocean, and discovered oscillations and patterns in the curves... that offered a noteworthy analogy.
>
> (2011, 3234–38)

The quasi-meteorological patterns of mimoids and symmetriads are thus equated with the invisible electrical currents sweeping through the human body and brain. (Incidentally, this equation explains how the ocean could have read the human characters' memories and recreated their "guests.") This equivalence between brain waves and the ocean's movements becomes tangible in Kelvin's dreams, which foreground a heavily affective experience of pattern crisscrossing the inner and the outer, the animate and the inanimate:

> I would run off in every direction at once and gather back together in the form of a suffering that was more vivid than any waking state, multiplied a hundredfold, concentrated in black and red distances, now hardening into rock, now rising to a crescendo somewhere in the glow of another sun or another world.
>
> (2011, 3311–13)

The affective contour of this passage offers a syntactic equivalent to the patterned nature of mind, alternating outward and inward motion ("run off" and "gather back," "multiplied" and "concentrated," "hardening" and "rising") in a way that interweaves the narrator's self and cosmic realities like "another sun or another world."

Because material pattern, mind, and affect go hand in hand, the novel suggests that the ocean's spectacular mimoids and symmetriads may *also* be affective in nature: although we may never know these feelings in detail, sensing their affective nature is a step toward grasping the ocean's otherness. Perhaps, then, the metaphorical somatization of the ocean serves to reveal this affective substrate, which pervades (and fuses together) the two sides of the novel's plot: the human drama of Kelvin's encounter with a creature that looks exactly like his dead wife; and the cosmic drama of humanity's encounter with a planet-sized, ocean-shaped mind. *Solaris* thus toys with a panpsychic conception of mental phenomena: the unimaginable complexity of the ocean's mind calls attention to how *any* kind of pattern in external reality may possess affective qualities. This is the conclusion reached by one of the thinkers associated with the nonhuman turn, Steven Shaviro, in *The Universe of Things* (2014): building on Alfred North Whitehead's philosophy, Shaviro argues that "all entities have insides as well as outsides, or first-person experiences as well as observable, third-person properties" (2014, 104). *Solaris* explores this philosophical position by way of a fictional situation: it deploys characters' bodies and a set of embodied metaphors (along with the affect they generate) to evoke—indirectly but no less powerfully—the possibility that an ocean might have a first-person perspective.

In this sense, *Solaris* takes Kelvin's vision of Harey's body as a landscape to its logical consequence: there is no fundamental difference between a living body and a seemingly inert landscape, because both pulsate with mind-like patterns. This realization goes against the grain of widespread ontological assumptions, particularly the cognitively basic distinction between sentient subjects and inanimate matter: normally, we attribute mind only in conjunction with organismic bodies.[17] The ocean lends itself to a panpsychic reading precisely by questioning these assumptions—and with them, everyday notions of embodiment. This is what Kelvin's final contact with the ocean signifies, succeeding where scientific efforts had failed. The ending portrays a deeply affective merging between the character's human body and the ocean's protean embodiment: "I was becoming one with this fluid unseeing colossus, as if—without the slightest effort, without words, without a single thought—I was forgiving it for everything" (2011, 3762–63). Jue (2014, 232) links this "becoming one" to the sensation of limitlessness that Sigmund Freud (1962, 11–12) referred to as "oceanic feeling." But while for Freud oceanic feelings are at the root of religious experiences, Lem's affective contact with the ocean appears entirely material: it doesn't imply transcendence but, on the contrary, a recognition of the pervasiveness of mind in the physical world. The novel's defamiliarization of everyday modes of embodiment makes that recognition possible.

***

In the case studies of my previous chapters, a cosmic perspective was introduced into the storyworld by a spatio-temporal framework or scientific theory external to the body. In the texts I have discussed in this chapter, the bodily defamiliarization that is triggered by the cosmic perspective comes "from the inside": readers are encouraged to imagine and empathize with bodies that already contain, in some form, a cosmic element. In *Under the Skin,* the departure from human embodiment is a matter of degree, and it is only the hybridity of the protagonist's body—the fact that she is half alien, half human—that sets in motion the defamiliarization. Lovecraft's Great Race is more obviously unsettling, with its conical body and tentacle-like appendages. However, hybridity figures prominently in "The Shadow Out of Time" as well, since the protagonist experiences a discrepancy between certain anthropocentric expectations surrounding the body and the alien body that he comes to inhabit. But this alien body is still recognizable as such: it has a trunk, limbs, a sensory apparatus, and so on. The aliens are biological organisms, even if their makeup is radically different from that of terrestrial animals. No such biological continuity is possible in Lem's *Solaris,* which imagines the alien body in more radical terms than either Faber or Lovecraft. The ocean is a full-blown cosmic entity in that it coevolved with a planet: its mind has no biological underpinnings but appears to emerge from inorganic matter, such as the waves or the quasi-meteorological phenomena that the ocean generates. Yet the novel invites us to understand this alien entity through the lens of embodied metaphors and—even more importantly—through recognizably somatic affect. This is what emerges in the final encounter between Kelvin and the ocean—a passage that prompts an embodied reading of the entire novel.

Solaris destabilizes a cognitively basic equation between biological life and mind; in this sense, it goes perhaps farther than the other narratives in interrogating the uneasy relationship between mind, bodies, and matter. However, similar questions are present in *Under the Skin* and "The Shadow Out of Time" as well. Isserley's dissolution into Scotland's inanimate landscape and its particle-like building blocks is poised on the same dividing line between phenomenology and the seemingly insentient "things" that surround us. Lovecraft attempts a similar operation not by spreading the body outward, into the external world, but by undermining phenomenology from the inside: the protagonist takes on an alien body horrifically gutted of first-person experience, a vague form whose very thinking is object-oriented and object-like.

Where these case studies converge, then, is in the attention they pay to the materiality of the body: human experience is collapsed into biological or physical processes, which are in turn collapsed into material realities—a narrative sleight-of-hand that leaves us wondering how experience could have disappeared in the process (once again, the hard problem of consciousness).[18] Seen from this cosmic perspective, the materiality of our body becomes a source of radical and as if ineliminable strangeness. In exploring this materiality and its disturbing implications, my case studies speak to the concerns of nonhuman theorists and speculative realists in contemporary philosophy—but they do so in a way that uses the body itself (the characters' and potentially the readers') as a springboard toward the nonhuman. The concept of pattern is key to this dynamic: as we know from the introduction, one of the core ideas of embodied (and, more specifically, enactivist) approaches to cognition is that mind arises from patterned coordination with the physical and social world. Thus, the body allows Isserley to experience the comforting texture of the nonhuman world in *Under the Skin*; vague kinetic patterns (such as the "floating" motion) mark the protagonist's adoption of an alien body in Lovecraft's novella; and wave-like structures bring together human brains and the ocean's inanimate mind in *Solaris*. Through the affective patterning of embodiment, characters and readers can thus become privy to the fabric of the cosmos itself, with all the existential anxieties that it entails for a human audience.

Notes

1 One of the clearest articulations of this link between life and mind in enactivist philosophy can be found in Evan Thompson's *Mind in Life* (2007b).
2 I further explore the possibilities of these narrative transformations of the body—from the human to the nonhuman—in an article co-authored with Shannon Lambert (Caracciolo and Lambert 2019).
3 "Vodsel" is a neologism, but it is likely related to the Dutch word "voedsel" (food). Michel Faber was born in the Netherlands and moved to Australia when he was seven.
4 For more on metaphorical language in *Under the Skin*, see Caracciolo (2017a, 211–14).

5 See Caracciolo (2017b) for a more extended discussion of the ethical quandaries at the heart of Faber's novel.

6 I have already addressed the role of disgust in character engagements in Caracciolo (2016a, Chap. 5).

7 For more on metaphor and the phenomenology of pain, see Caracciolo (2013a, 98–99).

8 Perhaps even more than professional critics, online reviewers of the novel have picked up on this environmentalist "message." Consider, for instance, these comments: "Michel Faber almost forces the reader to observe how we, as human beings and caretakers of the earth, protect our environment and each other" (Perskie 2003); "Male-female gender roles and sexuality, 'speciesism,' vegetarian vs. meat-eating ideologies, and environmental depletion by bad political behavior, are all vilified in the course of the story" (A Reading Shrink 2014).

9 The association between cleanness and the natural world emerges in a scene toward the end of the novel: after having decided to leave the farm once and for all, Isserley washes herself in "the icy shallows of [a] loch" (Faber 2000, 287). The uneasy environmentalism of Faber's novel casts its shadow on this episode, indicating that any human action is bound to contaminate a pristine natural world, as the final (and largely rhetorical) question suggests: "She hoped the shampoo wouldn't do any harm to the things that lived in the loch. A few drops of chemical soap into such a vast reservoir of natural purity wouldn't have much effect, surely?" (2000, 287).

10 For a discussion of the weird as a distinctive literary mode, see Luckhurst (2017).

11 Thus, Manfred Jahn (1996) argues that focalization can be more or less "strict," depending on how textually well-defined the focalizing character's position is.

12 In linguistics, a garden path sentence is a sentence that creates certain grammatical expectations but asks readers to revise these expectations on the fly, reinterpreting the syntax a posteriori. "The horse raced past the barn fell" is a classic example: the final verb forces us to reinterpret the grammatical function of the word "raced." Lovecraft's description does something similar with readers' mental imagery, encouraging them to revise their understanding of the narrator's body size at the end of the passage. For more on narrative and garden path sentences, see Abbott (2013, Chap. 3).

13 Here and throughout the numbers in the *Solaris* citations are references to "locations" in my Kindle edition of the novel (Lem 2011). The Kindle edition was translated from the Polish by Bill Johnston, in what is considered a major improvement over the previous translation by Joanna Kilmartin and Steve Cox, which was based on the French edition of the novel (see Flood 2011). However, the Johnson translation is currently available in digital format only.

14 For more on the philosophy of Lem's works, see the collection edited by Swirski (2006).

15 Johnson (2000) surveys psychological work on the developmental underpinnings of the distinction between subjects and things.

16 Stephan Besser (2017) has written an insightful article on the discourse of pattern in contemporary "neuroculture," arguing that pattern brings together the mental and the physical—an idea that Lem anticipates in *Solaris*.

17 Lisa Zunshine examines the narrative potential of violations of basic ontological distinctions in *Strange Concepts and the Stories They Make Possible* (2008).

18 For a more detailed discussion of narrative "sleights-of-hand" in relation to the hard problem of consciousness, see Caracciolo (2016b).

6   The Wide, Wide Cosmos

If this book started with the exploration of the microcosm, its last chapter turns to the farthest reaches of the universe and examines how the narrative imagination deals with very large scales. We'll see how literary narrative confronts the cosmos in the broadest sense of the term—the cosmos as the spatio-temporal totality that enfolds, and at the same time infinitely transcends, human existence. This is the project undertaken by the three narratives I will consider: Vladimir Nabokov's short story "Lance," first published in 1958 and Nabokov's only foray into science fiction; Olaf Stapledon's 1937 *Star Maker*, one of the most influential—and certainly among the most comprehensive—visions of the cosmos in science fiction; and Arthur C. Clarke's *2001: A Space Odyssey* (1968), the novel grown out of Clarke's collaboration with Stanley Kubrick. As in previous chapters, this order of presentation does not reflect the chronology of these texts' publication dates but rather a conceptual dialectic: while Nabokov infuses the cosmos with bodily qualities, Stapledon seeks to minimize the role of embodiment in his definitive account of cosmic history. Clarke negotiates a middle way (hence the dialectic): he retains the grandiose scope of Stapledon's narrative but also adopts embodied strategies similar to Nabokov's.

Confronting spatial greatness inevitably evokes the notion of the sublime. This book's argument about the interplay of embodiment and cosmic realities inscribes itself in a long intellectual tradition that asks what happens to the human imagination once it hits the wall of its own limitations. Theories of the sublime are, clearly, part of that tradition: sublime refers to objects that elicit emotions of awe and terror due to their incommensurability with the human, including the physical size of the human body. This incommensurability—literally, the lack of a common measure or proportion—between human beings and the natural world rose to prominence with eighteenth-century theorists of the natural sublime, particularly Edmund Burke; but it can be traced back to the influential treatise *On the Sublime* attributed to Cassius Longinus and composed in the first or third century CE (the exact identity of the author is debated):

> According to Longinus, although rhetoric is the primary determinate of the sublime, it is nature that seeds the idea of greatness in

man, and that inclines us to admire the grandeur of the Nile, the Rhine, or still more the ocean.

(Shaw 2006, 28)

While these examples—and many others contained in the works of the Romantics—are drawn from the natural landscape of our planet, the cosmos as a whole is bound to inspire sublime feelings as well.

Most theorists agree that the sublime is an affective phenomenon, or at least one that manifests itself affectively; yet how exactly these emotions are accounted for and interpreted varies significantly from commentator to commentator. Ecocritic Christopher Hitt discusses a fundamental tension within accounts of the sublime:

> the contradiction of the sublime is that it has tended to include *both* humbling fear *and* ennobling validation for the perceiving subject. Ever since the eighteenth century, critics and readers alike have generally paid more attention to the latter than to the former. But humility before nature has consistently been an elementary part of the natural sublime.
>
> (1999, 606; emphasis in the original)

Undoubtedly, the foremost advocate of the sublime as "ennobling validation" is philosopher Immanuel Kant. As Kant argues in his *Critique of the Power of Judgment*, the sublime depends on an impasse of our imagination, which is based on experience and therefore constrained by the senses. Yet, for Kant, human reason makes up for the breakdown of our imagination. The following analysis is worth quoting at length, because of how it appeals to a cosmic scale ("Milky Way systems"):

> A tree that we estimate by the height of a man may serve as a standard for a mountain, and, if the latter were, say, a mile high, it could serve as the unit for the number that expresses the diameter of the earth, in order to make the latter intuitable; the diameter of the earth could serve as the unit for the planetary system so far as known to us, this for the Milky Way, and the immeasurable multitude of such Milky Way systems...Now in the aesthetic judging of such an immeasurable whole, the sublime does not lie as much in the magnitude of the number as in the fact that as we progress we always arrive at ever greater units; the systematic division of the structure of the world contributes to this, representing to us all that is great in nature as in its turn small, but actually representing our imagination in all its boundlessness, and with it nature, as paling into insignificance beside the ideas of reason.
>
> (Kant 2002, 140)

Kant starts by calling attention to the possibility of converting the human body ("the height of a man") into a unit of measurement for a tree, the tree for a mountain, the mountain for the Earth, the Earth for the solar system, and so on. At every step, our sensory imagination struggles more and more to grasp the exact scale of the object we are trying to imagine: reality's commensurability with the human body becomes increasingly problematic. For Kant, the sublime does not lie in this sheer "magnitude of the number," but in the fact that—despite our faltering imagination—the mathematical system *works* unfalteringly: mathematics is able to reveal the "systematic division of the structure of the world" because it is the product of the "ideas of reason," which are not subject to the limitations of human experience (including the imagination). As Kant succinctly puts it, the sublime "demonstrates a faculty of the mind that surpasses every measure of the senses" (2002, 134). According to Hitt, Kant's analysis results in "the triumphant emergence of reason, revealing to us, finally, our 'pre-eminence over nature'" (Hitt 1999, 608; quotation from Kant 2002, 145).

Kant's conclusion runs counter to the fundamental premise of this book: namely, that *all* human cognition is derived from and dependent on the experiential knowledge of our embodied interactions with the world. From this perspective, Kant's trump card of disembodied "reason" becomes unavailable, and we are left with a paradox, which I will restate once again: how do we confront in our embodied imagination realities that are, as Kant and other theorists of the sublime rightly suggest, incommensurable with the human body? Considering this question shifts the balance toward what Hitt calls "the ecological sublime," which does not create a sense of "ennobling validation" but elicits feelings such as wonder and awe at the sheer scale of the cosmos. Insofar as these feelings are located in and felt through the body, they are a means of probing the cosmos—and its size—in embodied terms. Affect thus offers an opportunity to close the rift between the intermediate world (where our bodies are located) and the wide cosmos. To put the same point otherwise: faced with sublime landscapes, bodily defamiliarization follows a primarily affective route.[1]

This is a nonrepresentational opportunity: in responding affectively to the greatness of the cosmos, we do not attempt to form a conceptual equivalent of this greatness (we do not *directly* imagine or mentally represent the cosmos as a whole) but we only feel its overwhelming scale. This interest in moving beyond representation reflects the enactivist tenet that the world is "its own best model" (R. A. Brooks 1991; quoted in Noë 2004, 50). The upshot is that basic experience—such as perception and emotion—is not based on "internal" representations of the world but on patterns of sensorimotor as well as affective coordination (Hutto and Myin 2012). We should not drive a wedge between affect and representation, of course: in narrative, as I argued more at length elsewhere

(Caracciolo 2014d, Chap. 1), affective phenomena are always bound up with representation—where representation is defined as a semiotic reference to discrete events and existents (characters, locations). But part of the power of narrative is that it may, through representational means, draw on a level of our experience that is fundamentally affective, preverbal, and nonrepresentational.

This is what this chapter's case studies attempt to do: they start by asking readers to imagine cosmic realities, but then they dramatically pull the rug from under the feet of readers' imagination—a narrative gesture that prompts a specifically affective mode of engagement with the wide cosmos. However, the feelings involved are not the awe and terror generally associated with the sublime—nor do they point to the technological sublime often evoked by science fiction. The reader's embodied affect is defamiliarized precisely because these conventional emotional pathways for thinking about the scale of the cosmos are challenged at a fundamental level.[2] Nabokov resorts to his signature irony and indirection in recounting a young man's trip to a distant planet—an experience charged with ineffable affect. Stapledon, at the opposite end of the scale, chronicles a mind-boggling cosmic history in a dispassionate tone whose very nonchalance and humorlessness are a source of wonder. Clarke, finally, builds on metaphors related to play and games to reclaim the value of childlike wonder at cosmic realities. While the affective dimension of bodily defamiliarization was implicit in all my previous textual analyses, these final case studies place it front and center.

The Planet Turns Its Back

Vladimir Nabokov famously remarked in an essay on Gogol that "the difference between the comic side of things, and their cosmic side, depends upon one sibilant" (1989, 144). We've already seen this association at work in Calvino's *Cosmicomics*, but Nabokov's interpretation of this semantic proximity in "Lance" is subtler than Calvino's. As the reader may remember from Chapter 1, Calvino's comedy in "All at One Point" depends on overt incongruities and paradoxes—how can there be narrative, and anthropomorphic characters, before the birth of time and space itself? By contrast, Nabokov's irony derives from the tension between two dimensions of his short story: the sublime quest for a cosmic insight that affords escape from the limitations of the human condition and a keen sensitivity to the comic side of this condition.[3] While Calvino ultimately privileges the comic, Nabokov walks the line between sublimity and parody; he is interested in "the sensation of something ludicrous and at the same time stellar, lurking constantly around the corner," to quote again from the essay on Gogol (1989, 144). We will see that, in "Lance," this "lurking" takes on a distinctly embodied form: that of a planet turning its back on human explorers.

The short story is, in essence, an account of humanity's first contact with an alien planet. It begins with a description of this planet: "A rosy globe, marbled with dusky blotches, it is one of the countless objects diligently revolving in the infinite and gratuitous awfulness of fluid space" (Nabokov 1997, 632). The planet is depicted as a toy-like object floating in the void of "fluid space," here associated with a sense of scale ("infinite") and lack of purpose ("gratuitous"). These are well-known triggers of the sublime, but the narrator's tone tends to downplay them: the emphasis, in this passage, falls on the ordinary nature of this astronomical body, not on the "awfulness" of the surrounding cosmos. Even when the narrator converts the spatial distance of the planet into a temporal interval he comes across as slightly dismissive: the planet "may very well be separated from the earth by only as many miles as there are years between last Friday and the rise of the Himalayas—a million times the reader's average age" (1997, 632). If we don't gasp at the unimaginable temporality of "a million times the reader's average age," it is because the apparently casual references to "last Friday" and the age of the story's readers make the comparison sound more down-to-earth than it actually is. We thus begin to understand Nabokov's narrative strategy in this short story—an ironic strategy, insofar as the sublimity of the cosmos is evoked but at the same time subtly counterbalanced by humorous or parodic devices.

We can contrast this effect with the narrator's reflections on the tedium of reading science fiction. At the beginning of the story, the narrator brushes off science fiction as a formulaic genre, claiming to abhor its standard trappings: "clichés are...the same throughout all cheap reading matter, whether it spans the universe or the living room" (1997, 633). Science fiction is then compared to "'assorted' cookies that differ from one another only in shape and shade, whereby their shrewd makers ensnare the salivating consumer in a mad Pavlovian world" (1997, 633). The problem with science fiction is that it is too unsophisticated and predictable in its engagement with the cosmos; this results in an involuntary—and unintentionally humorous—conflation between the universe and the "living room." Nabokov's narrative aims to inhibit that Pavlovian reflex by actively *embracing* irony: paradoxically, it is by confronting the parochialism of the cosmos head-on that we may attune our minds to its sublimity. In "Lance," this ironic strategy results in a series of figurative mappings between cosmic entities and the body.

"Lance" is, as I pointed out above, the account of an expedition to a distant planet. The protagonist is one of the astronauts, Emery Lancelot Boke, nicknamed "Lance"; the narrator remains anonymous, but he claims that Lance is a "more or less remote descendant" of his (1997, 634). The other characters are Lance's apprehensive parents: Mr. Boke, an "old professor of history, a brilliant medievalist" (1997, 635), and his wife. Charles Nicol (1987, 13–14) reads this narrative setup through the lens of Nabokov's biography, arguing that Lance is none other than Nabokov's son, Dmitri, and that Mr. Boke's anxieties at Lance's interplanetary trip mirror Nabokov's own fears for Dmitri, an avid mountaineer. Not only is the cosmos experienced mostly from the perspective of Lance's parents, who remain on Earth, but it is shot through with their affective responses—namely, dreading the death of their son. In fact, death is so central to the narrative that the narrator explicitly links it to interplanetary travel:

> Deep in the human mind, the concept of dying is synonymous with that of leaving the earth. To escape its gravity means to transcend the grave, and a man upon finding himself on another planet has really no way of proving to himself that he is not dead—that the naive old myth has not come true.
>
> (1997, 640)

As in Ballard's "The Terminal Beach" (discussed in Chapter 4), the cosmos sets in motion archetypical meanings ("the naive old myth"). This mythical assimilation is clearly influenced by Mr. Boke's readings as a medievalist: Lance's space explorations are repeatedly equated with the adventures of Lancelot in medieval romance, and particularly in the twelfth-century *Lancelot, the Knight of the Cart* by Chrétien de Troyes (see Nicol 1987, 14–16). Consider, for instance, this passage, where the Bokes observe their son's progress from their balcony through a "field glass":

> The sidereal haze makes the Bokes dizzy—gray incense, insanity, infinity-sickness. But they cannot tear themselves away from the nightmare of space, cannot go back to the lighted bedroom, a corner of which shows in the glass door. And presently *the* planet rises, like a tiny bonfire.
>
> There, to the right, is the Bridge of the Sword leading to the Otherworld (*"dont nus estranges ne retorne"*). Lancelot crawls over it in great pain, in ineffable anguish. "Thou shalt not pass a pass that is called the Pass Perilous." But another enchanter commands: "You shall. You shall even acquire a sense of humor that will tide you over the trying spots." The brave old Bokes think they can distinguish Lance scaling, on crampons, the verglased rock of the sky or silently breaking trail through the soft snows of nebulae.
>
> (1997, 637; italics in the original)

At first, the Bokes can't see Lance—he is surrounded by a "sidereal haze" that serves as an equivalent of Lance's distance, depicted here as sickening and nightmarish. When the planet comes into sight, it is its diminutive size that is emphasized; further, the "planet as bonfire" metaphor evokes an ancestral association between fire and storytelling. This device introduces the mythical past of the Arthurian romance, with Lance being transfigured into Lancelot in the following paragraph. Here death emerges again (the "Otherworld"); the italicized sentence, lifted from Chrétien's *Lancelot*, "from which we return strange," is a first—but crucial—reference to the "strangeness" of this interplanetary trip, how it changes the traveler's view of the cosmos. It cannot be a coincidence that the next sentence marks a shift from the elevated language of the Arthurian romance to the comic repetition of the word "pass"; and that humor itself is thematized in the following sentence. What Nabokov is suggesting here is that irony may be uniquely able to disclose a new—and inherently "strange"—perspective on the cosmos. To be able to grasp that perspective, we must read against the grain of the Arthurian references woven through the short story. Those references provide sublimity by alluding to a mythical past. However, the sublime is offset by the comic distance introduced by the narrative situation—the apprehensive parents and the narrator's playful metaphors (such as the "tiny bonfire"). We are thus taken to a place between sublimity and humor—a place where Nabokov's cosmic irony dwells; and just like Lance, we may "return strange" from it.

How exactly this happens is a matter of embodied metaphors and of the feelings they elicit. This becomes particularly clear in the following passage, which is again centered on the Bokes ("the little spectators") and their view of the sky:

> The conjuror who displays the firmament has rolled up his sleeves and performs in full view of the little spectators. Planets may dip out of sight (just as objects are obliterated by the blurry curve of one's own cheekbone); but they are back when the earth turns its head. The nakedness of the night is appalling. Lance has left; the fragility of his young limbs grows in direct ratio to the distance he covers.
>
> (1997, 636)

The embodied image of the conjuror's rolling up his sleeves turns the firmament into a stage, reducing it to a lower (and more human-scale) level of reality. Yet because there is magic involved, and because the passage is at least suggestive of the glittering expanse of the night sky, the reduction to the intermediate world is only partial: something of the sublimity survives, tinging the language of the following sentences. At first, there is a simile comparing planets and objects being "obliterated by the blurry curve of one's own cheekbone." Once again, an embodied simile, but this works in the opposite direction to the image of the conjuror: while the latter tends to "scale down" the cosmos, the simile "scales up" the human body to a size comparable to astronomical objects. This strategy can be contrasted with how Joyce develops the parallel between his human characters and "celestial bodies" in "Ithaca"—for Joyce's characters, unlike the cheekbone evoked by Nabokov, remain anchored to the intermediate world. The metaphorical scaling up of the body becomes even more prominent in the following sentence, where the Earth itself is endowed with a head, as if the cheekbone of the previous simile was expanding into a full-fledged body. The metaphor "nakedness of the night" completes the process: now the night sky, our first point of access to the cosmos, is seen as having a body. Hence, while the Arthurian allusions of the previous quotations work by superimposing a mythical landscape onto the cosmic one, this passage projects embodied qualities onto cosmic entities.

The question is: how does Nabokov's short story pull off this feat of triangulation, bringing together the mythical, the embodied, and the cosmic? A first hint is provided by the sentence that concludes the last quotation: since the fragility of the human body increases with its distance from the intermediate world, the cosmic is linked with mortality, and this link is conceptualized in mythical terms—through a sophisticated (and ironic) mix of sublimity and humor. The association between the cosmos and the body is particularly complex, because the more the cosmos jeopardizes the survival of the human body, the more it takes on embodied qualities of its own. This is the core of "strangeness" that the narrative is exploring, or (put otherwise) the bodily defamiliarization that it performs in affective terms. This reading is confirmed when the narrator describes, with clear sexual overtones, Lance's passion for space exploration:

> When it comes to exploring a celestial body, his is the satisfaction of a passionate desire to feel with his own fingers, to stroke, and inspect, and smile at, and inhale, and stroke again—with that same smile of nameless, moaning, melting pleasure the never-before-touched matter of which the celestial object is made.
>
> (1997, 640)

Note how the metaphor of the "celestial body" inspires Lance's engagement with the planet, which becomes an object of quasi-sexual knowledge, in line with what we've seen in Chapter 3 (but much more overtly and systematically in this passage). This strategy gives rise to a back-and-forth between the embodied explorer and an equally (if paradoxically) embodied cosmos, with Lance's mortality being caught in between. The receptive reader's body becomes the site of this affective dynamic, which defamiliarizes our understanding of cosmic sublimity through its unexpected blend with irony.

Having established this ambivalent role of the body in the narrative, we can proceed to discuss the second half of the short story. Lance survives his interplanetary trip and makes it back to Earth. However, the narrator cannot adequately describe Lance's cosmic experience of landing on an alien planet. He thus resorts to recounting a recurrent dream of his, which—he claims—offers an approximation of Lance's experience:

> When I was a boy of seven or eight, I used to dream a vaguely recurrent dream set in a certain environment, which I have never been able to recognize and identify in any rational manner, though I have seen many strange lands. I am inclined to make it serve now, in order to patch up a gaping hole, a raw wound in my story.
>
> (1997, 640)

More embodied metaphors, this time for the narrative itself: the ineffability of Lance's experience is likened to a wound. This prepares the description of the dream landscape, where the body—again—figures prominently:

> There was nothing spectacular about that environment, nothing monstrous or even odd: just a bit of noncommittal stability represented by a bit of level ground and filmed over with a bit of neutral nebulosity; in other words, the indifferent back of a view rather than its face. The nuisance of that dream was that for *some* reason I could not walk *around* the view to *meet* it on equal terms. There lurked in the *mist* a mass of something—mineral matter or the like—oppressively and quite meaninglessly shaped, and, in the course of my dream, I kept filling some kind of receptacle (translated as "pail") with smaller shapes (translated as "pebbles"), and my nose was bleeding but I was too impatient and excited to do anything about it.
>
> (1997, 640–41; italics in the original)

The image of the pail and—even more clearly—the vague "receptacle" evoke the womb, with the narrator's "filling" action taking on sexual overtones. The nosebleed is also reminiscent of sexual intercourse, possibly through an intertextual reference to Chrétien's poem: as noted by Nicol, "Guinevere, waking up after a tryst with the wounded Lancelot, is puzzled by the blood on the sheets and mistakenly attributes it to a nosebleed" (1987, 17). These symbolic references to sexuality would seem to open the door to a Freudian reading of the dream—for instance, one that sees it as a manifestation of sexual drives or childhood traumas—but I believe there are reasons to resist this reading: these are only Freudian-sounding tricks that Nabokov, like a conjuror, uses to distract the reader who is unable, or unwilling, to attend to the alienness at the heart of the narrative. This interpretation is based on evidence both external and internal to the text. Externally, we know that Nabokov was always extremely critical of Freudian accounts of art. Brian Boyd, for instance, writes: "Taking issue with Freud, Nabokov claimed that 'sex is but the ancilla of art,' that the artfulness of nature lies behind the allures and the wiles of sex, as it lies behind so much else" (2001, 287). But the internal evidence is even more significant. We've seen that the cosmos has been repeatedly compared to a body. That is what emerges, although somewhat surreptitiously, from this passage, too. Consider the phrase "the indifferent back of a view rather than its face." While the word "back" may be interpreted loosely, the metaphor of the "face" clearly anthropomorphizes the dream land-scape or rather provides it with a body. The following sentence ex-presses the core of the dream experience, even if the narrator casually dismisses it as a "nuisance": it is an experience of not being able to face the planet ("*meet* it on equal terms")—and by extension, the body of the cosmos itself. In short, the dream expresses the narrator's inability to fully acknowledge the truth of his own metaphors: that the cosmos itself may have a body and that our knowledge of it may be embodied and even sexual—although the sexuality involved is fundamentally dif-ferent from the human (and human-scale) sexuality that plays a central role in Freud's theories.

To fully understand this point, we have to go back to the "oceanic feeling" outlined by Freud in *Civilization and Its Discontents* and dis-cussed briefly at the end of the previous chapter (in relation to Lem's *So-laris*). This feeling denotes a quasi-mystical experience of union with the nonhuman and the cosmic. Freud himself claimed to be unable to expe-rience it: "I cannot discover this 'oceanic' feeling in myself" (1962, 12). A hypothetical Freudian reading of the narrator's dream in "Lance" would thus focus on the sexual suggestions contained at the end of the passage; but these are only a blind to prevent a casual reader from see-ing the cosmic (and in a broad sense oceanic) feeling that the passage artfully probes. This is, in my view, the deeper meaning of the "mass of something—mineral matter or the like—oppressively and quite mean-inglessly shaped" that the narrator describes. This obscure mineral mass is the paradoxical embodiment of the cosmos itself, which Lance con-fronts but the narrator is unable to capture outside of the allusiveness and elusiveness of this dream.

This reading puts us in a position to understand the enigmatic, and anticlimactic, ending of the short story. After Lance's return, his parents visit him at the hospital where he is recovering from the trip. They are able to talk to him briefly, but they are shown out of the room by the nurse as soon as Lance begins telling them about his experiences on the planet. The text ends with the Bokes still making their way out of the hospital. These are the story's last words: "There are, in that elevator, two smiling women and, the object of their bright sympathy, a girl with a baby, besides the gray-haired, bent, sullen elevator man, who stands with his back to everybody" (1997, 642). At first sight, this ending looks extremely unusual. What is the significance of the elevator man, who has never been mentioned before in the short story? Why does the text end on such a seemingly trivial note? On reflection, it seems that the elevator man is important not for who he is or what he does—but for his bodily posture. In fact, he is turning his back to everyone, just like the landscape in the narrator's dream. The elevator man's body serves as a comic counterpoint to the body of the cosmos, as it is evoked by Nabokov's metaphorical language (at the stylistic level), and as it emerges from Lance's ineffable experience of the planet (at the affective level). What is especially striking about this ending is that it extends, and grounds in the embodied domain, the interplay of sublimity and parody we have already seen at work in Nabokov's intertextual references to Chrétien's poem. The sublime body of the cosmos, which can be sensed but never known directly, is contrasted with a body as ordinary as a gray-haired elevator man's. Nabokov's irony arises from this contrast, and with it a sense of insight into our relationship with nonhuman realities. Such insight cannot be easily pinned down or cashed out in words: the cosmic body is not represented but hinted at, obliquely, through affective responses over the course of the reading experience. For readers who are willing to play Nabokov's sophisticated game, this cosmic insight derives from an affective process of bodily defamiliarization—one in which the cosmos itself is invested, half sublimely half humorously, with a body that we can touch and even desire.

Snowballing Panpsychism

Among the cosmic visions examined in this book, the one offered by Olaf Stapledon in his 1937 *Star Maker* is the most uncompromising in its confrontation with the sheer scale of nonhuman realities—even as this radical approach comes with risks of its own: at times, Stapledon's prose reads more like an obscure philosophical treatise than a work of fiction, but this abstruseness is the logical consequence of Stapledon's painstaking efforts to disentangle the human imagination from the intermediate world. Stapledon was a British writer whose science fiction works—and particularly, along with *Star Maker*, the earlier *Last and First Men* (1930)—have had a major impact on the genre: as Leslie Fiedler puts it, "Stapledon's vast cosmological point of view widened once and for all the scale and scope of science fiction" (1983, 6). Yet the breadth of Stapledon's vision remains to a large extent unique and inimitable, with later writers—including Clarke, as we will see—drawing on Stapledon's cosmic imagination while exploring much more human-scale plots and situations.

Commentators have suggested parallels between *Star Maker* and Dante's *Divine Comedy*, arguing that Stapledon's text has the scope and grandeur of Dante's poem. Yet Dante's God becomes, in Stapledon's book, an agnostic's "Star Maker" who remains utterly indifferent to the fate of humankind. In a compelling book-length study of the cultural imagination of alien life, Mark Brake writes:

> Stapledon's account of life in the universe is a more morally ambiguous one [than Dante's *Divine Comedy*]. We are confronted with a more complex case in which we learn that the force behind the cosmos, the Star Maker, transcends the narrow bounds of good and evil.
> (2013, 232)

From this cosmic viewpoint, *Homo Sapiens* becomes one of the many intelligent species (and by far *not* the most intelligent or long-lived) in a universe of unimaginable proportions.

Stapledon builds on what was still, in the 1930s, a highly controversial theory about the universe—namely, the idea that the cosmos is expanding, which prompted scientists to posit a Big Bang. Referring to the Other Earth, a planet populated by anthropomorphic creatures, the narrator comments: "The startling nearness of so many galaxies in the astronomy of the Other Men could be explained on the theory of the 'expanding universe'" (2011, 44). Stapledon offers an equally remarkable anticipation of contemporary pluralist cosmologies (a hypothesis known as the "multiverse"; see Tegmark 2004), speculating that our cosmos is only one of the many universes brought into being by the Star Maker over the course of his creative experimentations with mind and matter. Stapledon's cosmic vision is a daring attempt at reconciling scientific knowledge about the universe with a deep-seated need for *meaning* as we come face to face with nonhuman realities. In that sense, the text (like Dante's poem) voices cosmological questions of a distinctly spiritual nature even as it rejects (unlike Dante's poem) the answers provided by religion.

Yet it all begins in the intermediate world. The first-person narrator, who remains anonymous throughout the book, leaves his home in the middle of the night, anxious about his marriage and the fate of a world overrun by fascism; this political dimension of the novel, here only implicit, is substantiated by a later nod to crowds "saluting the flood-lit Führer" or venerating the "mob's idol" in Mussolini's Italy (2011, 187). The narrator experiences a vague sense of "bitterness," in which marital issues and the historical juncture of the 1930s merge; his mind then turns to questions about the ultimate meaning of human life. As he grapples with these questions, he is caught between two opposite, and seemingly irreconcilable, impulses. On the one hand, he acknowledges that the human is only a tiny—and largely insignificant—drop in the cosmic ocean: "in such a universe as this what significance could there be in our fortuitous, our frail, our evanescent community?" (2011, 5). On the other hand, for all the overwhelming evidence of our irrelevance in the grand scheme of things, the narrator cannot completely shake off the intuition that his marriage, and perhaps human relations more generally ("our prized atom of community"), somehow matter: "Even the cold stars, even the whole cosmos with all its inane immensities could not convince me that this our prized atom of community, imperfect as it was, short-lived as it must be, was not significant" (2011, 6).

The apparently intractable problem of reconciling human meaning and cosmic scale constitutes the epistemological starting point of the narrator's voyage: the text becomes a thought experiment asking what would become of humankind once the viewpoint of the cosmos is taken up in the most radical terms. This is how the voyage begins: as he ponders on the mystery of human existence, the narrator uses his imagination to distance himself from Earth. Yet to our—and the narrator's—surprise this metaphorical flight of the imagination is followed by what looks and feels like actual presence in outer space: "Imagination was now stimulated to a new, strange mode of perception. Looking from star to star, I saw the heaven no longer as a jewelled ceiling and floor, but as depth beyond flashing depth of suns" (2011, 7). Note how Stapledon's language performs a shift from comparisons involving reassuringly ordinary objects ("jewelled," "ceiling and floor") to the metaphorical abstraction of the "depth beyond flashing depth of suns." This abstraction extends into the character's embodied experience, for the body does not seem to matter in this vision:

> I myself was seemingly disembodied, for I could neither see nor touch my own flesh. And when I willed to move my limbs, nothing happened. I had no limbs. The familiar inner perceptions of my body, and the headache which had oppressed me since morning, had given way to a vague lightness and exhilaration.
>
> (2011, 8)

How are we to interpret this feeling of disembodiment? Should we think that in Stapledon's prose the tension between embodiment and the cosmos we have explored throughout this book reaches a breaking point, with the cosmos finally leaving the body on the sidelines? Should we conclude that Stapledon's vision of the universe condemns embodied knowledge not just to biological insignificance but, much more worryingly, to epistemological irrelevance? So far the standard answer I've offered in this book has been "no, because…"—with various (but related) reasons filling the gap: how literary language and narrative always imply a minimum of embodied responses, how our imagination of nonhuman realities builds on the traces left by bodily interactions with the world (through embodied metaphors, for example), and so on. I believe this is true of *Star Maker* as well. Yet we must recognize that Stapledon's narrative raises a uniquely radical challenge to embodiment, perhaps even more radical than the "Ithaca" chapter of Joyce's *Ulysses* (analyzed in Chapter 2). However, in both cases the reader's body continues to matter: in *Ulysses*, it was through the activation of embodied patterns or image schemata; in *Star Maker*, as we will see, it is through an affective and rhythmic form of bodily defamiliarization.

We are repeatedly reminded that the narrator has no body and that his feelings are uncoupled from their normal bodily basis: "The featureless darkness...terrified me, if I may call 'terror' the repugnance and foreboding which I now experienced without any of the bodily accompaniments of terror, without any sensation of trembling, sweating, gasping, or palpitation" (2011, 13). This strategy is reminiscent of Lovecraft's probing of the divide between embodiment and phenomenology in "The Shadow Out of Time," but while Lovecraft foregrounds bodies without phenomenology, Stapledon's point of departure is precisely the opposite: a paradoxically disembodied subject. The same paradox surrounds the narrator's physical movement in space, which would imply some form of material existence; yet the speed of this movement is so high and the reference system (planets getting closer, stars vanishing) so vague that it is difficult to construe it as genuine physical motion. Stapledon calls it a "bodiless viewpoint" (2011, 12), and it results in descriptions as abstract as the following:

> Through the effect of my own passage the nearer stars appeared to drift across the background of the stars at greater distance. This drifting accelerated, till, for an instant, the whole visible sky was streaked with flying stars. Then everything vanished.
>
> (2011, 13)

Passages like this are deeply counterintuitive insofar as they blur any frame of reference we may have for understanding motion in space: the narrator's perception resembles an abstract composition of specks of light and background darkness.[4]

Soon enough, however, locomotion itself will become unnecessary:

> I...discovered that, by merely willing to approach a star, I could set myself in motion towards it, and at such a speed that I must have travelled much faster than normal light. This, as I knew very well, was physically impossible...I inferred that my motion must therefore be in some manner a mental, not a physical phenomenon.
>
> (2011, 14)

It would be difficult to find a more unambiguous case of mind-body dualism: because physics cannot explain the narrator's seemingly instantaneous displacements, then their nature must be mental, not physical—and the entire physical realm (to which the body clearly belongs) is made irrelevant or at least secondary to the narrator's disembodied vision of the cosmos. This irrelevance becomes increasingly clear as we read the narrative of the narrator's explorations. In later chapters, he masters a form of "telepathic" communication with alien species—a communication, in other words, that abstracts from any physical medium. Further, the narrator is joined by a number of alien intelligences he encounters in his travels: these intelligences augment his mental capacities through "the pooling or integration of our memories and of our temperaments" (2011, 47). The narrator also points out how joining forces with these alien beings helps him distinguish between the universal features of mental life and those that are mere accidents of evolution in a particular environment (2011, 47). This account of collective mind straightforwardly rejects embodiment as the precondition for mental processes: "Two disembodied minds, occupying the same visual position, possessing the same memories and desires, and often performing the same mental acts at the same time, can scarcely be conceived as distinct beings" (2011, 47).

In a key passage, the narrator adds that this collective mind will "prove itself a method, and a very potent method, of cosmological research" (2011, 48). The method works as follows: on every planet visited by the narrator, he and his companions enlist a local mind, which expands their imaginative reach through what is described as a "snowball" effect. We are also reminded that, while the narrator's account uses the grammatically singular "I," this pronoun signifies a "communal 'I' which was supported by the innumerable explorers" (2011, 50). Stapledon's experimentations with mind and matter continue throughout the novel. In the first five chapters, the link between living organisms and mental processes is to a large extent preserved, except for the fact that the alien species endowed with mind are increasingly divergent from the human bodily form. In Chapter 7, the equation between mind and the life of individual organisms is explicitly questioned; we read, for instance, about

> a host of individual [bird-like bodies that] were possessed together by a single individual mind of human rank. The body of this mind was multiple, but the mind itself was almost as firmly knit as the mind of a man.

> (2011, 79)

Starting from Chapter 9, *Star Maker* offers an even more striking example of dissociation between organic life and mind, through what the narrator calls "minded worlds." With this chapter, Stapledon's novel comes into its own: the narrator recounts the history not of individual creatures or even of entire alien species, but of "worlds" fighting against one another or forming galactic alliances. The language is clearly mentalistic, with the narrator distinguishing between "mad" and "sane" worlds and even pointing out that there are significant differences in the "mental development" of the "mad" ones (2011, 107). At first glance, this may look like a metonymic strategy: a world is "minded" when it houses an intelligent species that takes control of the planet and therefore shapes its interactions with neighboring planets. Perhaps then the phrase "minded world" is not unlike "Washington" in the sense of "the government of the United States": an inanimate entity stands in, metonymically, for the individuals responsible for making decisions in Washington. But a later discovery that stars themselves are minded makes the metonymic reading of "minded worlds" less likely: "It was not excessively difficult for us [the narrator and his companions] to enter telepathically into the star's perception of the gentle titillations, strokings, pluckings, and scintillations that came to it from the galactic environment" (2011, 139). What follows is a surprising description of "what it is like to be a star" that leaves no room for ambiguity: Stapledon is claiming that the inanimate matter of stars is endowed with mind-like experiences (here captured by vague and indeterminate feelings such as the "titillations," etc.). The stars' experiences are rendered in terms of dance-like, kinetic patterns: "The star's motor life is thus to be thought of almost as a life of dance, or of figure-skating, executed with perfect skill according to an ideal principle which emerges into consciousness from the depths of the stellar nature" (2011, 139). As many of the narratives we have examined in this book (from Levi's "Carbon" to Lem's *Solaris*), Stapledon's *Star Maker* employs the patterned experience of motion as a bridge between human-scale and nonhuman realities.

Brake comments on the ascription of mind to inanimate worlds as follows: "In a spiritual examination that began with Giordano Bruno's idea that planets and stars have souls, Stapledon makes the heavenly bodies mindful" (2013, 230). Like Lem's ocean, these worlds and stars are minds uncoupled from biological, organismic life. Yet what passes as an intractable mystery in *Solaris*—the very possibility of such a mind—is presented in *Star Maker* as a matter of course: despite the occasional caveats about the metaphorical nature of his account, the narrator sounds quite confident about the mentalistic nature of planets and stars. This degree of confidence is made possible, diegetically, by the "snowballing" of the narrator's telepathic abilities (thanks to his cosmic companions). In fact, the narrator even theorizes that his "communal I" augments his understanding of the cosmos, allowing him to sense mind in entities far beyond the intermediate world in which mind, embodiment, and individual life are closely bound up. The analogy he proposes is intriguing:

> just as, in the experience of *Homo Sapiens*, the Earth is now "shrinking" to the dimensions of a country, so, in this critical period of the life of our galaxy, the whole galaxy was "shrinking" to the dimensions of a world.
>
> (2011, 110; emphasis in the original)

This spatial "shrinking" is accompanied by an expansion of mind, which points to a panpsychist framework—that is, as seen in the last chapter, one in which the mind pervades the entire universe.

Stapledon's approach to the problem of interconnectivity is equally striking. The language of interpersonal relations is used systematically to describe interactions between worlds: "Between the minded planetary systems occurred infinite variations of personal intercourse...Between individual systems of worlds, as between symbiotic partners, there sometimes occurred relationships with an almost sexual flavour, though actual sex played no part in them" (2011, 124). We have seen a similar conflation between levels of reality—the social and the astronomical— in the Calvino short story examined in Chapter 1: in Calvino, the incongruity of the comparison between people and planets is a constant source of irony, while in Stapledon the attribution of quasi-intimate and even sexual experience to astronomical bodies is entirely earnest. The matter-of-fact tone goes hand in hand with the scale of Stapledon's account, which invites us to imagine the cosmos at such a level of generality that even anthropomorphizing metaphors do not come across as incongruous: the terms of comparison are not the cosmos and a specific scenario of human interaction (as in Calvino), but only the cosmos and generic notions of partnership or sexual intercourse. This abstraction eases the interconnectivity.

Yet the narrator's voyage does not end here. In fact, after examining mind as contingently realized in other (kinds of) bodies, and after seeing cosmic entities themselves as endowed with mind, the narrator and his companions merge their mental processes with those of entire galaxies:

> With grave joy we, the cosmical explorers, who were already gathered up into the communal mind of our own galaxy, now found ourselves in intimate union with a score of other galactic minds. We, or rather I, now experienced the slow drift of the galaxies much as a man feels the swing of his own limbs.
>
> (2011, 149)

This is a remarkable passage, and not only because of the nonchalance with which the narrator introduces the deeply perplexing notion of a "galactic mind." Even more intriguing is the closing reference to the human body, in a simile that associates the "slow drift of the galaxies" (as perceived by the narrator's expanded mind) with the kinesthetic experience of swinging one's limbs. After the narrator has taken great pains to distance the reader imaginatively from the human body, foregrounding a disembodied mind that can move unconstrained in space and time, why this sudden re-emergence of the body? The simile evokes the expansion of the narrator's mind, highlighting his progressive "incorporation" of the cosmos and how nonhuman realities have become part of him with the immediacy typical of embodied experience. As always, the narrator's comparison is straightforward, perhaps even naïve, in its simplicity; but it is precisely this naïveté that lends credibility to his account, giving us a sense that he has succeeded in moving beyond anthropocentric assumptions: from this cosmic viewpoint, there can be no incongruity or irony in comparing a human body with a "galactic mind," for both entities exist with the same degree of certainty. Thus, the body makes a (metaphorical) comeback when the narrator is so far removed from the intermediate world that there is no longer a risk that embodied experience may "provincialize" the cosmos: the realities that we are asked to accept are so enormous (in spatial scale) and astonishing (in terms of everyday plausibility) that interconnectivity ceases to be a problem, and an explicitly embodied simile can support our imagination of the narrator's galactic mind.

Eventually, the cosmos is shown to be entirely pervaded by mind, and the narrator becomes the interpreter of its mental activity: "I, the communal mind of a score of galaxies, seemed now to myself to be the abortive and crippled mind of the cosmos itself" (2011, 150). The narrator's mind is "abortive and crippled" because it cannot know fully its creator, the Star Maker. Only in the last two chapters of his account does the narrator come face to face with the Star Maker. Because the life story of the anonymous narrator has now merged with the history of the cosmos itself—through the "snowballing" expansion of his mind—this encounter is described as "the supreme moment of the cosmos" (2011, 159). Here all spatial and temporal distinctions break down. In a flash of insight, the narrator witnesses the birth of the universe and its eventual death, including the collapse of his own mind: "Looking forward from my station in the supreme moment of the cosmos, I saw myself, the cosmical mind, sink steadily towards death" (2011, 164). Yet the narrator also realizes that "our" cosmos is only one of the Star Maker's countless creations. The essence of this Star Maker, we are told, is not love—the fundamental attribute of God for Christianity and other religions—but contemplation: "All passions, it seemed, were comprised within the spirit's temper; but mastered, icily gripped within the cold, clear, crystal ecstasy of contemplation" (2011, 184). This contemplative detachment appears to trickle into the narrator's own affective stance from the very beginning of the text.

The Star Maker's creativity is prodigious: we see him experimenting with mind and matter, inventing nonspatial universes as well as musical ones where "creatures appeared to one another as complex patterns and rhythms of tonal characters" (2011, 171). The concept of rhythm is key to this creative activity: we read that the Star Maker's "first toy cosmos" was only "a temporal rhythm, as it were of sound and silence. From this first simple drumbeat, premonitory of a thousand creations, he developed with infantile but godlike zest a flickering tattoo, a changeful complexity of rhythm" (2011, 169). Further, just as the expansion of the narrator's communal mind has a certain periodicity (from individual minds to a single "cosmic" mind), the Star Maker's creative attempts fall into a rhythmic pattern of increasing "maturity," as the narrator puts it. Our own cosmos belongs to a relatively mature phase, but it precedes the "ultimate cosmos," captured through another rhythmical analogy: it is "like the last movement of a symphony" (2011, 181).

That the notion of rhythm should emerge in this final "hypercosmical apparition" (2011, 185) is highly significant. For rhythm, as I explained in Chapters 2 and 3, is a deeply embodied phenomenon: from our heartbeat to the cycle of day and night (which gives rise to the so-called "circadian rhythm"), our phenomenological experience is rich in temporal patterns that are felt in and through the body, as shifts in affective tone. While inconceivably more abstract and removed from the intermediate world, the rhythm of the Star Maker's creative endeavors is still linked to this embodied sense of rhythm via a quasi-geometrical process of expansion: the temporality of human life (from birth to maturity to death) is structurally analogous to the development of the cosmos itself, which culminates in the emergence of a "cosmic mind," the narrator's, able to foresee its own end; in turn, the history of the cosmos is structurally analogous to the progression of the Star Maker's creativity, which also goes from childlike experimentations to the symphonic perfection of the "ultimate cosmos."

In light of this musical parallel, the very narrative method adopted by Stapledon in *Star Maker* takes on rhythmic qualities. These are, for instance, literary critic John Huntington's words: "The narrator repeatedly returns to the beginning, each time encompassing a broader understanding of what constitutes the meaningful cosmos" (1981, 362). The closest visual equivalent to this progression—its "spatial form," to borrow Joseph Frank's (1945) influential concept—is a spiral, with every fold of the figure repeating the temporal structure of the underlying fold, but on a larger scale. *Star Maker* thus points up the structural similarity between levels of reality even as it calls attention—dramatically—to the different temporal and spatial scales involved. In describing Stapledon's peculiar narrative method, Huntington uses a kinetic (and embodied) simile, suggesting that the text reads like a "group dance in which each participant, while executing his own figure, comprises part of a continuous pattern in space and time that goes on despite the collapse of any separate individual" (1981, 364). Because of how the text foregrounds questions of rhythm and music, this "continuous pattern" must be perceived in rhythmical terms, as an affective contour, in the reading of the text: thus, while the human body loses its central role in the narrator's account, it remains implicitly active in the "group dance" traced by the cosmos itself. Further, the apparent emotionlessness of the narrative potentially *increases* the reader's affective involvement as he or she follows—with mounting wonder—the rhythmic patterning of this cosmic vision, whose ambition is only rivaled by its matter-of-factness.

It is significant that the spiral-like progression of the narrative closely resembles, in conceptual and spatial terms, the already discussed "snowballing" of the narrator's communal mind. During his travels, the narrator enlists new minds, which—like new folds in a spiral—increase exponentially the breadth and depth of his mental capacities. The augmentation of the narrator's mind is a necessary step toward understanding how matter and mind co-occur in the universe, in entities such as planets, stars, or even galaxies. Mind expands from the human to the cosmic scale; in this process, the narrator's mental experiences and the "external" history of the cosmos do not only converge but are ultimately revealed to be one.

This panpsychist conclusion sheds new light on the narrator's disembodiment. Perhaps the bracketing of the human body serves a strategic purpose: it is, in the narrator's own words, "a method...of cosmological research" (2011, 48) that enables readers to see how cosmic entities may be minded while possessing radically different "bodies" from the organisms that populate the intermediate world. To put the same point otherwise, the separation between mind and body in the narrator's persona is a heuristic tool intended to show that mind may emerge at other levels of reality than the world of human-scale bodies. As soon as we accept this conclusion, we are encouraged to see how the text's "movement" across levels of reality is defined by a periodicity—a rhythm—that is still in some ways dependent on our bodily experience, if only through the affective contour it engenders: while the body drops out of the picture in representational (that is, diegetic) terms, it is still the site of readers' affective responses to the narrator's account. The tension between the apparent disembodiment of the story and the implication of affective patterns in the abstract rhythm of its progression is a rich source of defamiliarization.

In the epilogue, the text reverts abruptly to the intermediate world. The narrator finds himself on Earth: he wakes up on the hill of the novel's first chapter, as if no time had passed during his cosmic visions. He returns to the existential questions that troubled him at the beginning. What is the significance of human life vis-à-vis the wide cosmos? One may expect the narrator's "hypercosmical" experiences to have aggravated these anxieties; but, strangely, this is not the case. He now seems to have found value in his "little treasure of community" (2011, 186), which refers primarily to his marriage but also—more generally—to human cooperation; he adds that this sense of community, "not the astronomical and hypercosmical immensity, nor even the planetary grain, this, this alone, was the solid ground of existence" (2011, 186). The narrator has discovered that community is not just an object of human striving, but the cosmic tendency that underlies the "snowballing" of his tale. Community can thus be found throughout the cosmos; it is produced through a historical process that is—Stapledon suggests—fundamentally rhythmic in nature. Yet as we move "up" in spatial scale, love as the underlying principle of community is replaced by what the narrator characterizes as the "crystal ecstasy" of contemplation (2011, 188). Community, in the broadest sense, becomes interchangeable with the totality coldly scrutinized by the Star Maker. And from this perspective, even something as deeply flawed and fragile as the human mind takes on poignancy and—therefore—emotional significance: "Strange that in this light, in which even the dearest love is frostily assessed, and even the possible defeat of our half-waking world is contemplated without remission of praise, the human crisis does not lose but gains significance" (2011, 188–89). Facing up to the cosmos and our physical limitations paves the way for this affect-laden realization, which carries enormous ethical as well as political resonance as the world braces itself for planetary conflict (foreshadowed here by "the young men...saluting the flood-lit Führer"; 2011, 187). Taking a cosmic viewpoint, as Stapledon attempts to do more vigorously than any other writer discussed in this book, does not necessarily lead to a pessimistic, nihilistic sense of human irrelevance. On the contrary, a keener awareness of our limitations can foster a sense of community and responsibility toward the nonhuman realities with which we are inescapably intertwined. I will take up this point again in the coda.

Playing with the Star Child

Arthur C. Clarke was already an established science fiction writer when Stanley Kubrick asked him, in 1964, to be part of his new project, which he wanted to become the "proverbial 'really good' science-fiction movie" (quoted in Wigley 2016). Kubrick's masterpiece, *2001: A Space Odyssey*, grew out of that invitation. And so did Clarke's homonymous novel, which came out one year later than the film, in 1968. It was the result of a close—and at times tense—collaboration in which, according to Clarke, "both novel and screenplay [had been] written simultaneously, with feedback in both directions" (1972, 31). Readers and commentators have tended to see Clarke's *2001* as a companion piece, which fills in many of the plot blanks of Kubrick's film but also sacrifices the elegant minimalism of Kubrick's style to lengthy exposition. Yet Clarke's novel is not devoid of interest, particularly when seen in the tradition of Stapledon's science fiction. *2001* is less radical and experimental than Stapledon's text—it is a full-fledged novel, with characters and a narrative arc, but it is fueled by many of the same themes and concerns that underlie *Star Maker*. The first and perhaps most significant of these thematic interests has to do with the emergence of mind, and particularly of intelligence, in the universe. While Stapledon asks this question top-down, by taking (or at least resolutely moving toward) a cosmic perspective from the outset, Clarke adopts a different tack: the first part of *2001* is set on Earth and shows a group of "man-apes" experiencing the leap from animal behavior to human-like intelligence and culture. This "great leap forward," to use the terminology coined by Jared Diamond (1993), is made possible by the apes' exposure to a "crystalline monolith" (2012, 12) of mysterious origins.

After this prologue in prehistory, the novel jumps forward to the space age, when another monolith is discovered on the Moon. This is the transition rendered by Kubrick's famous match cut between a bone and a spaceship, although in Clarke's novel this association between the man-apes' tools and advanced technology remains implicit.[5] A spaceship is sent to Japetus, one of Saturn's satellites, to investigate an unusually bright area that, scientists say, could be linked to the monolith on the Moon. The protagonist, David Bowman, is on this ship, the *Discovery*, although the crew doesn't know the real objective of their mission yet. Things go wrong, however, due to the malfunctioning of the spaceship's supercomputer, so that Bowman finds himself completing the mission alone. On reaching his destination, Bowman is afforded startling insights into the civilization that built the monolith, realizing that this alien race shaped not just life on Earth but the history of the universe across the board.

As this rundown of the plot shows, the novel moves from a terrestrial framework (the Earth of the "man-apes") to a cosmic one, but this transition is much more gradual than in Stapledon's text. Further, even in the later chapters of the novel the intermediate world never drops out of the picture, because Clarke constantly attempts to translate cosmic insights into concrete, human-scale terms: in this sense, *2001* adopts a number of metaphorical strategies reminiscent of Nabokov's "Lance." Nabokov and Clarke may seem like an improbable pair, but recall Nabokov's comparisons between the planet and a "rosy globe" or a "tiny bonfire": Clarke's prose is rich in similar parallels; while he does *not* ascribe a body to the cosmos, as Nabokov does, he turns cosmic entities into toy-like objects that afford direct embodied manipulation. This centrality of play paves the way for David Bowman's transformation into a "Star-Child" in the novel's last chapter, which marks the final stage of the process that had started with the apes' evolution into humans in the first pages. *2001* thus successfully marries Nabokov's focus on embodied experience with the staggering scope of Stapledon's narrative, which explains why I chose to place Clarke's novel at the end of this chapter. This strategy aims to evoke a particular affective state, whereby the sublimity of the cosmos is inflected with childlike wonder instead of Nabokovian irony.

To explore this affective dimension of *2001*, I will focus on the novel's last two parts, where Bowman—after reaching Japetus—is transported light-years away from our solar system. Stapledon's influence becomes particularly evident here, but the presence of a full-fledged (embodied) character like Bowman prevents the narrative from flying away into Stapledon's abstract theorizing. Consider the following description of Saturn's rings:

> It was as if Saturn was surrounded by scores of concentric hoops, all touching each other, all so flat that they might have been cut from the thinnest possible paper. The system of the rings looked like some delicate work of art, or a fragile toy to be admired but never touched. By no effort of the will could Bowman really appreciate its true scale, and convince himself that the whole planet Earth, if set down here, would look like a ball bearing rolling round the rim of a dinner plate.
>
> (2012, 231)

This passage achieves a form of interconnectivity in which large-scale entities (the planet and its rings) are metaphorically mapped on, and therefore reduced to, familiar human-scale objects: hoops, paper, a work of art or toy, a ball bearing, a dinner plate. At first, this strategy would seem to downplay Saturn's size, but the perspective abruptly changes in the last sentence, in which the narrator—distancing himself from Bowman—points out how small the Earth would look in comparison to Saturn. In a sense, then, the insistence on Saturn's toy-like appearance serves to underscore the diminutive size of our own planet—and therefore, a fortiori, of the human species that evolved on its surface.

This vision of Saturn marks the beginning of Bowman's cosmic trip. With the spaceship in orbit around Japetus, Bowman finally discovers the source of the incredible brightness that astronomers had seen from Earth: it is a monolith not unlike the one that had been found on the Moon. At this point, the narrator interrupts Bowman's narrative and opens a digression outlining the history of the civilization that built the monolith. In this chapter, called "The Experiment," we learn that this spacefaring race had "found nothing more precious [in the whole galaxy] than Mind"; therefore, "they encouraged its dawning everywhere. They became farmers in the fields of stars; they sowed, and sometimes they reaped" (2012, 243–44). The human species is one of these aliens' many experiments with mind, and a monolith was erected on the Moon in order to measure the success of this experiment: if and when the human species would reach the stage of technological evolution that would allow it to travel to the Moon and unearth the monolith. But the alien civilization, we read, continued to evolve, too: they abandoned their biological bodies, first to become cyborg-like entities ("They no longer built spaceships. They were spaceships"; 2012, 245), then to turn into "creatures of radiation, free at last from the tyranny of matter" (2012, 245).

While less grand in scope, this vision of the alien "lords of the galaxy" (2012, 245) is highly reminiscent of Stapledon's Star Maker, and Clarke's prose comes close to the stately philosophical tone of Stapledon's account. But the difference—and it is a crucial one—is that this is only a parenthesis in the narrative of an embodied human being, Bowman. This Stapledonesque chapter, then, sets the stage for Bowman's embodied encounter with the cosmos in the remainder of the novel.

Bowman decides to leave the spaceship and use one of the pods to approach and land on the monolith, which the narrator now calls the "Star Gate"; and a gate it is, as Bowman soon discovers. When the pod is about to touch down on the monolith, it starts behaving "like one of those optical illusions, when a three-dimensional object can, by an effort of will, appear to turn inside out—its near and far sides suddenly interchanging" (2012, 253). This simile works on several levels: it renders an abrupt change in the character's perception, and particularly how the monolith undermines what psychologists would call his "naïve physics"—that is, his intuitive grasp of basic image-schematic distinctions such as that between a solid surface and a hollow one (see Smith and Casati 1994). The mention of the optical illusion—perhaps something like a Necker cube—also evokes the abstraction of geometry, a domain that seems utterly incompatible with human embodiment. Hence, the simile prepares the reader for Bowman's discovery that the monolith is "full of stars" (2012, 254)—again challenging the dichotomy between inside (an enclosed space) and outside (where we imagine stars to be)—and for the paradoxical contraction of space as the Star Gate swallows up the astronaut: "Space turned and twisted upon itself" (2012, 256). These moves announce that Bowman's trip does not follow the logic of the intermediate world; yet the experience of space does not cease to matter, as it mostly does in *Star Maker*.

In fact, Bowman undergoes a hyperspace-like experience, with stars moving past him at incredible speed. He then arrives in a place that serves—the narrator points out—as a "cosmic switching device, routing the traffic of the stars through unimaginable dimensions of space and time. [Bowman] was passing through a Grand Central Station of the galaxy" (2012, 265). This place is described as follows:

> all the surface that Bowman could see was tessellated into obviously artificial patterns that must have been miles on a side. It was like the jigsaw puzzle of a giant that played with planets; and at the centers of many of those squares and triangles and polygons were gaping black shafts—twins of the chasm from which he had just emerged.
> (2012, 262)

Here are more geometrical shapes but also—remarkably—another simile drawing on the domain of play and games ("like the jigsaw puzzle"), which reintroduces embodiment in a scaled-up form ("a giant"). Thus, this passage—and indeed this whole section of the novel—bring together perceptual abstraction, counterintuitive physics, and play, a device that eases the reader's imagination by implicating the sensorimotor schemata of bodily experience (such as rearranging the pieces of a jigsaw puzzle). The association between the cosmos and play is strengthened after a few lines, when the "softly glowing milkiness" of the "sky" is compared to "being inside a ping-pong ball" (2012, 262).

Why does play become so salient in this final portion of *2001*? Cognitive scientists Di Paolo, Rohde, and De Jaegher (2010) can help us answer this question. Working within the paradigm of embodied cognition, and more specifically of enactivist approaches to the mind (see Introduction), Di Paolo, Rohde, and De Jaegher argue that play is cognitively and developmentally significant because it allows us to generate and experiment with meanings not given in our immediate situation. Here is how Di Paolo, Rohde, and De Jaegher describe this process:

> Once objects in the environment are imbued with meaning by actions that in turn demand from the child an (adaptive) interpretation, these objects become toys—would-be cars, houses, and creatures. The child is now acting at the pinnacle of his or her enactive capabilities, because he or she is bringing forth an alienated meaning through gestural schemas and then—and here lies the equally radical trick—submitting to the reality thus created through adaptive equilibration.
> (2010, 77)

In Di Paolo, Rohde, and De Jaegher's terminology, a meaning is "alienated" when it is not available in the immediate situation without the child's imaginary intervention: for instance, a tree stump is not dangerous per se, but if a child engaging in a game of make-believe sees it as a bear it will take on an additional, "alienated" meaning of danger.[6] However, this imaginary reinterpretation of the stump is not just a mental act: because play is a highly embodied activity, the child's make-believe will inspire patterns of embodied engagement ("gestural schemas"), such as attacking or running away from the bear-stump, which would make little sense in the literal stump scenario. These new embodied behaviors are what the authors call "adaptive equilibration" at the end of the quotation. Di Paolo, Rohde, and De Jaegher thus emphasize the role of bodily patterns in the creation of novel meanings: in development, play is the first activity that enables humans and other animals to transcend the here and now, moving beyond their immediate surroundings in a way that, however, remains fundamentally embodied. Play thus lays the groundwork for activities that combine imaginative, embodied involvement and meaning generation, such as our engagement with art (see Boyd 2009; Caracciolo 2014d, Chap. 3).

This account of play casts new light on Clarke's use of toy-like or playful imagery throughout *2001*, and especially at the height of the protagonist's cosmic vision at the end of the novel. On the one hand, the text constructs a highly counterintuitive scenario in which a character experiences interstellar space in ways that would seem impossible for an embodied creature:

> He was now so close to the red sun that he would have been burned up in a moment if its radiation had not been held at bay by some invisible screen. And during his voyage he had been subjected to accelerations that should have crushed him instantly—yet he had felt nothing.
>
> (2012, 274)

The inherent limitations of biological beings are here transcended. On the other hand, the text retains a link with embodied experience by appealing to the semantic domain of play. Hence the bodily defamiliarization at work in this text: the cosmos is transfigured into an embodied playground, just as the stump can be transformed into a bear by a child's creativity. Yet, due to the counterintuitive dimension of the space represented by Clarke, this cosmic playground resists complete reduction to the human-scale, intermediate world: "It seemed that space had been turned inside out: this was not a place for Man" (2012, 263). Just as play enables children to rise above the meanings given in their immediate surroundings, Clarke's playful metaphors create a cosmic vision that is posthuman—like Stapledon's—and nevertheless strongly suggests the possibility of direct embodied engagement. Going beyond human embodiment involves, surprisingly, not a forward movement—toward new technologies, for example—but a reversion to the roots of embodied creativity. In turn, this strategy calls for a particular affective stance toward the cosmos, a feeling of childlike wonder uncomplicated by apprehension over human littleness and fragility.

Nowhere is this point made clearer than in the novel's last chapter. Bowman's interstellar trip ends in a place that is eerily reminiscent of a hotel suite on Earth. This is clearly an environment designed by the alien civilization to put Bowman at ease, with the goal of entering his mind and preparing him for a "realm of consciousness that no man had experienced before" (2012, 290). This process triggers a metaphorical motion in time: "He was retrogressing down the corridors of time, being drained of knowledge and experience as he swept back toward his childhood" (2012, 290–91). Bowman's "retrogressing" or "sweeping back" are kinetic images for a process that is more than just mnemonic: Bowman is physically going back to the roots of that embodied creativity first discovered in childhood, through play. The outcome is Bowman's evolution into a posthuman being—a "Star-Child," as the narrator calls him.

The chapter ends with the words: "In an empty room, floating amid the fires of a double star twenty thousand light-years from Earth, a baby opened its eyes and began to cry" (2012, 291). Surely, this is but a stage in Bowman's transformation into a being capable of embracing, in his boundless imagination, the whole cosmos: "for all his powers, he knew that he was still a baby. So he would remain until he had decided on a new form, or had passed beyond the necessities of matter" (2012, 293). But Clarke's choice of a child for this ending is strategic, because it ties in with the playful or toy-like metaphors for cosmic entities deployed throughout the novel. Thus, in the last chapter the Star-Child is presented with the following vision of Earth: "There before him, a glittering toy no Star-Child could resist, floated the planet Earth with all its peoples" (2012, 297).

In this final scene, the Earth itself is transformed into a "glittering toy," with a dramatic reduction of the planetary scale to the size of an object that affords direct, embodied interaction. This ending completes the novel's movement from the intermediate world to the cosmic perspective—a movement initiated in the first part, where the "man-apes" learned to use material objects as tools. But there is a fundamental difference between the apes' stones and clubs and the Earth as a "glittering toy": since a toy is not merely a utilitarian artifact, it signals an affective relationship to the cosmos that is not marked by the desire to exploit but by the open-ended freedom of play. The novel's final words are: "For though [the Star-Child] was master of the world, he was not quite sure what to do next. But he would think of something" (2012, 297). The character's apparent detachment from Earth reflects his embracing a cosmic perspective, from which even being "master of the world" does not inspire immediate, practical action but only contemplation. Yet the potential for bodily action *is* there, because of the embodied dimension of play; in this sense, Clarke's strategies come closer to Nabokov's ironic conflation of the cosmos and the body than to the stark abstraction of Stapledon's prose.

However, the scope of Clarke's bodily defamiliarization is much wider than in Nabokov's "Lance": while Nabokov's protagonist only catches an ineffable glimpse of the cosmos, Bowman, now transformed into a Star-Child, fuses with the aliens' cosmic mind and embodies it by taking a stance analogous to that of a playing child. Affectively, this stance resembles the sublime, but only in the sense of childlike marvel at the universe and its boundless creative potential. Although the cosmos dwarfs the human species, the Star-Child no longer experiences fear over its scale: "the cold, dark waste of cosmic dust which he had once feared seemed no more than the beat of a raven's wing across the face of the Sun" (2012, 296). The suggestiveness of the association between a wing beat and the dark expanse of the cosmos illustrates the power of poetic creativity, which has its developmental roots in play. The affect evoked in this way is radically different from Kant's version of the sublime, which consists—as seen in the first section of this chapter—in affirming human reason *in spite of* our physical limitations. Instead, Clarke's narrative suggests that these limitations can be sidestepped only by embracing our littleness—our being but "the beat of a raven's wing" in front of cosmic realities—while reclaiming the value of childlike creativity, including the marvelous promise of unfettered embodied engagement. Clarke's toy-like metaphors for cosmic entities outline this utopian promise and enable willing readers to experience it affectively.

***

Narrative, despite its limited means and its bias for the human scale, can serve as an imaginative probe into cosmic realities. That is one of the core ideas of this book, and this final chapter has taken that line of thinking to its logical extreme, looking at how narrative engages with the most expansive meaning of the word "cosmos"—namely, the universe in its spatio-temporal totality. I have argued that affective patterns play a key role in that cosmic confrontation.

Nabokov, Stapledon, and Clarke all attempt to *represent* the cosmos in some way, rendering it in human-scale language: hence, Nabokov's "tiny bonfire," Stapledon's intergalactic "partnerships," and Clarke's toy-like Earth. But direct verbal figuration can only take us so far, because the interconnectivity it establishes is inevitably reductive: downsizing the cosmos to objects or social interactions grounded in the intermediate world may be useful as a heuristic device, but it also carries a risk of misrepresenting what science tells us about the spatio-temporal scale of the universe and the so-called "mediocrity" of the human. Stephen Hawking expresses this point very pithily in an interview with Ken Campbell: "The human race is just a chemical scum on a moderate-sized planet, orbiting around a very average star in the outer suburb of one among a hundred billion galaxies" (quoted in Deutsch 1997, 177–78). Any direct comparison between human-scale objects and the cosmos as a whole carries a risk of sidelining the mediocrity of the human—of making the human sound more important than it really is. To avoid that risk, the authors discussed in this chapter skillfully exploit the affective potential of our imagination of the cosmos. Affective involvement compensates for the insufficiency of language, inviting us to *feel* our mediocrity where representational strategies may inadvertently foster false beliefs in the commensurability of the human and the cosmic—or, even more dangerously, in the metaphysical superiority of human mind and reason over "brute" nonhuman matter. It is precisely this blind logic that has led to the indiscriminate exploitation of natural resources on our planet. Indeed, the critique of representation has broad resonance in the environmental humanities, where scholars such as Emily Potter invite us to "emphasise more-than-textual ways of knowing the world; knowledge emergent from embodied process and material practices" (2009, 3). Thus, Nabokov, Stapledon, and Clarke combine conceptual interconnectivity with affective and embodied patterns that aim to preserve the *distance* between the human scale and the cosmic, unsettling any sense of human mastery.

This significance of realities beyond the human is often captured under the time-honored heading of the "sublime." Our imagination of objects or scenes of great physical size is bound up with feelings of fear, awe, and wonder—sublime feelings that, despite their partly shared phenomenological qualities, have been interpreted by commentators in substantially different ways. This is, to a large extent, true for the texts examined in this chapter as well. Nabokov favors irony and ambiguity, suggestively associating the cosmos with bodily realities in Lance's expedition to a far-off planet: here the sublime is seemingly undercut by the narrator's humor, but in the last analysis this affective mix fuels the reader's imagination, creating a sense of intense (if ultimately ineffable) union with the cosmos. Stapledon's prose is equally striking, although its effectiveness depends on a total *lack* of humor or overt affect: the narrator's cosmic vision is all-encompassing, and yet rendered in a dispassionate tone almost reminiscent of a philosophical treatise. Readers are thus given the chance to experience what we may think of as second-order marvel at the cosmos—marvel at the narrator's utterly nonchalant account of how his personal history blends with the history of the cosmos as a whole. Finally, Clarke's *2001* taps into the affective value of childlike play—with its inebriating freedom and creativity—to envision humanity's passing beyond itself: through Bowman's transformation into a Star-Child, readers can experience the marvel of the cosmos in a form that is unconstrained by awareness of our biological and cognitive limitations.

None of these moves would be possible without our being embodied creatures capable of affective attunement to the physical realities that surround us. Affect thus complements the representational strategies of bodily defamiliarization we've seen at work in previous chapters, in which the form of the human body was evoked but at the same time challenged at the level of the diegesis. Of course, affective responses to the cosmos are by no means exclusive to my case studies in this chapter, since they can be found in virtually *all* previous textual analyses. Yet affect becomes more salient in "maximalist" texts that engage with the cosmos as a totality: arguably, the larger the distance between the human-scale world and the cosmic realities to be incorporated into narrative, the more significant and central to readers' experiences affective phenomena are bound to become. In a sense, these texts successfully exploit the affective foundations of *any* narrative—the way in which narrative, despite being a representational art, has its roots in more basic, affective patterns. From a developmental perspective, Ellen Dissanayake (2011) argues that the three narrative universals of suspense, curiosity, and surprise build on the affective patterns that run through preverbal exchanges between mothers and infants. This theory brings us back to the sphere of childhood and to the creative play that characterizes it. Nabokov's irony, Stapledon's contemplative detachment, and Clarke's childlike wonder explore different aspects of this affectivity of play, placing it center stage in their narratives and using it as a tool to trigger bodily defamiliarization and thus question anthropocentric assumptions.

Notes

1 Interestingly, this focus on the embodiment of the sublime dovetails with Edmund Burke's materialist account in his 1757 *Philosophical Enquiry*: for Burke, the sublime involves "an unnatural tension and certain violent emotions of the nerves" (1990, 121). Burke's sublime is in many ways opposed to Kant's intellectualized discussion. For more on the materialism of Burke's vision, see Alan Richardson's *The Neural Sublime* (2010).

2 In Chapter 5 of *The Seven Beauties of Science Fiction* (2008), Istvan Csicsery-Ronay offers a helpful discussion of the sublime—particularly, but not exclusively, in the technological mode—as a staple element of science fiction.

3 I won't pursue this line of thinking in this context, but it's important to note that Nabokov's focus on the cosmic goes hand in hand with the latent mysticism of his works. This dimension has been discussed by Nabokov scholars under the heading of the "beyond" or "otherworld" (see, e.g., Alexandrov 1991).

4 Thanks to *Star Trek*'s "warp drive" and similar effects in other science fiction franchises, this visual abstraction has become a cliché of space travel. I am grateful to one of the anonymous readers of this manuscript for raising this point.

5 I read Clarke's flashforward alongside its equivalent in Kubrick's *2001* in Caracciolo (2015).

6 This example is inspired by Kendall Walton's (1990, 38) account of mimesis, which uses a similar tree stump scenario.

Coda
And So What?

This book's argument comes down to a simple idea: literary fiction can take readers beyond the human-scale reality of ordinary experience, inviting them to imagine things and processes that far exceed the range of human perception. In the twentieth-century novels and short stories I have examined in the previous chapters, this feat is made possible by fiction's dialogue with scientific models of reality. The main concern of these texts is not communicating scientific knowledge, or even doing justice to it. In fact, the science they draw upon is frequently partial or outdated. Rather, these narratives imagine the ramifications of the near-invisible realities of science for readers' intermediate world. They are interested in how it all comes together: how the cosmos trickles down (or "up," in the case of the infinitesimally small) and inflects the objects and entities that populate everyday life. In the eons of evolutionary history, our embodied minds have become attuned to certain kinds of realities, particularly those that afford physical interaction and those of human intersubjectivity. Yet human cultures have developed conceptual and technological tools to sidestep this evolutionary bias, affording access to levels of reality that we cannot perceive with the naked eye. Science is one of the practices that make the cosmos legible, and it undoubtedly plays a central role in Western modernity.

By leveraging our imagination in creative ways, twentieth-century fiction has sought to fill the gap between what we can know scientifically about the cosmos and what we can experience directly. We have seen in this book that the embodiment of our cognitive makeup is both a constraint and an opportunity as we imagine worlds beyond the human: traces and patterns arising from our interaction with human-scale reality can be uncoupled from it and recombined—via bodily defamiliarization—into novel, heuristically potent imagery. Thus, the texts I have examined in this book tap into readers' embodied experience in an attempt to put them in touch with the cosmos. Whether through kinetic, affective, or thematic strategies, these fictional narratives use readers' familiarity with the body against the grain of their own cognitive biases and limitations. When this operation is successful—and it is a matter of *both* the writer's skill and readers' predispositions—fiction discloses a cosmic perspective on human affairs. If we reject the lure of metaphysical and religious systems that place the human at the center of the universe, if—put otherwise—we face up to the revelations of science, we realize that human superiority over other living species and the inanimate world (also known as "human exceptionalism") is little more than wishful thinking: human communities are subject to the same evolutionary and environmental pressures as any other animal species, and humankind has been around for what is, in evolutionary terms, a mere blink of an eye. Even our most outstanding achievements pale in comparison with the dizzying spatio-temporal scale of the cosmos. Fiction of the kind I have tackled in this book leaves us with this startling realization by inviting us to take on a cosmic perspective on human affairs.

The question is, then: once we have attained, temporarily and partially of course, this cosmic vantage point, what do we do with it? To phrase the question otherwise: and so what? It is not a trivial concern. For surely, ethical action in the human domain depends on recognizing the value of human life and society. In the grand (cosmic) scheme of things, our species is physically insignificant and parochial—remember Stephen Hawking's remark, discussed at the end of the previous chapter, that the human race is "just a chemical scum on a moderate-sized planet" (quoted in Deutsch 1997, 177–178). Surely, if that is what our bodies are, our embodied minds cannot be much different, because—unless we want to go down the problematic route of dualism—they are material through and through. Thus, doesn't the cosmic perspective encourage a dangerous form of nihilism? Doesn't acknowledging our irrelevance undercut any value judgment and, therefore, the possibility of finding moral bearings in the vast landscape of human behavior? In the context of the current ecological crisis, does it make sense to act in less wasteful ways in the interest of "saving the environment" (which amounts, in many if not most cases, to ensuring our own survival), if our individual and collective existence is only a tiny drop in the cosmic ocean? Stapledon's *Star Maker*, as we have seen, toys with such questions. The protagonist's cosmic voyage affords him new insight into the importance of community, the only institution that—the narrative suggests—can partially offset our biological and cognitive limitations. Yet the reasons for this affirmation of community are never spelled out by Stapledon.

Another cosmic narrative, a short story by contemporary American writer Jenny Hollowell, can help me further articulate this problem.[1] It is titled "A History of Everything, Including You" (2007), and—like Stapledon's text—it sees romantic partnerships as a fundamental building block of community. Stapledon's narrative begins, as the reader will remember, with a conflict between the narrator and his wife. The "You" in Hollowell's title also refers to the narrator's partner, but we find out about the identity of the addressee only after a cosmic prologue—an ironic, and remarkably agnostic, retelling of the Book of Genesis:

> First, there was God or gods or nothing, then synthesis, space, the expanse, explosions, implosions, particles, objects, combustion, and fusion. Out of the chaos came order. Stars were born and shone and died. Planets rolled across their galaxies on invisible ellipses and the elements combined and became.
>
> (2007, 25)

The narrator jumps forward to the emergence of life on Earth and the birth of our own species—again, ironically, shrugging off the divisive question of creationism: "Life evolved or was created" (2007, 25). Developments in human culture and technology are then surveyed with the amused tone of an alien anthropologist: "We invented lipstick, vaccines, Pilates, solar panels, interventions, table manners, firearms, window treatments, therapy, birth control, tailgating, status symbols, palimony, sportsmanship, focus groups, Zoloft, sunscreen, landscaping, Cessnas, fortune cookies, chemotherapy, convenience foods, and computers" (2007, 26). The apparent haphazardness of this list evens out the difference between, say, fortune cookies and chemotherapy, along with their respective emotional connotations. This strategy is responsible for the peculiar humor of the narrative, which combines a cosmic vantage point with a lighthearted, almost nonchalant tone. The cosmic and the comic, we know from Nabokov, go hand in hand.

At this point, a "you" emerges from the collective "we" of humankind. It is the narrator's partner; the story of their courtship and marriage is told in a strikingly abbreviated and accelerated fashion:

> We fought and made up and got good jobs and got married and bought an apartment and worked out and ate more and talked less. I got depressed. You ignored me. I was sick of you. You drank too much and got careless with money. I slept with my boss. We went into counseling and got a dog.
>
> (2007, 27)

The syntax creates a fast, staccato pace that buffers the immediate emotional significance of the narrated events, as if the nonchalant cosmic perspective of the beginning infiltrated the narrator's evaluations. As seen multiple times in this book (for instance, in my reading of Calvino's "All at One Point" or Winterson's *Gut Symmetries*) rhythm can serve as a bridge between human-scale and cosmic realities: here this rhythmic connection is established by Hollowell's style, which brings together "the history of everything" and a couple's romantic relationship by applying the same syntactic treatment (short sentences, lack of subordination, etc.) to both levels of reality. But while this narrative method filters out some of the emotions that we would normally associate with romantic bonds, the overall effect is not completely unemotional: the rhythm of the narrative becomes an affective contour. In fact, the cosmic perspective introduces a particular poignancy, which complicates the already mentioned humor and becomes more distinct as soon as the narrative situation reveals itself: after the partner's death, the narrator looks back on the events of their life together. In the final episode, we read:

> There was that time on the porch when you said, "Can you believe it?" This was near the end, and your hands were trembling. I think you were talking about everything, including us. Did you want me to say it, so that it would not be lost?
>
> (2007, 27)

The partner's question signals disbelief at the breadth and depth of life, and perhaps at the speed with which it has passed by. This feeling ties in with the sense of sheer multiplicity evoked by the lists of material objects that constellate present-day human life. The emotional poignancy I have talked about originates in a deeply compassionate view of life as the narrator acknowledges—implicitly, but no less powerfully—how frail and fleeting it is, and yet how staggeringly varied.

Thus, the narrator rejoices at the ability to salvage particular moments from oblivion: "It's a victory to remember how the jellyfish stung you and you ran screaming from the water. It's a victory to remember dressing the wound with meat tenderizer and you saying I made it better" (2007, 28). It is the rich sensory texture of these memories that emerges, and it is presented as something inherently valuable *because* of its fleetingness. The variety of human experience mirrors—and offers an imaginative point of entry into—the unimaginable diversity of the cosmos itself. The narrative's final, melancholic sentence points to the beauty of the inanimate world as a sensory counterpoint to the partner's death: "A storm was moving in. I did not think of heaven, but I saw that the clouds were beautiful and I watched them cover the sun" (2007, 28). There is cosmic detachment at work here, but it is detachment that leads to heightened attention and care for lived experience, not to indifference.

Hollowell's "History of Everything, Including You" thus shows how we may bring the cosmic perspective to bear on our everyday lives while avoiding the pitfalls of nihilism. The narrative has a tongue-in-cheek quality: telling "the history of everything" and one's romantic life in the same breath is a bold project, and that boldness is made possible only by the strength of the two protagonists' relationship. Meaning is a social phenomenon created in the dance of intersubjective interactions, as enactivist philosophers like Di Paolo and De Jaegher (2007) teach us: only by embracing and cultivating interpersonal bonds can we fully come to grips with our cosmic insignificance, and even playfully shrug it away. Moreover, understanding the fragility of human life—in both individual and species-wide terms—puts us in a better position to honor it.

Finally, and crucially, only reflecting on the cosmos and the parochiality of our own species can foster the humility that is necessary to act more respectfully toward the nonhuman realities that surround us. It is perhaps inevitable for humans to think in anthropocentric terms; but confronting the cosmic perspective through the narratives I have examined in this book (and, no doubt, countless other narratives) can temper that anthropocentrism, shifting our attention away from ourselves and our in-groups on a local or national level, toward the human species as a whole. In a seminal essay, Dipesh Chakrabarty writes that there "could be no phenomenology of us as a species" (2009, 220). Imagining a perspective that is as radically distant from the human-scale world as that of the cosmos can, perhaps, deepen our awareness of how we share the texture of lived experience with our conspecifics as well as other animals. If we follow this route, something akin to a phenomenology of the human can come into view. Exploring that feeling of community is, on my reading, the central preoccupation of Hollowell's short story, which echoes and enriches the cosmic voyage related in Stapledon's *Star Maker*. I hope to have shown in this book that only sustained attention to formal patterns—in the related practices of close reading, narratological analysis, and cognitive literary studies—can fully reveal the multifaceted affective impact of narrative's confrontation with nonhuman realities.[2] The human imagination is limited in its representational range; but our bodies can resonate—affectively and nonrepresentationally—with phenomena far beyond the intermediate world of day-to-day experience. Developing a sensitivity to form can reinforce, and bring to consciousness, this affective and embodied resonance.

Ultimately, however, we should not expect fiction to offer any definitive answers to cosmic anxieties. For even the best kind of fiction cannot, and does not aim to, solve problems; on the contrary, it taps into the emotional energies those problems mobilize, and in doing so it invites readers to nuance and clarify their thinking. It is up to each reader to accept or decline that invitation. The task of those who read literature professionally, like this writer and (presumably) the readers of this book, is to make sure that the invitation will "not be lost."

Notes

1 I would like to thank Emily Bald for bringing Hollowell's story to my attention at the 2015 conference of the Pacific Ancient and Modern Language Association in Portland, Oregon.
2 I develop this line of thinking on narrative form and nonhuman realities in *Narrating the Mesh* (forthcoming).

References

A Reading Shrink. 2014. "Well-Written Horror Story." *Amazon.com Customer Reviews:* Under the Skin. April 9, 2014. http://www.amazon.com/review/RPI2R400YWEGJ.

Abbott, H. Porter. 2003. "Unnarratable Knowledge: The Difficulty of Understanding Evolution by Natural Selection." In *Narrative Theory and the Cognitive Sciences,* edited by David Herman, 143–62. Stanford, CA: CSLI Publications.

———. 2013. *Real Mysteries: Narrative and the Unknowable.* Columbus: Ohio State University Press.

Abecassis, Jack I. 2000. "The Eclipse of Desire: L'Affaire Houellebecq." *MLN* 115 (4): 801–26.

Aït-Touati, Frédérique. 2011. *Fictions of the Cosmos.* Chicago, IL and London: University of Chicago Press.

Alaimo, Stacy. 2010. *Bodily Natures: Science, Environment, and the Material Self.* Bloomington: Indiana University Press.

Alexandrov, Vladimir. 1991. *Nabokov's Otherworld.* Princeton, NJ: Princeton University Press.

Anderson, Michael L. 2003. "Embodied Cognition: A Field Guide." *Artificial Intelligence* 149 (1): 91–130.

Antonello, Pierpaolo. 2007. "Primo Levi and 'Man as Maker.'" In *The Cambridge Companion to Primo Levi,* edited by Robert S. C. Gordon, 89–104. Cambridge: Cambridge University Press.

Arnheim, Rudolf. 1969. *Visual Thinking.* Berkeley: University of California Press.

Askin, Ridvan. 2015. "Prolegomenon to a Differential Theory of Narrative." *SubStance* 44 (3): 155–70.

Bakhtin, Mikhail. 1981. *The Dialogic Imagination: Four Essays.* Edited by Michael Holquist. Austin and London: University of Texas Press.

———. 1984. *Rabelais and His World.* Bloomington: Indiana University Press.

Ballard, J. G. 1996. "Which Way to Inner Space?" In *A User's Guide to the Millennium: Essays and Reviews,* 195–98. London: HarperCollins.

———. 2009. *The Complete Stories.* New York and London: Norton.

Barad, Karen. 2007. *Meeting the Universe Halfway: Quantum Physics and the Entanglement of Matter and Meaning.* Durham, NC and London: Duke University Press.

Baroni, Raphaël. 2013. "Tellability." In *The Living Handbook of Narratology,* edited by Peter Hühn. Hamburg: Hamburg University Press. http://www.lhn.uni-hamburg.de/article/tellability.

Barsalou, Lawrence W. 2003. "Situated Simulation in the Human Conceptual System." *Language and Cognitive Processes* 18 (5–6): 513–62.

Bartusiak, Marcia. 2009. *The Day We Found the Universe*. New York: Vintage.

Belpoliti, Marco. 1998. *Primo Levi*. Milan: Bruno Mondadori.

Bennett, Jane. 2010. *Vibrant Matter: A Political Ecology of Things*. Durham, NC and London: Duke University Press Books.

Bergen, Benjamin K. 2012. *Louder Than Words: The New Science of How the Mind Makes Meaning*. New York: Basic Books.

Berlina, Alexandra. 2015. "Art, as Device: Introduction." *Poetics Today* 36 (3): 151–74.

Bernaerts, Lars, Dirk De Geest, Luc Herman, and Bart Vervaeck, eds. 2013. *Stories and Minds: Cognitive Approaches to Literary Narrative*. Lincoln and London: University of Nebraska Press.

Besser, Stephan. 2017. "How Patterns Meet: Tracing the Isomorphic Imagination in Contemporary Neuroculture." *Configurations* 25 (4): 415–45.

Bixler, Andrea. 2007. "Teaching Evolution with the Aid of Science Fiction." *American Biology Teacher* 69 (6): 337–40.

Bleich, David. 2013. *The Materiality of Language: Gender, Politics, and the University*. Bloomington: Indiana University Press.

Bleiler, Everett F. 1990. *Science-Fiction, the Early Years*. Kent, OH: Kent State University Press.

Bogost, Ian. 2012. *Alien Phenomenology, or What It's Like to Be a Thing*. Minneapolis: University of Minnesota Press.

Bolens, Guillemette. 2012. *The Style of Gestures: Embodiment and Cognition in Literary Narrative*. Baltimore, MD: The Johns Hopkins University Press.

Borges, Jorge Luis. 2000. "The Immortal." In *The Aleph and Other Stories*, translated by Andrew Hurley, 3–19. New York: Penguin Books.

———. 2007. "A New Refutation of Time." In *Labyrinths: Selected Stories and Other Writings*, translated by James E. Irby, 217–34. New York: New Directions.

Boroditsky, Lera. 2000. "Metaphoric Structuring: Understanding Time through Spatial Metaphors." *Cognition* 75 (1): 1–28.

Boroditsky, Lera, and Jesse J. Prinz. 2008. "What Thoughts Are Made Of." In *Embodied Grounding: Social, Cognitive, Affective, and Neuroscientific Approaches*, edited by G. R. Semin and Eliot R. Smith, 98–115. Cambridge: Cambridge University Press.

Bossart, W. H. 2003. *Borges and Philosophy: Self, Time, and Metaphysics*. New York: Peter Lang.

Boyd, Brian. 2001. *Nabokov's Ada: The Place of Consciousness*. Second edition. Christchurch: Cybereditions.

———. 2009. *On the Origin of Stories: Evolution, Cognition, and Fiction*. Cambridge, MA: Harvard University Press.

Brake, Mark. 2013. *Alien Life Imagined: Communicating the Science and Culture of Astrobiology*. Cambridge: Cambridge University Press.

Brooks, Peter. 1984. *Reading for the Plot: Design and Intention in Narrative*. New York: Knopf.

Brooks, Rodney A. 1991. "Intelligence without Reason." Artificial Intelligence Laboratory Report 1293. Cambridge, MA: MIT. http://people.csail.mit.edu/brooks/papers/AIM-1293.pdf.

Brown, John Seely, Allan Collins, and Paul Duguid. 1989. "Situated Cognition and the Culture of Learning." *Educational Researcher* 18 (1): 32–42.

Budgen, Frank. 1972. *James Joyce and the Making of* Ulysses. Oxford: Oxford University Press.

Burke, Edmund. 1990. *A Philosophical Enquiry into the Origin of Our Ideas of the Sublime and Beautiful.* Edited by Adam Phillips. Oxford: Oxford University Press.

Butler, Rex. 2012. "Infinity and One: On Jorge Luis Borges's 'El Inmortal.'" *The Modern Language Review* 107 (1): 182–97.

Butterworth, George. 1995. "An Ecological Perspective on the Origins of Self." In *The Body and the Self,* edited by José Luis Bermúdez, Anthony J. Marcel, and Naomi Eilan, 87–106. Cambridge, MA: The MIT Press.

Calvino, Italo. 1984. *Cosmicomiche vecchie e nuove.* Milan: Garzanti.

———. 2009. *The Complete Cosmicomics.* Translated by Martin McLaughlin, Tim Parks, and William Weaver. London: Penguin Books.

Caracciolo, Marco. Forthcoming. *Narrating the Mesh: Form and Story in the Anthropocene.* Charlottesville: University of Virginia Press.

———. 2011. "The Reader's Virtual Body: Narrative Space and Its Reconstruction." *Storyworlds* 3: 117–38.

———. 2013a. "Blind Reading: Toward an Enactivist Theory of the Reader's Imagination." In *Stories and Minds: Cognitive Approaches to Literary Narrative,* edited by Lars Bernaerts, Dirk De Geest, Luc Herman, and Bart Vervaeck, 81–106. Lincoln and London: University of Nebraska Press.

———. 2013b. "Embodiment at the Crossroads: Some Open Questions between Literary Interpretation and Cognitive Science." *Poetics Today* 34 (1–2): 233–53.

———. 2013c. "Narrative Space and Readers' Responses to Stories: A Phenomenological Account." *Style* 47 (4): 425–44.

———. 2013d. "Phenomenological Metaphors in Readers' Engagement with Characters: The Case of Ian McEwan's *Saturday*." *Language and Literature* 22 (1): 60–76.

———. 2014a. "Embodied Cognition and the Grotesque in Calvino's *La giornata d'uno scrutatore* and Sanguineti's *Capriccio italiano*." *CLCWeb: Comparative Literature and Culture* 16 (1). http://docs.lib.purdue.edu/clcweb/vol16/iss1/9/.

———. 2014b. "Interpretation for the Bodies: Bridging the Gap." *Style* 48 (3): 385–403.

———. 2014c. "Tell-Tale Rhythms: Embodiment and Narrative Discourse." *Storyworlds* 6 (2): 49–73.

———. 2014d. *The Experientiality of Narrative: An Enactivist Approach.* Berlin: de Gruyter.

———. 2015. "Bones in Outer Space: Narrative and the Cosmos in *2001: A Space Odyssey* and Its Remediations." *Image & Narrative* 16 (3): 73–89.

———. 2016a. *Strange Narrators in Contemporary Fiction: Explorations in Readers' Engagement with Characters.* Lincoln: University of Nebraska Press.

———. 2016b. "'The Bagatelle of Particle Waves': Facing the Hard Problem of Consciousness in Houellebecq's *Les Particules Élémentaires* and Mitchell's *Ghostwritten*." *Critique: Studies in Contemporary Fiction* 57 (5): 487–501.

———. 2017a. "Creative Metaphor in Literature." In *Routledge Handbook of Metaphor and Language*, edited by Elena Semino and Zsófia Demjén, 206–18. London: Routledge.

———. 2017b. "Murky Mercy: Michel Faber's *Under the Skin* and the Difficulty of Reality." *College Literature* 44 (4): 589–612.

———. 2018. "Degrees of Embodiment in Literary Reading: Notes for a Theoretical Model, with *American Psycho* as a Case Study." In *Expressive Minds and Artistic Creations: Studies in Cognitive Poetics*, edited by Szilvia Csábi. Oxford: Oxford University Press.

———. 2019. "Ungrounding Fictional Worlds: An Enactivist Perspective on the 'Worldlikeness' of Fiction." In *Possible Worlds Theory and Contemporary Narratology*, edited by Alice Bell and Marie-Laure Ryan, 113–31. Lincoln: University of Nebraska Press.

———. 2020. "Object-Oriented Plotting and Nonhuman Realities in DeLillo's *Underworld* and Iñárritu's *Babel*." In *Environment and Narrative: New Directions in Econarratology*, edited by Erin James and Eric Morel, 45–64. Columbus: Ohio State University Press.

Caracciolo, Marco, and Shannon Lambert. 2019. "Narrative Bodies and Nonhuman Transformations." *SubStance* 48 (3): 45–63.

Carasso, Françoise. 2009. *Primo Levi. La scelta della chiarezza*. Translated by Daniela Napoli. Turin: Einaudi.

Chakrabarty, Dipesh. 2009. "The Climate of History: Four Theses." *Critical Inquiry* 35 (2): 197–222.

———. 2014. "Climate and Capital: On Conjoined Histories." *Critical Inquiry* 41 (1): 1–23.

Chalmers, David J. 1995. "Facing Up to the Problem of Consciousness." *Journal of Consciousness Studies* 2 (3): 200–219.

Chatman, Seymour. 1978. *Story and Discourse*. Ithaca, NY and London: Cornell University Press.

Christ, Roland. 1969. *The Narrow Act: Borges' Art of Allusion*. New York: New York University Press.

Clark, Andy. 1997. *Being There: Putting Brain, Body, and World Together Again*. Cambridge, MA: MIT Press.

Clark, Andy, and David J. Chalmers. 2010. "The Extended Mind." In *The Extended Mind*, edited by Richard Menary, 27–42. Cambridge, MA: MIT Press.

Clark, Timothy. 2015. *Ecocriticism on the Edge: The Anthropocene as a Threshold Concept*. London: Bloomsbury.

Clarke, Arthur C. 1972. *The Lost Worlds of 2001: The Ultimate Log of the Ultimate Trip*. New York: Signet Books.

———. 2012. *2001: A Space Odyssey*. Kindle Edition. New York: RosettaBooks.

Clute, John. 2014. "Zoline, Pamela." In *SFE: The Encyclopedia of Science Fiction*. http://www.sf-encyclopedia.com/entry/zoline_pamela.

Coale, Samuel Chase. 2012. *Quirks of the Quantum: Postmodernism and Contemporary American Fiction*. Charlottesville: University of Virginia Press.

Cook, Guy. 1994. *The Discourse of Literature: The Interplay of Form and Mind*. Oxford: Oxford University Press.

Coplan, Amy. 2004. "Empathic Engagement with Narrative Fictions." *The Journal of Aesthetics and Art Criticism* 62 (2): 141–52.

Crist, Eileen. 2013. "On the Poverty of Our Nomenclature." *Environmental Humanities* 3 (1): 129–47.

Crutzen, Paul J., and Eugene F. Stoermer. 2000. "The Anthropocene." *Global Change Newsletter* 41: 17–18.

Csicsery-Ronay, Istvan. 2008. *The Seven Beauties of Science Fiction*. Middletown, CT: Wesleyan University Press.

Cummings, Ray. 2005. *The Girl in the Golden Atom*. Lincoln and London: University of Nebraska Press.

Czachesz, István. 2009. "Metamorphosis and Mind: Cognitive Explorations of the Grotesque in Early Christian Literature." In *Metamorphoses: Resurrection, Body and Transformative Practices in Early Christianity*, edited by Turid Karlsen Seim and Jorunn Økland, 207–30. Berlin and New York: de Gruyter.

Damasio, Antonio. 2000. *The Feeling of What Happens: Body and Emotion in the Making of Consciousness*. London: William Heinemann.

Dannenberg, Hilary P. 2008. *Coincidence and Counterfactuality: Plotting Time and Space in Narrative Fiction*. Lincoln and London: University of Nebraska Press.

Dawkins, Richard. 1996. *The Blind Watchmaker: Why the Evidence of Evolution Reveals a Universe without Design*. New York: Norton.

De Certeau, Michel. 1984. *The Practice of Everyday Life*. Translated by Steven F. Rendall. Berkeley and Los Angeles: University of California Press.

De Jaegher, Hanne, and Ezequiel A. Di Paolo. 2007. "Participatory Sense-Making: An Enactive Approach to Social Cognition." *Phenomenology and the Cognitive Sciences* 6 (4): 485–507.

Dennett, Daniel C. 1991. *Consciousness Explained*. London: Penguin.

Deutsch, David. 1997. *The Fabric of Reality: Towards a Theory of Everything*. London: Penguin.

Di Paolo, Ezequiel A., Marieke Rohde, and Hanne De Jaegher. 2010. "Horizons for the Enactive Mind: Values, Social Interaction, and Play." In *Enaction: Toward a New Paradigm for Cognitive Science*, edited by John Stewart, Olivier Gapenne, and Ezequiel A. Di Paolo, 33–87. Cambridge, MA: MIT Press.

Diamond, Jared M. 1993. *The Third Chimpanzee: The Evolution and Future of the Human Animal*. New York: Harper Perennial.

Dicken, Thomas M. 2004. "God and Pigment: John Updike on the Conservation of Meaning." *Religion & Literature* 36 (3): 69–87.

Dillon, Sarah. 2011. "'It's a Question of Words, Therefore': Becoming-Animal in Michel Faber's *Under the Skin*." *Science Fiction Studies* 38 (1): 134–54.

Dissanayake, Ellen. 2011. "Prelinguistic and Preliterate Substrates of Poetic Narrative." *Poetics Today* 32 (1): 55–79.

Dolphijn, Rick, and Iris van der Tuin, eds. 2012. *New Materialism: Interviews & Cartographies*. Ann Arbor, MI: Open Humanities Press.

Easterlin, Nancy. 2012. *A Biocultural Approach to Literary Theory and Interpretation*. Baltimore, MD and London: The Johns Hopkins University Press.

Eliot, T. S. 1997. "Hamlet and His Problems." In *The Sacred Wood and Major Early Essays*, 55–59. New York: Dover.

Ellmann, Maud. 2008. "*Ulysses*: The Epic of the Human Body." In *A Companion to James Joyce*, edited by Richard Brown, 54–70. Malden, MA: Blackwell.

Esrock, Ellen J. 2004. "Embodying Literature." *Journal of Consciousness Studies* 11 (5–6): 79–89.

———. 2007. "Tendencies toward Embodiment in Word and Image Studies." *Poetics Today* 28 (1): 165–68.

Evans, Vyvyan, and Melanie Green. 2006. *Cognitive Linguistics: An Introduction*. Edinburgh: Edinburgh University Press.

Faber, Michel. 2000. *Under the Skin*. Edinburgh: Canongate.

Farwell, Marilyn. 1996. *Heterosexual Plots and Lesbian Narratives*. New York: New York University Press.

Fauconnier, Gilles, and Mark Turner. 2002. *The Way We Think: Conceptual Blending and the Mind's Hidden Complexities*. New York: Basic Books.

Fiedler, Leslie A. 1983. *Olaf Stapledon: A Man Divided*. Oxford: Oxford University Press.

Fleishman, Avrom. 1967. "Science in Ithaca." *Wisconsin Studies in Contemporary Literature* 8 (3): 377–91.

Flood, Alison. 2011. "First Ever Direct English Translation of *Solaris* Published." *The Guardian Online*. June 15, 2011. https://www.theguardian.com/books/2011/jun/15/first-direct-translation-solaris.

Fludernik, Monika. 1996. *Towards a "Natural" Narratology*. London: Routledge.

———. 2003. "Scene Shift, Metalepsis, and the Metaleptic Mode." *Style* 37: 382–400.

Foote, Kenneth E., and Maoz Azaryahu. 2009. "Sense of Place." In *International Encyclopedia of Human Geography*, edited by Rob Kitchin and Nigel Thrift, 10: 96–100. Amsterdam: Elsevier.

Frank, Joseph. 1945. "Spatial Form in Modern Literature: An Essay in Three Parts." *The Sewanee Review* 53 (4): 643–53.

Freese, Peter. 2009. *The Clown of Armageddon: The Novels of Kurt Vonnegut*. Heidelberg: Winter.

Freud, Sigmund. 1962. *Civilization and Its Discontents*. Translated by James Strachey. New York: Norton.

Fromm, Harold. 2009. *The Nature of Being Human: From Environmentalism to Consciousness*. Baltimore, MD: The Johns Hopkins University Press.

Fuller, Robert C. 2008. *Spirituality in the Flesh: Bodily Sources of Religious Experiences*. Oxford and New York: Oxford University Press.

Gallese, Vittorio. 2005. "Embodied Simulation: From Neurons to Phenomenal Experience." *Phenomenology and the Cognitive Sciences* 1: 23–48.

Gerrig, Richard J. 1993. *Experiencing Narrative Worlds: On the Psychological Activities of Reading*. New Haven, CT and London: Yale University Press.

Gibbs, Raymond W. 2005. *Embodiment and Cognitive Science*. Cambridge: Cambridge University Press.

———. 2006. "Metaphor Interpretation as Embodied Simulation." *Mind and Language* 21: 434–458.

———. 2013. "Walking the Walk While Thinking About the Talk: Embodied Interpretation of Metaphorical Narratives." *Journal of Psycholinguistic Research* 42 (4): 363–78.

Gibson, James J. 1983. *The Senses Considered as Perceptual Systems.* Westport, CT: Greenwood Press.

———. 1986. *The Ecological Approach to Visual Perception.* New York: Psychology Press.

Gilbert, Stuart, ed. 1957. *Letters of James Joyce.* London: Faber and Faber.

Glenberg, Arthur M., and Michael P. Kaschak. 2002. "Grounding Language in Action." *Psychonomic Bulletin & Review* 9 (3): 558–65.

Glover, Edward. 1947. *War, Sadism, and Pacifism.* London: Allen & Unwin.

Goatly, Andrew. 2011. *The Language of Metaphors.* Second edition. New York and London: Routledge.

Goldman, Alan. 2002. "Plain Sex." In *The Philosophy of Sex: Fourth Edition,* edited by Alan Soble, 39–55. Lanham, MD: Rowman & Littlefield.

Goldstein, Martin, and Inge F. Goldstein. 1995. *The Refrigerator and the Universe: Understanding the Laws of Energy.* Cambridge, MA: Harvard University Press.

Gomel, Elana. 2010. *Postmodern Science Fiction and Temporal Imagination.* London: Continuum.

———. 2014. *Narrative Space and Time: Representing Impossible Topologies in Literature.* New York: Routledge.

Gould, Stephen Jay. 1987. *Time's Arrow, Time's Cycle: Myth and Metaphor in the Discovery of Geological Time.* Cambridge, MA: Harvard University Press.

Grandy, Walter T., Jr. 2012. *Entropy and the Time Evolution of Macroscopic Systems.* Oxford: Oxford University Press.

Grice, Helena, and Tim Woods. 1998. "Grand (Dis)Unified Theories? Dislocated Discourses in *Gut Symmetries.*" In *"I'm Telling You Stories": Jeanette Winterson and the Politics of Reading,* edited by Helena Grice and Tim Woods, 117–26. Amsterdam: Rodopi.

Griffin, Clive. 2013. "Philosophy and Fiction." In *The Cambridge Companion to Jorge Luis Borges,* edited by Edwin Williamson, 5–15. Cambridge: Cambridge University Press.

Grusin, Richard. 2015a. "Introduction." In *The Nonhuman Turn,* edited by Richard Grusin, vii–xxix. Minneapolis: University of Minnesota Press.

———. ed. 2015b. *The Nonhuman Turn.* Minneapolis: University of Minnesota Press.

Gymnich, Marion, and Alexandre Segao Costa. 2006. "Of Humans, Pigs, Fish and Apes: The Literary Motif of Human-Animal Metamorphosis and Its Multiple Functions in Contemporary Fiction." *L'Esprit Créateur* 46 (2): 68–88.

Hampe, Beate, and Joseph E. Grady. 2005. *From Perception to Meaning: Image Schemas in Cognitive Linguistics.* Berlin: Walter de Gruyter.

Harding, Jennifer Riddle. 2017. *Similes, Puns and Counterfactuals in Literary Narrative.* New York: Routledge.

Harman, Graham. 2008. "On the Horror of Phenomenology: Lovecraft and Husserl." *Collapse* IV: 3–34.

Hauk, Olaf, Ingrid Johnsrude, and Friedemann Pulvermüller. 2004. "Somatotopic Representation of Action Words in Human Motor and Premotor Cortex." *Neuron* 41 (2): 301–7.

Heidegger, Martin. 1996. *Being and Time.* Translated by Joan Stambaugh. Albany: State University of New York Press.

Henchman, Anna. 2014. *The Starry Sky Within: Astronomy and the Reach of the Mind in Victorian Literature*. Oxford and New York: Oxford University Press.

Herman, David. 2002. *Story Logic: Problems and Possibilities of Narrative*. Lincoln: University of Nebraska Press.

———. 2003. "Stories as a Tool for Thinking." In *Narrative Theory and the Cognitive Sciences*, 163–92. Stanford, CA: CSLI Publications.

———. 2013. *Storytelling and the Sciences of Mind*. Cambridge, MA: MIT Press.

———. 2014. "Narratology beyond the Human." *DIEGESIS* 3 (2). https://www.diegesis.uni-wuppertal.de/index.php/diegesis/article/view/165.

———. 2018. *Narratology Beyond the Human: Storytelling and Animal Life*. Oxford: Oxford University Press.

Hewitt, Elizabeth. 1994. "Generic Exhaustion and the 'Heat Death' of Science Fiction." *Science Fiction Studies* 21 (3): 289–301.

Hitt, Christopher. 1999. "Toward an Ecological Sublime." *New Literary History* 30 (3): 603–23.

Hofstadter, Douglas R. 1999. *Gödel, Escher, Bach: An Eternal Golden Braid*. New York: Basic Books.

———. 2007. *I Am a Strange Loop*. New York: Basic Books.

Hogan, Patrick Colm. 2011. *Affective Narratology: The Emotional Structure of Stories*. Lincoln and London: University of Nebraska Press.

Hollowell, Jenny. 2007. "A History of Everything, Including You." In *New Sudden Fiction: Short-Short Stories from America and Beyond*, edited by Robert Shapard and James Thomas, 25–28. New York: Norton.

Holt, Jim. 2013. *Why Does the World Exist? An Existential Detective Story*. New York: Liveright.

Holton, Gerald James, and Stephen G. Brush. 2001. *Physics, the Human Adventure: From Copernicus to Einstein and Beyond*. New Brunswick, NJ: Rutgers University Press.

Horkheimer, Max, and Theodor W. Adorno. 2002. *Dialectic of Enlightenment: Philosophical Fragments*. Translated by Edmund Jephcott. Stanford, CA: Stanford University Press.

Houellebecq, Michel. 2000. *The Elementary Particles*. Translated by Frank Wynne. New York: Knopf.

———. 2006. *H. P. Lovecraft: Against the World, Against Life*. Translated by Dorna Khazeni. London: Weidenfeld and Nicolson.

Hume, Kathryn. 1982. "Science and Imagination in Calvino's 'Cosmicomics.'" *Mosaic* 15 (4): 47–58.

Huntington, John. 1981. "Olaf Stapledon and the Novel about the Future." *Contemporary Literature* 22 (3): 349–65.

Hutto, Daniel D. 2008. *Folk Psychological Narratives: The Sociocultural Basis of Understanding Reasons*. Cambridge, MA: MIT Press.

Hutto, Daniel D., and Erik Myin. 2012. *Radicalizing Enactivism: Basic Minds without Content*. Cambridge, MA: MIT Press.

Iovino, Serenella. 2014. "Storie dell'altro mondo. Calvino post-umano." *MLN* 129 (1): 118–38.

Jahn, Manfred. 1996. "Windows of Focalization: Deconstructing and Reconstructing a Narratological Concept." *Style* 30 (2): 241–67.

James, Erin. 2015. *The Storyworld Accord: Econarratology and Postcolonial Narratives*. Lincoln: University of Nebraska Press.

Jameson, Fredric. 2005. *Archaeologies of the Future: The Desire Called Utopia and Other Science Fictions*. London and New York: Verso.

Jamieson, Dale. 2014. *Reason in a Dark Time: Why the Struggle Against Climate Change Failed—And What It Means for Our Future*. Oxford: Oxford University Press.

Johnson, Mark. 2008. "What Makes a Body?" *The Journal of Speculative Philosophy* 22 (3): 159–68.

Johnson, Sheila K. 1988. *The Japanese through American Eyes*. Stanford, CA: Stanford University Press.

Johnson, Susan C. 2000. "The Recognition of Mentalistic Agents in Infancy." *Trends in Cognitive Sciences* 4 (1): 22–28.

Joshi, S. T. 1990. *The Weird Tale*. Austin: University of Texas Press.

Joyce, James. 1992. *A Portrait of the Artist as a Young Man*. London: Penguin.

———. 2008. *Ulysses*. Edited by Jeri Johnson. Oxford: Oxford University Press.

Jue, Melody. 2014. "Churning Up the Depths: Nonhuman Ecologies of Metaphor in *Solaris* and 'Oceanic.'" In *Green Planets: Ecology and Science Fiction*, edited by Gerry Canavan and Kim Stanley Robinson, 226–41. Middletown, CT: Wesleyan University Press.

Jung, Carl Gustav, and Wolfgang Pauli. 2001. *Atom and Archetype: The Pauli/Jung Letters, 1932–1958*. Edited by Carl Alfred Meier. Translated by David Roscoe. Princeton, NJ: Princeton University Press.

Kafka, Franz. 2011. "A Message from the Emperor." Translated by Mark Harman. *The New York Review of Books*, 2011. http://www.nybooks.com/blogs/nyrblog/2011/jul/01/message-emperor-new-translation/.

Kant, Immanuel. 2002. *Critique of the Power of Judgment*. Edited by Paul Guyer. Translated by Paul Guyer and Eric Matthews. Cambridge: Cambridge University Press.

Karttunen, Laura. 2008. "A Sociostylistic Perspective on Negatives and the Disnarrated: Lahiri, Roy, Rushdie." *Partial Answers* 6 (2): 419–41.

Kimmel, Michael. 2005. "From Metaphor to the 'Mental Sketchpad': Literary Macrostructure and Compound Image Schemas in *Heart of Darkness*." *Metaphor and Symbol* 20 (3): 199–238.

———. 2009. "Analyzing Image Schemas in Literature." *Cognitive Semiotics* 5: 159–188.

Klinkowitz, Jerome. 2004. *The Vonnegut Effect*. Columbia: University of South Carolina Press.

Kohlmann, Benjamin. 2014. "What Is It Like to Be a Rat? Early Cold War Glimpses of the Post-Human." *Textual Practice* 28 (4): 655–75.

Kövecses, Zoltán. 2000. *Metaphor and Emotion: Language, Culture, and Body in Human Feeling*. Cambridge: Cambridge University Press.

Kristeva, Julia. 1989. *Language: The Unknown: An Initiation into Linguistics*. Translated by Anne M. Menke. New York: Columbia University Press.

Kukkonen, Karin. 2013. "Form as a Pattern of Thinking: Cognitive Poetics and New Formalism." In *New Formalisms and Literary Theory*, edited by Verena Theile and Linda Tredennick, 159–76. London: Palgrave Macmillan.

Kukkonen, Karin, and Marco Caracciolo. 2014. "Introduction: What Is the 'Second Generation'?" *Style* 48 (3): 261–74.

Kukkonen, Karin, and Sonja Klimek, eds. 2011. *Metalepsis in Popular Culture.* Berlin: De Gruyter.

Kuzmičová, Anežka. 2012. "Presence in the Reading of Literary Narrative: A Case for Motor Enactment." *Semiotica* 189 (1/4): 23–48.

Lakoff, George, and Mark Johnson. 1980. *Metaphors We Live By.* Chicago and London: University of Chicago Press.

———. 1999. *Philosophy in the Flesh: The Embodied Mind and Its Challenge to Western Thought.* New York: Basic Books.

Lakoff, George, and Rafael E. Núñez. 2001. *Where Mathematics Comes From: How the Embodied Mind Brings Mathematics Into Being.* New York: Basic Books.

Lapidot, Ema. 1991. "Borges y Escher: Artistas contemporáneos." *Revista Iberoamericana* 57 (155–156): 607–15.

Latour, Bruno. 2005. *Reassembling the Social: An Introduction to Actor-Network-Theory.* Oxford and New York: Oxford University Press.

Lawrence, Karen R. 1980. "Style and Narrative in the 'Ithaca' Chapter of Joyce's *Ulysses*." *ELH* 47 (3): 559–74.

Leary, David E. 1990. "Psyche's Muse: The Role of Metaphor in the History of Psychology." In *Metaphors in the History of Psychology*, 1–78. Cambridge: Cambridge University Press.

Lem, Stanisław. 2011. *Solaris.* Translated by Bill Johnston. Northridge, CA: Premier Digital Publishing.

Leslie, John. 2001. *Infinite Minds: A Philosophical Cosmology.* Oxford: Clarendon Press.

Levi, Primo. 1982. *Il sistema periodico.* Turin: Einaudi.

———. 1984. *The Periodic Table.* Translated by Raymond Rosenthal. New York: Schocken Books.

Levine, Caroline. 2015. *Forms: Whole, Rhythm, Hierarchy, Network.* Princeton, NJ: Princeton University Press.

Levinson, Stephen C. 2003. *Space in Language and Cognition: Explorations in Cognitive Diversity.* Cambridge: Cambridge University Press.

Leys, Ruth. 2011. "The Turn to Affect: A Critique." *Critical Inquiry* 37: 434–72.

London, Jack. 1998. "To Build a Fire." In *The Call of the Wild, White Fang and Other Stories*, edited by Earle Labor and Robert C. Leitz III, 341–57. Oxford: Oxford University Press.

Longair, Malcolm S. 2013. *The Cosmic Century: A History of Astrophysics and Cosmology.* Cambridge: Cambridge University Press.

Louwerse, Max, and Patrick Jeuniaux. 2008. "Language Comprehension Is Both Embodied and Symbolic." In *Symbols and Embodiment: Debates on Meaning and Cognition*, edited by Manuel de Vega, Arthur M. Glenberg, and Arthur C. Graesser, 309–26. Oxford and New York: Oxford University Press.

Lovecraft, H. P. 2004. "The Shadow Out of Time." In *The Dreams in the Witch House and Other Weird Stories*, edited by S. T. Joshi, 335–97. London: Penguin.

Lovejoy, Arthur O. 2001. *The Great Chain of Being: A Study of the History of an Idea.* Cambridge, MA: Harvard University Press.

Luckhurst, Roger. 2017. "The Weird: A Dis/Orientation." *Textual Practice* 31 (6): 1041–61.

Makinen, Merja. 2005. *The Novels of Jeanette Winterson*. Houndmills: Palgrave Macmillan.

Malina, Debra. 2002. *Breaking the Frame: Metalepsis and the Construction of the Subject*. Columbus: Ohio State University Press.

Mar, Raymond A., and Keith Oatley. 2008. "The Function of Fiction Is the Abstraction and Simulation of Social Experience." *Perspectives on Psychological Science* 3 (3): 173–92.

Markoff, John. 2015. "Sorry, Einstein. Quantum Study Suggests 'Spooky Action' Is Real." *The New York Times*, October 21, 2015. https://www.nytimes.com/2015/10/22/science/quantum-theory-experiment-said-to-prove-spooky-interactions.html.

Massumi, Brian. 2002. *Parables for the Virtual: Movement, Affect, Sensation*. Durham, NC: Duke University Press.

Matheson, Richard. 2012. "The Shrinking Man." In *American Science Fiction: Four Classic Novels 1953–1956*, edited by Gary K. Wolfe, 585–774. New York: The Library of America.

Maxwell, Nicholas. 2000. "The Mind-Body Problem and Explanatory Dualism." *Philosophy* 75: 57–60.

McClellan, Ann. 2004. "Science Fictions: British Women Scientists and Jeanette Winterson's *Gut Symmetries*." *Women's Studies* 33 (8): 1057–81.

McGurl, Mark. 2012. "The Posthuman Comedy." *Critical Inquiry* 38 (3): 533–553.

McHale, Brian. 1987. *Postmodernist Fiction*. London and New York: Routledge.

McInnis, Gilbert. 2005. "Evolutionary Mythology in the Writings of Kurt Vonnegut, Jr." *Critique: Studies in Contemporary Fiction* 46 (4): 383–96.

Menary, Richard. 2010. "Introduction to the Special Issue on 4E Cognition." *Phenomenology and the Cognitive Sciences* 9 (4): 459–463.

Merleau-Ponty, Maurice. 2002. *Phenomenology of Perception*. Translated by Colin Smith. London and New York: Routledge.

Michael, Israel, Jennifer Riddle Harding, and Vera Tobin. 2005. "On Simile." In *Language, Culture, and Mind*, edited by Suzanne Kemmer and Michel Achard, 123–35. Stanford, CA: CSLI Publications.

Miller, George A. 2003. "The Cognitive Revolution: A Historical Perspective." *Trends in Cognitive Sciences* 7 (3): 141–44.

Miller, Gerald Alva. 2012. *Exploring the Limits of the Human through Science Fiction*. New York: Palgrave Macmillan.

Montell, Conrad. 2002. "On Evolution of God-Seeking Mind: An Inquiry into Why Natural Selection Would Favor Imagination and Distortion of Sensory Experience." *Evolution and Cognition* 8 (1): 1–19.

Mullen, R. D. 1999. "Two Early Works by Ray Cummings: 'The Fire People' and 'Around the Universe.'" *Science Fiction Studies* 26 (2): 295–302.

Mustazza, Leonard. 1991. "A Darwinian Eden: Science and Myth in Kurt Vonnegut's 'Galápagos.'" *Journal of the Fantastic in the Arts* 3 (2): 55–65.

Nabokov, Vladimir. 1989. *Nikolai Gogol*. Oxford: Oxford University Press.

———. 1997. "Lance." In *The Stories of Vladimir Nabokov*, 632–42. New York: Vintage.

Nagel, Thomas. 2012. *Mind and Cosmos: Why the Materialist Neo-Darwinian Conception of Nature Is Almost Certainly False*. New York: Oxford University Press.

Nicholls, Peter. 2015. "New Wave." In *SFE: The Encyclopedia of Science Fiction.* http://www.sf-encyclopedia.com/entry/new_wave.

Nicol, Charles. 1987. "Nabokov and Science Fiction: 'Lance' (Nabokov et Science-Fiction: 'Lance')." *Science Fiction Studies* 14 (1): 9–20.

Noë, Alva. 2004. *Action in Perception.* Cambridge, MA: MIT Press.

Oatley, Keith. 2011. *Such Stuff as Dreams: The Psychology of Fiction.* Malden, MA: Wiley.

Penrose, Roger. 1997. *The Large, the Small and the Human Mind.* Edited by Malcolm Longair. Cambridge: Cambridge University Press.

Perlis, Alan David. 1982. "The Newtonian Nightmare of *Ulysses.*" In *The Seventh of Joyce,* edited by Bernard Benstock, 191–97. Bloomington: Indiana University Press.

Perskie, Jana L. 2003. "Take a Surreal Ride with Isserley on Highway A9!" *Amazon.ca Customer Reviews: Under the Skin.* December 28, 2003. http://www.amazon.ca/gp/aw/cr/rRTW2HBSGOGHST.

Pier, John. 2010. "Metalepsis." In *The Living Handbook of Narratology,* edited by Peter Hühn. Hamburg: Hamburg University Press. http://hup.sub.uni-hamburg.de/lhn/index.php/Metalepsis.

Pordzik, Ralph. 2012. "The Posthuman Future of Man: Anthropocentrism and the Other of Technology in Anglo-American Science Fiction." *Utopian Studies* 23 (1): 142–61.

Potter, Emily. 2009. "Climate Change and the Problem of Representation." *Australian Humanities Review* 46: 67–78.

Prince, Gerald. 1988. "The Disnarrated." *Style* 22 (1): 1–8.

Pulvermüller, Friedemann. 2005. "Brain Mechanisms Linking Language and Action." *Nature Reviews. Neuroscience* 6 (7): 576–82.

Punday, Daniel. 2003. *Narrative Bodies: Toward a Corporeal Narratology.* New York: Palgrave Macmillan.

Reber, Arthur S. 1992. "The Cognitive Unconscious: An Evolutionary Perspective." *Consciousness and Cognition* 1 (2): 93–133.

Richardson, Alan. 2010. *The Neural Sublime: Cognitive Theories and Romantic Texts.* Baltimore, MD: Johns Hopkins University Press.

Rigby, Kate. 2013. "Confronting Catastrophe: Ecocriticism in a Warming World." In *The Cambridge Companion to Literature and the Environment,* edited by Louise Westling, 212–25. Cambridge: Cambridge University Press.

Ritchie, L. David. 2009. "Relevance and Simulation in Metaphor." *Metaphor and Symbol* 24 (4): 249–62.

Rohrer, Tim. 2007. "Embodiment and Experientialism." In *The Oxford Handbook of Cognitive Linguistics,* edited by Dirk Geeraerts and Hubert Cuyckens, 25–47. Oxford: Oxford University Press.

Rosenheim, Shawn. 1995. "Extraterrestrial: Science Fictions in 'A Brief History of Time' and 'The Incredible Shrinking Man.'" *Film Quarterly* 48 (4): 15–21.

Ross, Charlotte. 2011. *Primo Levi's Narratives of Embodiment: Containing the Human.* New York: Routledge.

Ryan, Marie-Laure. 1991. *Possible Worlds, Artificial Intelligence, and Narrative Theory.* Bloomington: Indiana University Press.

———. 2001. *Narrative as Virtual Reality: Immersion and Interactivity in Literature and Electronic Media.* Baltimore, MD and London: Johns Hopkins University Press.

————. 2006. "From Parallel Universes to Possible Worlds: Ontological Pluralism in Physics, Narratology, and Narrative." *Poetics Today* 27 (4): 633–74.

Ryan, Marie-Laure, Kenneth Foote, and Maoz Azaryahu. 2016. *Narrating Space/Spatializing Narrative: Where Narrative Theory and Geography Meet.* Columbus: Ohio State University Press.

Sagan, Carl. 1980. *Cosmos.* New York: Random House.

Samolsky, Russell. 2011. *Apocalyptic Futures: Marked Bodies and the Violence of the Text in Kafka, Conrad, and Coetzee.* New York: Fordham University Press.

Scarry, Elaine. 2001. *Dreaming by the Book.* Princeton, NJ: Princeton University Press.

Schiff, James A. 1992. "Updike's 'Roger's Version': Re-Visualizing 'The Scarlet Letter.'" *South Atlantic Review* 57 (4): 59–76.

Schooler, Jonathan W., and Tonya Y. Engstler-Schooler. 1990. "Verbal Overshadowing of Visual Memories: Some Things Are Better Left Unsaid." *Cognitive Psychology* 22: 36–71.

Senn, Fritz. 1996. "'Ithaca': Portrait of the Chapter as a Long List." In *Joyce's "Ithaca,"* edited by Andrew Gibson, 31–76. Amsterdam: Rodopi.

Shaviro, Steven. 2014. *The Universe of Things: On Speculative Realism.* Minneapolis and London: University of Minnesota Press.

Shaw, Philip. 2006. *The Sublime.* London and New York: Routledge.

Sheets-Johnstone, Maxine. 2011. *The Primacy of Movement.* Expanded second edition. Philadelphia, PA and Amsterdam: John Benjamins.

Shklovsky, Viktor. 1991. "Art as Device." In *Theory of Prose,* translated by Benjamin Sher, 1–14. Champaign, IL and London: Dalkey Archive Press.

Slingerland, Edward. 2008a. *What Science Offers the Humanities: Integrating Body and Culture.* Cambridge: Cambridge University Press.

————. 2008b. "Who's Afraid of Reductionism? The Study of Religion in the Age of Cognitive Science." *Journal of the American Academy of Religion* 76 (2): 375–411.

Smith, Barry, and Roberto Casati. 1994. "Naive Physics." *Philosophical Psychology* 7 (2): 227–247.

Snow, C. P. 1990. "The Two Cultures." *Leonardo* 23 (2/3): 169–73.

Söffner, Jan. 2017. "Embodying Technologies of Disability." In *Culture – Theory – Disability: Encounters between Disability Studies and Cultural Studies,* edited by Anne Waldschmidt, Hanjo Berressem, and Moritz Ingwersen, 152–59. Bielefeld: transcript Verlag.

Spolsky, Ellen. 2001. *Satisfying Skepticism: Embodied Knowledge in the Early Modern World.* Aldershot: Ashgate.

Stableford, Brian M., and David Langford. 2019. "Great and Small." In *SFE: The Encyclopedia of Science Fiction.* http://www.sf-encyclopedia.com/entry/great_and_small.

Stableford, Brian M., Peter Nicholls, Mike Ashley, and David Langford. 2015. "New Worlds." In *SFE: The Encyclopedia of Science Fiction.* http://www.sf-encyclopedia.com/entry/new_worlds.

Stapledon, Olaf. 2011. *Star Maker.* London: Orion Publishing Group.

Stern, Daniel N. 2010. *Forms of Vitality: Exploring Dynamic Experience in Psychology, the Arts, Psychotherapy, and Development.* Oxford: Oxford University Press.

Sternberg, Meir. 2001. "How Narrativity Makes a Difference." *Narrative* 9 (2): 115–22.

Stewart, Jon. 1993. "Borges on Immortality." *Philosophy and Literature* 17: 295–301.

Stockwell, Peter. 2009. *Texture: A Cognitive Aesthetics of Reading*. Edinburgh: Edinburgh University Press.

Stoljar, Daniel. 2009. *Physicalism*. Abingdon: Routledge.

Suvin, Darko. 1979. *Metamorphoses of Science Fiction: On the Poetics and History of a Literary Genre*. New Haven, CT: Yale University Press.

Swinburne, Richard. 2003. "The Argument to God from Fine-Tuning Reassessed." In *God and Design: The Teleological Argument and Modern Science*, edited by Neil A. Manson, 106–24. London: Routledge.

Swirski, Peter, ed. 2006. *The Art and Science of Stanislaw Lem*. Montreal: McGill-Queen's University Press.

Tan, Ed S. 1996. *Emotion and the Structure of Narrative Film: Film as an Emotion Machine*. Mahwah, NJ: Lawrence Erlbaum.

Tegmark, Max. 2004. "Parallel Universes." In *Science and Ultimate Reality: Quantum Theory, Cosmology, and Complexity*, edited by John D. Barrow, Paul C. W. Davies, and Charles L. Harper Jr., 459–91. Cambridge: Cambridge University Press.

Thiher, Allen. 2005. *Fiction Refracts Science: Modernist Writers from Proust to Borges*. Columbia: University of Missouri Press.

Thomas, Nigel J. T. 2014. "Mental Imagery." In *The Stanford Encyclopedia of Philosophy*, edited by Edward N. Zalta, Fall 2014. http://plato.stanford.edu/archives/fall2014/entries/mental-imagery/.

Thompson, Evan. 2007a. "Look Again: Phenomenology and Mental Imagery." *Phenomenology and the Cognitive Sciences* 6: 137–70.

———. 2007b. *Mind in Life: Biology, Phenomenology, and the Sciences of Mind*. Cambridge, MA: Harvard University Press.

Troscianko, Emily. 2010. "Kafkaesque Worlds in Real Time." *Language and Literature* 19 (2): 151–71.

Tuan, Yi-Fu. 1977. *Space and Place*. Minneapolis and London: University of Minnesota Press.

Updike, John. 1979. *Problems and Other Stories*. New York: Random House.

———. 2006. *Roger's Version*. London: Penguin.

van Dijk, Teun A., and Walter Kintsch. 1983. *Strategies of Discourse Comprehension*. New York: Academic Press.

Varela, Francisco J., Evan Thompson, and Eleanor Rosch. 1991. *The Embodied Mind: Cognitive Science and Human Experience*. Cambridge, MA: MIT Press.

Velleman, J. David. 2003. "Narrative Explanation." *The Philosophical Review* 112 (1): 1–25.

Vint, Sherryl. 2014. *A Guide for the Perplexed: Science Fiction*. London: Bloomsbury.

Vonnegut, Kurt. 2011. *Galápagos*. New York: RosettaBooks.

Walton, Kendall. 1990. *Mimesis as Make-Believe: On the Foundations of the Representational Arts*. Cambridge, MA: Harvard University Press.

Weik von Mossner, Alexa. 2017. *Affective Ecologies: Empathy, Emotion, and Environmental Narrative*. Columbus: Ohio State University Press.

Weissert, Thomas P. 1992. "Stanislaw Lem and a Topology of Mind." *Science Fiction Studies* 19 (2): 161–66.

Wigley, Samuel. 2016. "The Letter from Stanley Kubrick That Started *2001: A Space Odyssey*." British Film Institute. June 9, 2016. http://www.bfi.org.uk/news-opinion/news-bfi/features/letter-stanley-kubrick-started-2001-space-odyssey.

Wilson, Elizabeth A. 2015. *Gut Feminism*. Durham, NC: Duke University Press.

Winterson, Jeanette. 1997. *Gut Symmetries*. New York: Random House.

Wolfe, Gary K. 2006. "Let's Get Small! Review of Ray Cummings's *The Girl in the Golden Atom*." *Science Fiction Studies* 33 (3): 528–31.

Woods, Derek. 2014. "Scale Critique for the Anthropocene." *Minnesota Review* 83: 133–42.

Wulf, Andrea. 2016. *The Invention of Nature: Alexander von Humboldt's New World*. New York: Vintage.

Zabriskie, Beverley. 2001. "Jung and Pauli: A Meeting of Rare Minds." In *Atom and Archetype: The Pauli/Jung Letters, 1932–1958*, edited by Carl Alfred Meier, xxvii–l. Princeton, NJ: Princeton University Press.

Zoline, Pamela. 1988. "The Heat Death of the Universe." In *The Heat Death of the Universe and Other Stories*, 13–28. New York: McPherson & Company.

Zunshine, Lisa. 2008. *Strange Concepts and the Stories They Make Possible: Cognition, Culture, Narrative*. Baltimore, MD and London: Johns Hopkins University Press.

———. ed. 2015. *The Oxford Handbook of Cognitive Literary Studies*. New York: Oxford University Press.

Zwaan, Rolf A. 2004. "The Immersed Experiencer: Towards an Embodied Theory of Language Comprehension." In *The Psychology of Learning and Motivation*, edited by Brian H. Ross, 35–63. San Diego, CA and London: Elsevier Academic Press.

Zwaan, Rolf A., and Lawrence J. Taylor. 2006. "Seeing, Acting, Understanding: Motor Resonance in Language Comprehension." *Journal of Experimental Psychology* 135 (1): 1–11.

Index

Note: Page numbers followed by "n" denote endnotes.

Abbott, H. Porter 112, 124, 168n12
abstraction 2, 11, 55–57; and conceptual categories 78; and Gestalt psychology 57; and interconnectivity 185; and rhythm 97, 188; and style 181; *see also* geometry
affect: affective contour 12; affective involvement in narrative 11–15; and the cosmos 171–72; and bodily defamiliarization 172, 197–98; forms of vitality 67, 101; and natural patterns 165; and psychological development 198; *vs.* emotion 23n10; *see also* emotion; rhythm
affordance 42
Alaimo, Stacy 75, 96, 144
Aldiss, Brian 64
alien phenomenology *see* phenomenology
allegory 134, 159; *see also* symbol
animals 42, 140n1, 145
Anthropocene 17, 23n13, 26, 122, 158; *see also* climate change
anthropocentrism 17, 29, 159–60, 186; *see also* human exceptionalism; parochialism of the human
anthropomorphism 34, 73, 112; and the divine 87–88; and narrative 17; and the nonhuman 29–30
Artificial Intelligence 5–6

Bakhtin, Mikhail 114, 135, 145
Ballard, J. G. 64, 112–21
Barsalou, Lawrence 78
Bennett, Jane 29–30

Big Bang 21, 27–34, 84, 89–90, 180; *see also* cosmology; scientific knowledge
bodily defamiliarization 3–4; and affect 171; and the cosmos 20; degrees 26, 34, 49; and immersion 48; and the mind-body problem 138; and the nonhuman 18; *see also* defamiliarization
Bogost, Ian 29
Bolens, Guillemette 15
Borges, Jorge Luis 37, 129–38
Boroditsky, Lera 2, 11, 134, 140n9
Burke, Edmund 169, 198n1

Calvino, Italo 27–34, 49, 73–74, 172, 185
catastrophe 127; and the Cold War 113, 140n10; and ecocriticism 139
Chakrabarty, Dipesh 17, 158, 203
childhood 193–94, 198
chronotope 114, 135
Clarke, Arthur C. 189–98
climate change 17, 26, 49, 196, 200
cognition 4, 7; conscious *vs.* unconscious 6–7; situated cognition 78; *see also* embodied cognition
cognitive literary studies 9, 15, 36
comedy *see* humor
conceptual knowledge 58, 78; *see also* image schema
consciousness 9–10; and embodied simulation 56; hard problem of consciousness 110–11, 124, 129, 149, 161, 168n18; and strange loops 131; *see also* dualism
contemplation 130, 186, 195

Cosmicomics (by Italo Calvino) 27–34
cosmology 19, 24n16, 47, 50n4, 50n7,
    93; *see also* Big Bang; scientific
    knowledge
cosmos 19–20; benefits of a cosmic
    perspective 202–3; coupling with
    bodily defamiliarization 49–50;
    difficulty of imagining the cosmos
    3–4; history of imagining the
    cosmos 20, 24n15; *see also* Big
    Bang; cosmology
Crutzen, Paul 17
Cummings, Ray 34–40, 154

dance *see* movement
Darwin, Charles 112, 122, 128
De Certeau, Michel 52
De Jaegher, Hanne 6, 193, 203
defamiliarization 3, 23n1; *see also*
    bodily defamiliarization
Descartes, René 19, 77, 97, 111, 116,
    129, 138
description 42–43, 134–35; and
    scale 35–36, 154–56; and visual
    recognition 59
Di Paolo, Ezequiel A. 6, 193, 203
disaster *see* catastrophe
disgust 135, 145–46, 163, 168n6
divine 19, 33, 85–89, 179, 186, 201;
    see also religion
dualism 111, 117, 120, 128, 151,
    200; *see also* consciousness; New
    Materialism

Easterlin, Nancy 18
ecocriticism 18, 26, 139, 170; *see also*
    econarratology
ecological crisis *see* climate change
ecological psychology *see* affordance;
    intermediate world
econarratology 18, 48
The Elementary Particles (by Michel
    Houellebecq) 98–105
embodied cognition 2–3, 7–15, 56; *see
    also* embodied simulation; extended
    mind
embodied simulation 8–10, 23n6, 33,
    56; and concepts 78; and metaphor
    10–11, 28
embodiment; alien embodiment
    141–42; five dimensions of 15; *see
    also* embodied cognition; mortality;
    sexuality; transcorporeality
emotion 11–12; *vs.* affect 23n10; and
    metaphor 11; and the nonhuman

148, 169–72; and sense of place
    115; *see also* affect
empathy 31, 44, 50n9, 115, 144, 147
enactivism 4–7, 23n3, 36, 167n1,
    203; and the critique of mental
    representations 171–72; and play
    193; and sensorimotor patterns
    23n5, 79, 97, 142
entropy 65–69, 71
Esrock, Ellen 9, 13, 29
estrangement *see* defamiliarization
ethics 105, 139, 143, 147, 168n5,
    189; and the cosmos 50n4, 200;
    and literary engagements with
    science 82–83, 107
evolutionary theory 112, 121–24,
    150–51
extended mind 118, 140n3
extinction 113, 121, 127, 139,
    140n1, 155

Faber, Michel 142–50
Fludernik, Monika 17, 24n14, 140n8
form *see* narrative; patterns
forms of vitality *see* affect
Freud, Sigmund 166, 177–78

Galápagos (by Kurt Vonnegut)
    121–29
garden path sentences 154, 168n12;
    see also syntax
geometry 83, 89–90, 102–3, 192; *see
    also* abstraction
Gibbs, Raymond W. 10–11, 23n4,
    27–28
Gibson, James J. 2–3, 42
The Girl in the Golden Atom (by Ray
    Cummings) 34–40
God *see* divine
great chain of being 19, 145, 149–50
grotesque 135, 140n10, 145–46
Grusin, Richard 4, 16, 18, 139
Gut Symmetries (by Jeanette
    Winterson) 91–98

hard problem of consciousness *see*
    consciousness
Harman, Graham 142, 151, 156, 158
Hawking, Stephen 196, 200
"The Heat Death of the Universe"
    (by Pamela Zoline) 64–71
Herman, David 4, 18, 23n3, 48
"A History of Everything, Including
    You" (by Jenny Hollowell) 200–3,
    204n1

Hofstadter, Douglas R. 130–31, 133, 137
Hogan, Patrick Colm 11
Hollowell, Jenny 200–3
Houellebecq, Michel 98–105, 150
human exceptionalism 5, 17, 122, 200; *see also* anthropocentrism; parochialism of the human
humor 30, 127, 201–2; lack of humor in literary style 42, 197; and the sublime 172–76
Hutto, Daniel D. 6, 17, 171

image schema 11–14, 23n8, 57–58, 70, 80n10, 130; and bodily defamiliarization 62; and naïve physics 192
imagination 2, 16, 33, 36, 153–54; environmental imagination 48; visual *vs.* haptic imagination 86, 162–63; *see also* mental imagery
immersion 10, 48, 115–16, 135
"The Immortal" (by Jorge Luis Borges) 129–38
interconnectivity 11, 51; and abstraction 185; and affect 196–97; interconnectivity anchor 52, 58, 62–63, 69–71, 78, 80n1; and metaphor 90; and T. S. Eliot's objective correlative 79
intermediate world 2–3; and cosmic perspective-taking 20; narrative's bias toward the intermediate world 18
intersubjectivity 32, 45, 98, 104, 185, 203; *see also* love
irony *see* humor

James, Erin 18, 48
Johnson, Mark 7, 10–11, 15, 23n4, 25, 57, 134
Joyce, James 51–65, 76, 175–76, 181
Jung, Carl Gustav 91–92

Kafka, Franz 13–14, 101
Kant, Immanuel 170–71
Kimmel, Michael 12–13
Kubrick, Stanley 169, 189
Kukkonen, Karin 24n18, 78, 140n8
Kuzmičová, Anežka 10, 39, 80n5, 116

Lakoff, George 2, 7, 10–11, 15, 23n4, 25, 57, 134
"Lance" (by Vladimir Nabokov) 172–79

Latour, Bruno 16
Lem, Stanisław 158–66
Levi, Primo 71–78
lists 33, 51, 68, 78, 201
lived experience *see* phenomenology
London, Jack 1–2
love 119, 186, 189, 200; and the origin of the universe 32–33; and plot 89; as unifying principle 104–5; *see also* intersubjectivity; sexuality
Lovecraft, H. P. 150–58, 182
Lovejoy, Arthur O. 19, 145

Mar, Raymond 17
materiality: of the body 119, 167; of the cosmos 113; of language 5; of the mind 110–11, 117–18, 139; of the nonhuman 63, 69, 139; *see also* New Materialism
Matheson, Richard 40–47, 115
McHale, Brian 136
mental imagery 36, 48–49, 57, 59, 114; and spatial scale 38–39, 154, 168n12; vividness of mental imagery 115; *see also* imagination
Merleau-Ponty, Maurice 15, 151
metalepsis 77, 133, 136–37, 140n8
metaphor 10–11, 27–28, 50n2, 61; conceptual metaphor 25, 134; embodied metaphor for the nonhuman 28–29, 68, 75, 87, 161, 176–78; and interconnectivity 90; phenomenological metaphor 44–45, 168n7
metonymy 184
mind *see* cognition; consciousness
mind-body problem *see* dualism
mortality 2, 103, 133–34, 176
motion *see* movement
motor resonance *see* embodied simulation
movement 8–9, 27–28, 59–60, 76–77, 182, 187; and somatic perspective-taking 39; uncoupled from phenomenology 158; *see also* image schema; rhythm

Nabokov, Vladimir 108n5, 172–79, 190, 201
Nagel, Thomas 111, 119, 137
narrative 3–4, 6; and affect 11–15; and anthropocentrism 17–18; and the constitution of the self 135–36; narrative form 22–23, 65, 187, 203,

204n2; as a problem-posing tool
107, 139; as a tool for thinking 112
narrative theory 18, 48, 125; *see also*
econarratology
narratology *see* econarratology;
narrative theory
natural evolution *see* evolutionary
theory
nature *see* nonhuman
New Formalism 22–23, 24n18;
see also narrative; patterns
New Materialism 139
new wave 64, 112, 121; *see also*
science fiction
New Worlds 64, 80n7, 112; *see also*
science fiction
Newton, Isaac 19, 81
Noë, Alva 6, 171
nonhuman 16–18; and
anthropomorphism 29–30; and the
cosmic 20; and human subjectivity
139, 165; immersion in nonhuman
environments 48; and panpsychism
165, 186; and transcorporeality
75–76

Oatley, Keith 17
ostranenie *see* defamiliarization

panpsychism 165, 186
parochialism of the human 121,
151, 196, 200, 203; *see also*
anthropocentrism; human
exceptionalism
patterns 22, 29–31, 57–58, 79, 142,
168n16; and affect 197–98; and
enactivism 6, 23n5, 171, 193; and
movement 62, 76, 79, 184, 187–88;
and narrative 12, 36; and the nature
of reality 95–97, 104, 148, 164–65
Pauli, Wolfgang 91–92
perception 18, 39, 42, 57, 153, 171
The Periodic Table (by Primo Levi)
71–78
perspective-taking *see* cosmos;
empathy
phenomenology 15, 55, 70, 115,
146–49; alien phenomenology 29,
156; body as object *vs.* body as
subject 151; and the climate crisis
26; of humankind as a species 203;
and metaphorical language 44–45,
101, 168n7; and value 202; *see also*
perception; proprioception

physics 21, 66, 109; classical
(Newtonian) mechanics 81; naïve
physics 192; quantum physics
91–92, 99–100; subatomic physics
50n6; *see also* entropy
place *see* space
play 192–95
plot 14, 41, 82–83, 88–90, 100,
140n5; and human intentionality
24n14, 124–25; and sexual desire
106
posthuman 4, 29; posthuman
narrators 99, 105, 122; posthuman
temporality 110–13, 139n1; *see
also* nonhuman
proprioception 137, 153; *see also*
perception; phenomenology
Punday, Dan 15

religion 5, 83, 128–29, 180; *see also*
divine
representation 9–10, 18, 78, 188,
197–98; critique of representation
in enactivist philosophy 6, 171–72;
critique of representation in the
environmental humanities 196–97
rhythm 12–14, 76, 97, 186–88,
201–2; *see also* movement; syntax
Roger's Version (by John Updike)
83–90
Rohde, Marieke 193
romantic relationships *see*
intersubjectivity; love
Rosch, Eleanor 5–6
Ryan, Marie-Laure 10, 24n14, 48,
50n7, 125

satire *see* humor
scala naturae *see* great chain of being
scale 2–3, 62, 126, 138, 169–72;
asymmetry between spatial and
temporal scale 109–10; and the
climate crisis 17, 25–26, 80n1; *see
also* interconnectivity; intermediate
world; space; temporality
Scarry, Elaine 36, 39
schema refreshment 27, 29
science fiction 4, 23n2, 173, 179,
198n4; and the posthuman 139n1;
and the sublime 198n2; *see also*
new wave; *New Worlds*
scientific knowledge 54, 81–82,
91–92, 106–7; distance from
the intermediate world 19–20;

limitations of science 151, 159; and literature 20, 72, 80n11; *see also* Big Bang; cosmology; cosmos
selfhood 131–32, 135
sensation *see* perception; phenomenology; proprioception
sexuality 31–32, 81–82, 105–7, 176–78; *see also* love
The Shadow Out of Time (by H. P. Lovecraft) 150–58
Shaviro, Steven 142, 165
Shklovsky, Viktor 3, 23n1
The Shrinking Man (by Richard Matheson) 40–47
simile 50n2, 50n3; *see also* metaphor
simulation *see* embodied simulation
Slingerland, Edward 15, 111, 128
Snow, C. P. 72
Solaris (by Stanisław Lem) 158–66
space 25–26, 169; before the Big Bang 32–34; in narrative 9, 35–36, 48–49, 152–54; sense of place and sense of presence 115–16; *see also* scale
Spolsky, Ellen 15
Stapledon, Olaf 179–89, 192, 200
Star Maker (by Olaf Stapledon) 179–89
Stern, Daniel 67, 71, 101
Sternberg, Meir 11–12
storyworld 23n3; and plot 125; and the reader's embodiment 36, 48, 116
subjectivity *see* cognition; consciousness
sublime 127, 169–72, 198n1; and humor 175, 179; and marvel 195–96

Suvin, Darko 4, 23n2
symbol 78, 88, 116–17, 120
syntax 165, 201–2; and image schemata 62; and rhythm 14, 33–34, 98; *see also* garden path sentences

Tan, Ed 11
temporality 109–11, 124, 129–30, 139n1; deep time 140n2; immortality 133; of natural evolution 112; and spatial metaphors 134; *see also* scale
"The Terminal Beach" (by J. G. Ballard) 112–21
Thompson, Evan 5–6, 36, 142, 167n1
transcorporeality 75, 96–97, 144, 164
two cultures *see* scientific knowledge
2001: A Space Odyssey (by Arthur C. Clarke) 189–96

Ulysses (by James Joyce) 52–64
Under the Skin (by Michel Faber) 142–50
Updike, John 83–90

Varela, Francisco 5–6, 142
Velleman, David 12
verbal overshadowing 59, 80n5
virtual body *see* embodied cognition

Weik von Mossner, Alexa 18, 48
weird fiction 151, 168n10
Winterson, Jeanette 91–98

Zoline, Pamela 64–71, 112
Zunshine, Lisa 4, 168n17
Zwaan, Rolf A. 7, 9, 28